Living with the Dead
in the Middle Ages

ႸႩჂ

Living with the Dead in the Middle Ages

ഗൻ

Patrick J. Geary

Cornell University Press

Ithaca and London

First published 1994 by Cornell University Press
First printing, Cornell Paperbacks, 1994

Library of Congress Cataloging-in-Publication Data
Geary, Patrick J., 1948–
    Living with the dead in the Middle Ages / Patrick J. Geary.
        p. cm.
    Includes bibliographical references and index.
    ISBN-13: 978-0-8014-8098-0 (pbk. : alk. paper)
    ISBN-10: 0-8014-8098-1 (pbk. : alk. paper)
        1. Death—Religious aspects—Christianity—History of doctrines—Middle Ages,
600–1500. 2. Europe—Church history—Middle Ages, 600–1500. I. Title.
BT825.G36 1994
235—dc20   94-18873

Paperback printing 10 9 8 7 6 5

Contents

ဢ

vi   Contents

Living

Acknowledgments

I thank Suki Lewin and Elaine Hyams for their assistance in preparing the manuscript, Celeste Newbrough for her work in preparing the indexes, and the editorial staff of Cornell University Press for their patience and cooperation at every stage of the preparation of this book.

The following chapters are revised versions of essays that originally appeared in various North American and European journals and volumes. I thank the editors for permission to use this material here.

Chapter 1, "Saints, Scholars, and Society: The Elusive Goal," in *Sancta, Sanctus: Studies in Hagiography,* ed. Sandro Sticca (Binghamton: CEMERS, in press).

Chapter 2, "Zur Problematik der Interpretation archäologischer Quellen für die Geistes- und Religionsgeschichte," *Archaeologia Austriaca* 64 (1980): 111–118.

Chapter 3, "Germanic Tradition and Royal Ideology in the Ninth Century: The *Visio Karoli Magni,*" *Frühmittelalterliche Studien* 21 (1987): 274–294.

Chapter 4, "Echanges et relations entre les vivants et les morts dans la société du haut Moyen Age," *Droit et Cultures* 12 (1986): 3–18.

Chapter 5, "L'humiliation des saints," *Annales: ESC* 34 (1979): 27–42.

Chapter 6, "La coercition des saints dans la pratique religieuse médiévale," in *La culture populaire au Moyen Age,* ed. Pierre Boglioni (Montreal: L'Aurore, 1979), 146–161.

Chapter 7, "Vivre en conflit dans une France sans état: Typologie des méchanismes de règlement des conflits, 1050–1200," *Annales: ESC* 41 (1986): 1107–1133.

Chapter 8, "The Saint and the Shrine: The Pilgrim's Goal in the

Middle Ages," in *Wallfahrt kennt keine Grenzen,* ed. Lenz Kriss-Retten-beck and Gerda Möhler (Munich: Schnell & Steiner, 1984), 265–274.

Chapter 9, "The Ninth-Century Relic Trade—A Response to Pop-ular Piety?" in *Religion and the People, 800–1700,* ed. James Obel-kevich (Chapel Hill: University of North Carolina Press, 1979), 8–19.

Chapter 10, "Sacred Commodities: The Circulation of Medieval Relics," in *Commodities and Culture,* ed. Arjun Appadurai (Cambridge: Cambridge University Press, 1986), 169–191.

Chapter 11, "Saint Helen of Athyra and the Cathedral of Troyes in the Thirteenth Century," *Journal of Medieval and Renaissance Studies* 7 (1977): 149–168.

Chapter 12, "I Magi e Milano," in *Il millennio Ambrosiano: La città del vescovo dai carolingi al Barbarossa,* ed. Carlo Bertelli (Milan: Electa, 1988), 274–287.

Living with the Dead
in the Middle Ages

❧❧

Introduction

For all its fascination with violence and killing, death and dying, modern society is uneasy with death and still more with the dead. Much has been written, both serious and frivolous, about our intense desire to avoid facing death, our own and that of others. Death seems unnatural, a failure of our technological society, of our medical system, of our quest for personal fulfillment. Death is the ultimate evil, the supreme indictment of our inability to control the universe or even ourselves. Perhaps for that reason we tend to look on the dead as failures in a certain sense, unfortunates to be left behind as we move toward our own goal of avoiding the lapses and failures of diet, character, or caution which caused them to falter. The vast literature on death and dying ignores the dead to focus exclusively on the dying and then on the survivors. After the hasty funeral or memorial service and the brief obituary, the dead slip from our consciousness. It is not that an infinite gulf separates them from the living but rather that they simply no longer exist.

Thus the dead are banished from our society. No movement in support of the dead's rights has joined those demanding greater women's rights, children's rights, minorities' rights, and even animals' rights. In "developed" societies, the tombs of the dead, if they have them at all, are not usually maintained and cultivated with loving care by their survivors, nor their personal effects preserved as mementos, nor their actions and words studied and learned by subsequent generations. Mourning, no longer externalized by dress or activity, is not expected to extend much beyond a few weeks, and survivors who prolong their grief are rebuked by family, friends, and associates for failing to get on with life. Never before has the biblical injunction "Leave the dead to bury the dead" been embraced in so wholehearted a manner.

The present abandonment of the dead is the end result of a gradual process in Western society. It began perhaps in the High Middle Ages, when specialists (monks or canonesses) were entrusted with the care and remembrance of the dead, and experienced a major transformation with the Protestant Reformation, when reformers rejected the involvement of the dead in the affairs of the living. It has reached its culmination in the presentist world of the late twentieth century: never before have humans been able to kill so many people so efficiently or to forget them so completely.

Everything about this attitude is quite alien to the world on which this book focuses. In this world, which is essentially those regions of Europe under direct influence of the Frankish political and cultural traditions, death was omnipresent, not only in the sense that persons of all ages could and did die with appalling frequency and suddenness but also in the sense that the dead did not cease to be members of the human community. Death marked a transition, a change in status, but not an end. The living continued to owe them certain obligations, the most important that of *memoria*, remembrance. This meant not only liturgical remembrance in the prayers and masses offered for the dead for weeks, months, and years but also the preservation of the name, the family, and the deeds of the departed. For one category of the dead, those venerated as saints, prayers *for* changed to prayers *to*. These "very special dead" in the phrase of Peter Brown, could act as intercessors on behalf of the living before God.[1] But this difference was one of degree, not of kind. All the dead interacted with the living, continuing to aid them, to warn or admonish them, even to chastise them if the obligations of *memoria* were not fulfilled.

The dead were present among the living through liturgical commemoration, in dreams and visions, and in their physical remains, especially the tombs and relics of the saints. Omnipresent, they were drawn into every aspect of life. They played vital roles in social, economic, political, and cultural spheres. That such continuity ap-

---

1. Peter Brown, "Relics and Social Status in the Age of Gregory of Tours," in *Society and the Holy in Late Antiquity* (Berkeley, Calif., 1982), 222–250, and *The Cult of the Saints: Its Rise and Function in Latin Christianity* (Chicago, 1981), 69–85.

pears alien to our world is precisely the point of this book, which is intended, first, to show how very different the past was from the present and, second, to demonstrate the inner logic and reasonableness of this past.

The chapters in the first section, entitled "Reading," are methodological and historiographic, suggesting how scholars have gone about discussing the dead and the living and how perhaps this discussion could be advanced. By "reading" I mean a triple process of historical evaluation. First is the interpretation of traditional written sources in order to understand the past. Second, but equally important, is how one reads objects and actions as texts. Third is how one reads the growing literature on these issues, a literature less united by theme than fragmented by historiographic and methodological suppositions.

The second section, "Representing," explores how the dead form an important category in the representation of reality, that is, in the construction of a world in which the living and the dead are still a community. These chapters examine not just what is said about the horizons of this society but the implicit suppositions concerning the rights and roles of the dead in the control of property, in the continuation of family, and in the direction of individual and group goals. Chapter 3, which is an examination of a Carolingian vision account, suggests that the role of the dead as intermediaries between this world and the next, a role common to both Germanic and classical traditions, is progressively challenged by alternative Christian ways of communicating between these two worlds.

The third section, "Negotiating," presents the involvement of the dead and particularly of saints in the political sphere of conflict, arbitration, and negotiation. Claims and counterclaims involve the dead both as parties to conflicts and as sources of authority in their resolution. At the same time, interest groups, lay and clerical, attempt to enlist the dead as allies in advancing their claims, which are as much statements about how the world should be ordered as about the particulars of individual disputes. Here the dead are not always the central topic but, rather, form one part of the world of dispute processing.

The fourth section, "Reproducing," discusses the production and reproduction of those special dead who were the saints. How cults of saints developed, how specific locations became centers of sacred power, and how authorities attempted to readjust the landscape of the sacred all raise questions about the integration of Christian saints' cults into the lives of ordinary people. The "impresarios" of cults (to use another of Peter Brown's terms) worked with and within a broad field of meaning over which they had little control.

The final part, "Living," presents case studies of how different communities enlisted the assistance of new patrons in solving their problems. These two chapters suggest how one might "read" the broader issues of representing, negotiating, and reproducing as one analyzes the entry of specific saints into two different urban centers.

Implicit throughout are questions as to how one goes about studying the otherness of past societies and, in particular, how one gets beyond the explicit, formalized statements of values in order to read action, ritual, and practice on an equal footing with texts. The earliest portions of this book were written when the debates on the nature of "popular religion" were still flourishing and some scholars, at least, hoped to be able to distinguish clearly between "popular" and "elite" religions as parts of largely separate cultural systems. Little here supports such a dichotomous view of society. Still less, however, do I wish to suggest a harmonious and ordered culture conforming to the articulated beliefs of an ecclesiastical elite, an alternative way of understanding "medieval Christendom" which has since been proposed.[2] Rather I am examining a complex society characterized by tensions and contradictions in the varied practices and articulations that made up its system of social and cultural organization.

The fault lines in this society are not easy to trace. Clerics worked to articulate their existence within an inherited cultic language of late antique Latin, an existence that had at least as much in common with the lives of their lay brethren as with those of the church fathers. Thus their language, far from presenting a unified and unifying system of understanding, represents a fragmented attempt both to order the world by inherited categories and to express new concerns, fears, and claims at variance with this inheritance. Lacking a vernacular matrix within which to situate this discourse, I turn to descriptions

2. Representative of this tendency to define Christianity in terms of articulated belief systems is John Van Engen, "The Christian Middle Ages as an Historiographical Problem," *American Historical Review* 91 (1986): 519–552. See the pertinent criticisms by Jean-Claude Schmitt, *Religione, folklore e società nell'Occidente medievale* (Bari, 1988), 1–27.

of actions and the analysis of surviving material elements of their culture in order to establish the relationship between formal articulation and lived experience. If text is not privileged over act, and explicit meaning is taken as a point of departure, not as a destination, then understanding medieval society becomes a rather different enterprise from that in which most intellectual historians engage.

Most of these chapters originally appeared in European journals or collections. Four were published in French, one in Italian, and one in German. In making them available to a general English-language audience, I have revised them slightly, correcting or elaborating on their arguments and bringing notes and references up to date. The volume does not aim to present a comprehensive image of the dead and the living in the Middle Ages but, rather, to suggest some of the ways in which these two social groups once formed a single community.

Reading

ဆ

1 Saints, Scholars, and Society: The Elusive Goal

ಌಌ

Around 1965, scholars began to turn to the legends of the saints with high hopes and enormous effort in an attempt to breathe new life into a long-ignored body of religious texts.[1] Hagiography seemed to promise a new window into medieval religious ideals and into the lives of ordinary people. New approaches and new questions have indeed generated a tremendous growth of interest in the cult of saints among scholars across a wide spectrum of disciplines. And yet the promise of such studies remains partly unfulfilled.

The old nineteenth-century debate between scientific free thinkers and pious defenders of the legends of the saints has largely ended. Those few who continue to write cynical, debunking comments about medieval credulity or who poke fun at the seven sacred foreskins or the various heads of Saint John the Baptist venerated across Europe, seem as quaint as the pious defenders of the Provençal legends of Mary Magdalene or the miraculous transport of Saint James to Compostela. Likewise the positivist concern to separate "fact" from "fiction" in hagiography, which gave birth to the great Bollandist undertaking, has largely subsided in modern hagiographic studies. For decades it has simply not been accurate to begin a study of hagiography, as did Thomas Heffernan in an otherwise excellent book, with

1. Comprehensive discussions of the literature of hagiography, something this chapter does not aim to offer, are the bibliographic essay by Sofia Boesch Gajano in her *Agiografia altomedioevale* (Bologna, 1976), 261–300, and the introduction and bibliography prepared by Stephen Wilson in his *Saints and Their Cults: Studies in Religious Sociology, Folklore and History* (Cambridge, 1983). I am grateful to Barbara Rosenwein for her criticisms of a preliminary draft of this chapter.

the rhetorical *planctus* that until very recently hagiography has "fallen through the net of scholarly research, avoided by the historians because it lacks 'documentary' evidential status and by the literary historians because saints' lives are rarely works of art."[2] Not only have hagiographic texts received frequent, close scrutiny from medievalists for years, but they have moved from the periphery to the center of the scholarly enterprise. Perhaps the most striking example of this trend can be seen in the two books by one of America's most outstanding medievalists, Caroline Walker Bynum. In the preface to her 1982 collection *Jesus as Mother,* she defended her concentration on formal treatises on spirituality in contrast to the growing attention to artifacts, charters, and rituals attended by the laity, saying:

> The new history of spirituality is therefore in a curious situation. It has abandoned detailed study of most of the material medieval people themselves produced on the subject of religion in favor of far more intractable sources. It has done this partly from the admirable desire to correct the concentration of earlier scholarship on mainline groups . . . but partly, I suspect, from boredom and frustration with the interminable discussions of the soul's approach to God, which is the major subject of medieval religious writing. We cannot, however, afford to abandon what will always be the bulk of our information on medieval religion.[3]

Interestingly enough, her 1987 book, *Holy Feast and Holy Fast,* is based primarily on some of the most "intractable" of medieval sources, the hagiographic dossiers of late medieval saints.[4] Bynum's growing interest in hagiographic sources may reflect a realization that hagiography, rather than formal treatises and commentaries, provides "what will always be the bulk of our information on medieval religion." As Heffernan accurately points out, "The sheer number of lives of saints which survived in manuscript"[5] is enormously impressive. If, to the

2. Thomas J. Heffernan, *Sacred Biography: Saints and Their Biographers in the Middle Ages* (New York, 1988), 17.
3. Caroline Walker Bynum, *Jesus as Mother: Studies in the Spirituality of the High Middle Ages* (Berkeley, Calif., 1982), 5–6. Although Bynum includes saints' lives in her list of traditional sources, her sources for the essays in *Jesus as Mother,* in contrast to the works she characterizes as the "new approach," make little use of hagiography.
4. Caroline Walker Bynum, *Holy Feast and Holy Fast: The Religious Significance of Food to Medieval Women* (Berkeley, Calif., 1987).
5. Heffernan, vii.

lives, one adds liturgical calendars, collections of miracles, accounts of translations, martyrologies, liturgies celebrating saints' feasts, and the like, it is obvious that "most of the material medieval people themselves produced on the subject of religion" is not "interminable discussions of the soul's approach to God" but innumerable biographies of saints approaching God.

It is perhaps the large number of hagiographic sources, as much as anything else, that has led historians, increasingly concerned with the representativeness of evidence and statistical approaches to the past, to turn to them. The volumes of the *Acta Sanctorum* lure scholars with the promise of a mass of evidence not simply about saints, but about their society, if only they can find a way to use it. Anyone who has suffered over the sparseness of historical, epistolary, theological, and legal sources from the Merovingian world, for example, can appreciate the temptation to dive into the five fat volumes of saints' lives which make up the bulk of literary production from that age. But it is not only the quantity of texts that is appealing. As historians turn increasingly from the history of events to that of perceptions and values, hagiography appears a kind of source superior to almost any other, because it seems to offer images of societies' ideal types. For both reasons we have thrown ourselves into the study of these texts. The results however have, quite frankly, been disappointing. Enormous efforts have been expended, but much of what we produce is somehow vaguely unsatisfying. We should stop and take stock of where we are, what has happened in hagiography since 1965, and what formal and conceptual problems have prevented us from achieving the great promise this material seems to offer. I put forward here an admittedly subjective review of medieval Continental history focusing on hagiography, which makes no pretense to comprehensiveness.

New Directions

I date the new historical interest in hagiography to 1965 because in that year appeared František Graus's magnificent *People, Lord, and Saint in the Kingdom of the Merovingians: Studies in the Hagiography of the Merovingian Period*, a work he had completed some three years earlier. Graus is one of the last representatives of a lost world: the Germanophone Jewish Prague of high culture and scholarship. In this book, dedicated to his grandfather, "murdered at Auschwitz," and his brother, "murdered during the evacuation of Buchenwald," Graus, fully in command of a century of scholarship in German, French, Russian, and English and informed by the Marxist critique of cultural production, focuses a perceptive mind on the hagiographic literature of the early Frankish period. Two methodological perspectives mark his work as a new departure. The first is his understanding of the importance of hagiography for the study not simply of religion but of society: "For modern historiography the social function and the teaching of the legends are of particular interest. Thus the primary focus of this study concentrates especially on the attitude of the hagiographers toward the people and toward the rulers. This is a somewhat unusual point of departure for the study of hagiography. As far as I know, an exhaustive analysis of this sort has not been previously attempted, although the results will show that even the legends of the saints, and in many instances especially and only they, can become an important source of our knowledge."[6] In other words, not only can hagiography be used for incidental historical information, but it can and must be a privileged source for the study of social values. The second is his recognition that while investigating the social function of hagiography, one must never forget the essential literary nature of these texts. Understanding the formal components and traditions of this literary genre is an essential requirement for proper historical exploitation of hagiography. And a primary aspect of this literature is that it is, in part, consciously propaganda.[7] The implications of this second Grausian perspective are two. First, historians cannot avoid dealing with the formal literary tradition of the hagiographic texts with which they work; for these texts are anything but a transparent window into the everyday life of medieval people. Not only what they say about the virtues and miracles of the saints but

---

6. František Graus, *Volk, Herrscher und Heiliger im Reich der Merowinger: Studien zur Hagiographie der Merowingerzeit* (Prague, 1965), 11: "Für die moderne Historiographie sind besonders die gesellschaftliche Funktion und die Lehre der Legende von Interesse. Das Hauptaugenmerk der Untersuchung konzentriert sich also demgemäß besonders auf die Einstellung der Hagiographen zum Volk und zu den Herrschern. Das ist ein etwas ungewohnter Ausgangspunkt zur Untersuchung der Hagiographie; meines Wissens ist eine eingehendere Analyse dieser Art bisher noch nicht versucht worden, obzwar das Ergebnis lehren wird, daß auch die Legenden, und in manchen Fällen gerade und nur sie, eine wichtige Quelle unserer Kenntnisse werden können."

7. Ibid., 39.

even their presentation of ordinary people, even of the most mundane elements of the hagiographer's world, reflect other hagiographic texts and traditions that cannot be ignored. Historians thus
must be formalists. But second and equally important, literary
scholars cannot ignore the propagandistic nature of this literature.
Hagiography has an essential political dimension that escapes the
intertextuality of the literary dimension. Formalists thus must be
historians.

With these prolegomena in mind, I offer first my review of what I
see as important trends in the literature since the appearance of
Graus's book and then some suggestions for where we need to look to
solve some of the problems this cascade of work has left us. I see four
major trends in hagiographic scholarship. The first is a tendency to
move from the study of saints to that of society. Here Graus is clearly
the pioneer. Around the same time, Byzantinists such as François
Halkin and Evelyne Patlagean were opening late classical and Byzantine hagiography to use by social historians.[8] The work that gave the
greatest impetus to the functionalist tradition of hagiographic research in the English-speaking world, however, was Peter Brown's
"The Rise and Function of the Holy Man in Late Antiquity," which
appeared in 1971.[9] By placing at the very center of late antique life
figures whom political and social historians had long dismissed as
"marginal," by connecting their "religious" meaning to issues recognizable to the most secular twentieth-century intellectual, Brown not
only invented "the world of late antiquity" as a fashionable area of
research and inspired studies of holy men around the world, but he
made hagiography respectable to a generation of historians trained in
the traditions of the social sciences.

Graus and Brown were able to use hagiography for social and
political history because they broadened their perspective, examining, instead of a particular saint, many saints and their hagiographic
dossiers. This move from individual to collective is the second, related
trend in hagiographic scholarship. It has near predecessors in the
pioneering work of the Belgian Pierre Delooz which appeared in a

---

8. François Halkin, "L'hagiographie byzantine au service de l'histoire," *XIIIth International Congress of Byzantine Studies* [Oxford, 1966], (London, 1967), 11, 345–354;
Evelyne Patlagean, "A Byzance: Ancienne hagiographie et histoire sociale," *Annales: ESC* 23 (1968): 106–126.
9. Peter Brown, *Journal of Roman Studies* 61 (1971): 80–101.

series of publications between 1962 and 1969.[10] Excellent mono-
graphs on individual cults continue to be produced, such as David W.
Rollason's *The Mildrith Legend*,[11] the essays on Elizabeth of Thuringia
published by the University of Marburg in 1981,[12] and Dominique
Iogna-Prat's work on the hagiographic dossier of Saint Maïeul.[13] The
trend toward broader documentary bases is clear, however, and is not
an entirely new phenomenon. In 1908, Ludwig Zoepf published his
book on tenth-century saints' lives, in which he sought to understand
the *Zeitideen* of the age through a systematic analysis of its hagiography.[14] Like Zoeph, some of these more recent historians are looking
for social ideals in hagiographic production. Joseph-Claude Poulin,
in his work on Carolingian hagiography in Aquitaine, puts it thus:
"By their actual lives or by the deeds attributed to them, the saints
incarnated the moral ideals of their epoch. Thus their lives can serve
as an attempt to reconstitute the ideal model of a given society."[15] In
his book on thirteenth-century saints, Michael Goodich sought the
same kind of ideal: "The present study of thirteenth century sainthood, on the other hand, is more concerned with the saint himself as
an ideal cultural type. While his character was presented to youth as
an object worthy of emulation, whose life embodies the noblest ideals
of his age, at the same time the saint's development reflects the social
and political conflicts which engaged his contemporaries."[16] André

10. Pierre Delooz, "Pour une étude sociologique de la sainteté canonisée dans l'Eglise
    catholique," *Archives de sociologie des religions* 13 (1962): 17–43, "Notes sur les
    canonisations occitanes à l'époque de la croisade des Albigeois," *Annales de l'Institut
    d'études occitanes* 4, em. ser. 1 (1965): 106–112, and *Sociologie et canonisations* (Liège,
    1969).
11. David W. Rollason, *The Mildrith Legend: A Study in Early Medieval Hagiography in
    England* (Leicester, 1982).
12. *Sankt Elisabeth: Fürstin, Dienerin, Heilige Aufsätze, Dokumentation, Katalog* (Sigma-
    ringen, 1981). Other important studies of particular saints are found in Sofia
    Boesch Gajano and Lucia Sebastiani, eds., *Culto dei santi. Istituzioni e classi sociali in
    età preindustriale* (Aquila, 1984).
13. Dominique Iogna-Prat, *Agni immaculati: Recherches sur les sources hagiographiques
    relatives à Saint Maïeul de Cluny, 954–994* (Paris, 1988).
14. Ludwig Zoepf, *Das Heiligen-Leben im 10. Jahrhundert* (Leipzig, 1908), esp. chap. 3,
    "Das Heiligen-Leben, ein Spiegel der Zeitideen."
15. Joseph-Claude Poulin, *L'idéal de sainteté dans l'Aquitaine carolingienne d'après les
    sources hagiographiques, 750–950* (Laval, 1975), 3–4: "Par leur vie réelle ou par les
    hautes faits qu'on leur prête, les saints ont incarné l'idéal morale de leur époque.
    Leurs biographies peuvent donc servir à un essai de reconstitution du modèle idéal
    d'une société donnée."
16. Michael Goodich, *Vita Perfecta: The Ideal of Sainthood in the Thirteenth Century* (Stutt-
    gart, 1982), 3.

Vauchez too was searching in his book on canonizations for the saint as "the person who is the eminent illustration of the ideas of sanctity that the Christians of a given time held."[17] In contrast, whereas Goodich and Vauchez announced the ideal as their focus, Donald Weinstein and Rudolph Bell attempted in 1982 to assess 864 saints spanning seven hundred years of Western Christian sanctity, asking who they were, how they came to pursue spiritual perfection, and how their society dealt with them.[18] What distinguishes all these works from those of earlier scholars such as Zoepf is the prosopographic methodology these historians apply; their reliance, to at least some extent, on statistics; and their attempts to recover not simply religious, but social, ideals.

Third, as historians have gone beyond research on individual saints, they have also gone beyond the study of *vitae* and *passiones*, what Heffernan, perhaps after Zoepf, terms "sacred biography." They now examine additionally, or even particularly, other kinds of texts such as collections of miracles; accounts of translations, *adventus*, and elevations; liturgies; and hymns, on the one hand, and sanctorales, martyrologies, legendaries, exempla collections, and other collective works on the other. As Martin Heinzelmann explains, the first group differs from *vitae* and *passiones* in that while "the rule of the *exemplum* of a life in accord with the standards of sanctity is at the center of hagiographic biography, the *testimonium* of miracles, that is, the glory of the patron in eternity, stands at the center of *translationes*."[19] Some of these works such as Benedicta Ward's *Miracles and the Medieval Mind* or the more comprehensive and enlightening work on some five thousand miracles by Pierre-André Sigal, *Man and Miracle in Medieval France*, focus primarily on the meaning of miraculous in medieval society.[20] As Sigal expresses it, "To the study of the miraculous according to theoretical definitions, one must add a study

17. André Vauchez, *La sainteté en Occident aux derniers siècles du Moyen Age d'après les procès de canonisation et les documents hagiographiques* (Rome, 1981), 8: ". . . un homme qui est l'illustration éminente des idées que les chrétiens d'un temps donné se sont fait de la sainteté."
18. Donald Weinstein and Rudolph M. Bell, *Saints and Society: The Two Worlds of Western Christendom, 1000–1700* (Chicago, 1982), 1.
19. Martin Heinzelmann, *Translationsberichte und andere Quellen des Reliquienkultes*, Typologie des sources du Moyen Age occidental, 33 (Turnhout, 1979), 102.
20. Benedicta Ward, *Miracles and the Medieval Mind: Theory, Record and Event, 1000–1215*, 2d ed. (Philadelphia, 1987); Pierre-André Sigal, *L'homme et le miracle dans la France médiévale, XIe–XIIe siècle* (Paris, 1985).

of the miraculous in its daily reality through the testimony of those who were the object or the witness of a miracle."[21] Henri Platelle has shown the ways miracle collections reflect legal practice and disputing mechanisms.[22] Others, such as Michel Rouche and especially Ronald C. Finucane, have attempted to use miracle collections to study physical and psychological health in medieval society.[23] Vauchez's monumental work on sanctity is based largely on yet another kind of serial record, the inquisitions *de fama et sanctitate,* or canonization cases, conducted from the thirteenth through fifteenth centuries. Erika Laquer has drawn on the rich dossier compiled in the course of an extended legal process to examine the cult of Saint Eloi of Noyon during the thirteenth century.[24] William Christian's *Local Religion in Sixteenth-Century Spain,* perhaps the most successful examination of truly popular relationships between people and their patrons, is based entirely on the questionnaires sent by Philip II to the towns and villages of New Castile to investigate local religious and historical traditions.[25]

Just as these nonbiographical texts are receiving new attention, so too are collective texts, which are being analyzed not simply in terms of their components but as units. An outstanding example is Alain Boureau's *Golden Legend,* in which the author undertakes to examine a type of hagiographic genre, the vulgar Dominican legendary, which must be read, as he says, "both in its banality and in its singularity."[26]

21. Sigal, 10: "A l'étude du miracle selon des définitions théoriques il faut donc ajouter une étude du miracle dans sa réalité quotidienne à travers les témoignages de ceux qui ont été l'objet ou le témoin d'un miracle."

22. Henri Platelle, *Terre et ciel aux anciens Pays Bas: Recueil d'articles de . . . Platelle publié à l'occasion de son élection à l'Académie royale de Belgique* (Lille, 1991).

23. Michel Rouche, "Miracles, maladies et psychologie de la foi à l'époque carolingienne en Francie," in *Hagiographie cultures et sociétés, IVᵉ–XIIᵉ siècles,* Proceedings of a symposium at Nanterre and Paris, May 2–5, 1979 (Paris, 1981), 319–337; Ronald C. Finucane, *Miracles and Pilgrims: Popular Beliefs in Medieval England* (London, 1977).

24. Erika J. Laquer, "Ritual, Literacy and Documentary Evidence: Archbishop Eudes Rigaud and the Relics of Saint Eloi," *Francia* 13 (1985): 625–637.

25. William Christian, *Local Religion in Sixteenth–Century Spain* (Princeton, N.J., 1981). Other studies of hagiography in the context of local religion are Paolo Golinelli's *Culto dei santi e vita cittadina a Reggio Emilia, secoli IX–XII* (Modena, 1980), and *Indiscreta sanctitas: Studi sui rapporti tra culti, poteri e società nel pieno medioevo* (Rome, 1988). My own *Furta Sacra: Thefts of Relics in the Central Middle Ages,* 2d ed. (Princeton, N.J., 1990) also focuses on nonbiographical hagiography.

26. Alain Boureau, *La Légende dorée: Le système narratif de Jacques de Voraigne (†1298)*

Boureau's systematic study of the *Golden Legend* from formal, structural, and rhetorical perspectives brings us to the fourth trend in recent hagiographic work, the recognition of the critical problems of genre, of rhetoric, and especially of intertextuality. As Gabrielle Spiegel points out, the "linguistic turn" leads directly to the "prisonhouse of language."[27] We should not pretend that Jacques Derrida has revealed something radically new to us: that hagiography reproduces hagiography rather than some putative reality. Hippolyte Delehaye pointed this out in 1905 in his *Legends of the Saints*,[28] although because he wrote in plain, comprehensible language, his message was perhaps not as clear as that of Derrida. Medievalists have returned to this warning with a vengeance, deconstructing hagiographic texts into their constituent literary and rhetorical echoes until little remains. Perhaps the most thoroughgoing example of this is Friedrich Lotter's life of Severinus of Noricum (†482).[29] Under his careful analysis the *Vita Severini*, long considered the most important document for the history of late fifth-century Noricum, proves a pure tissue of rhetorical topoi and textual borrowings, incapable of telling us anything, not only about Severinus, but about Noricum in the fifth century.

In brief, then, and with many omissions, this appears to be the general trajectory of work by historians on saints and society: a focus away from the saints and toward the society in which they were sanctified; a focus shifted from *vitae* to other sorts of hagiographic texts; a tendency to study collectivities and serial records; and a growing recognition that these texts are not transparent windows into the saints' lives, their society, or even the spirituality of their age.

(Paris, 1984), 12. Also showing appreciation of the importance of legendaries both in Latin and in the vernacular are the 1983 conference proceedings from Montréal: Brenda Dunn-Lardeau, ed., *Legenda aurea, sept siècles de diffusion: Actes du colloque international sur la Legenda aurea, texte latin et branches vernaculaires* (Montreal, 1986); and Sherry L. Reames, *The Legenda Aurea: A Reexamination of Its Paradoxical History* (Madison, Wis., 1985).

27. For a survey of the implications of the new historicism for medieval history, see Gabrielle Spiegel, "History, Historicism and the Social Logic of the Text in the Middle Ages," *Speculum* 65 (1990): 59–86.

28. Hippolyte Delehaye, *Les légends hagiographiques* (Brussels, 1905).

29. Friedrich Lotter, *Severinus von Noricum: Legende und historische Wirklichkeit*, Monographien zur Geschichte des Mittelalters 12 (Stuttgart, 1976).

New Problems

What has gone wrong, then, with this effort? Even as we have pursued the saints and their society, we have too often lost sight of what a
hagiographic text is, what an author is, and what the society—whose
values an author is purportedly reflecting in his or her text—is. We
have reconceived the hagiographic genre according to modern classi-
fications and divisions. We have lumped hagiographers into a fairly
homogeneous group of authors whose collective "mind" we purport
to study, and we are seduced by our created text and invented author
into thinking that they represent an equally fictitious society.[30]

To rediscover what a hagiographic text is, one begins not with the
Acta Sanctorum or even the *Monumenta Germaniae Historica* but with
the manuscript collections of major European libraries. Before we
talk about the content of these texts or impose on them our own
systems of classification and organization, we need to understand the
systems of organization, use, and categorization of those who wrote,
copied, and collected them. Let me offer a few examples from
eighth-, ninth-, and tenth-century hagiographic manuscripts I have
studied in Paris, Brussels, and Munich. A codicological examination
of these manuscripts as artifacts suggests some important hypotheses
about the diverse nature of hagiographic production and its meaning
in the early Middle Ages.

Some, a minority, are prepared by a single hand or as a single
program and contain interrelated texts, for example: the ninth-
century Bibliothèque nationale MS lat. 5387, a manuscript of 191
folios containing, in order, *Sermones sancti patrum*, *Correctiones patrum*,
and the *Sententiae patrum;* or Bibliothèque royale (Brussels) MS.
8216-18, a copy of the *Vitae patrum* written in 819, begun "in hunia in
exercitu anno d. 819" and finished at Saint Florian. CLM (Munich)
1086 is an early ninth-century manuscript from the diocese of Eich-
stätt containing the lives of Bonifatius, Wynnebald, and Willibald.

---

30. It is to reestablish the nature of hagiographic texts in the context of their production, use, and circulation that François Dolbeau, Martin Heinzelmann, and
Joseph-Claude Poulin have initiated the project Sources hagiographiques de la
Gaule (SHG). See their preliminary report, "Les sources hagiographiques narra-
tives composées en Gaule avant l'an mil (SHG): Inventaire, examen critique,
datation," *Francia* 15 (1987): 701–731. The first example of the results of this
project is the remarkable study by Heinzelmann and Poulin, *Les vies anciennes de
sainte Geneviève de Paris: Etudes critiques* (Paris, 1986).

More common are manuscripts composed of miscellaneous portions of originally separate books or pamphlets bound together sometime between the ninth and eleventh centuries. For example, CLM 18546b from Tegernsee is composed of at least two manuscripts: the first, written in southern Germany in the ninth century, contains the *passio* of Cosmas and Damian, the *Visio Wettini*, the *Passio viti Modesti et Crescentiae*, while folios 37 through 197 contain hagiographic texts written in Tegernsee in the eleventh century.[31] Bibliothèque nationale MS lat. 1796 contains, in its first 75 folios, Saint Jerome's *Adversus Jovinianum;* then two folios of a treatise on the seven deadly sins; followed by a *Vita Fulgentii* that, from its faded condition, obviously spent considerable time as the first folio of a different manuscript containing the *vita* and the epistles of Fulgentius. Bibliothèque nationale MS lat. 5596, although entirely of the ninth century, contains the life of Saint Remigius, the *Liber historiae Francorum*, and then a miscellaneous series of texts including excerpts from Jerome, Augustine, Gregory the Great, and others. One could go on endlessly. The point is that hagiographic manuscripts were created in a wide variety of ways that suggests a spectrum of uses and purposes as well as modes of production. Passionaries and lectionaries, more or less connected to the development of the Roman martyrology or regional martyrologies, provide one kind of structure within which texts found their meaning. Some collections, such as Bibliothèque nationale MS lat. 2204, contain hagiographic texts by a single author, in this case Gregory of Tours; or lives of types of saints, such as the lives of female saints in Bibliothèque nationale in MS lat. 2994a; or single saints, as in the same collection's MS lat. 13759, which concerns Martin of Tours. In his analysis of manuscript collections containing Merovingian saints' lives, Wilhelm Levison found still other principles of organization, including regional collections and visions.[32] Still other hagiographic texts appear in manuscripts we would consider primarily historical or even medical. Bibliothèque nationale MS lat. 11218 begins with the "passions of Saints Cosmas and Damian, physicians" and announces, "The Lord will have mercy on whomever is ill

---

31. C. E. Eder, "Die Schule des Klosters Tegernsee im frühen Mittelalter im Spiegel der Tegernseer Handschriften," *Studien und Mitteilungen zur Geschichte des Benediktiner-ordens und seine Zweige* 83 (1972): 8–155.

32. Wilhelm Levison, "Conspectus codicum hagiographicorum," *MGH SSRM* 7:529–706.

and has this passion read above them." The passion is followed by a medical treatise attributed to the saints' mother.[33] Some manuscripts, such as Bibliothèque nationale MS lat. 2832, which contains the *Translatio SS Cypriani Sperati, et Pantaleonis,* contain florilegia collected by individuals and intended for their own use. In this case, the *translatio* is one of a series of texts in a manuscript that belonged to Bishop Florus of Lyons.[34] Others, as indicated by the division of texts into readings, were obviously used for liturgical purposes, probably in chapter, although they would not be classified today as liturgical manuscripts.[35]

These associations, these contexts, within which hagiographic texts are embedded must be our points of departure for understanding one level of meaning of hagiography in medieval society. We cannot understand the "ideal of sanctity" purportedly espoused by such texts if we separate them from these specific contexts. If we want to understand values reflected in the hagiography of a period, texts must be seen in relation to the other texts with which they were associated, read, or gathered, not in relation either to timeless views of Christian perfection or simply to other contemporary hagiographic texts. The meanings of texts change over time. The meaning, for example, of the lives of saints Euphrosyna and Pelagia preserved along with thirty-four other ascetic texts intended for a female monastic community of the ninth century is different from the meaning of these same *vitae* when contained within a lectionary. The *passio* of Cosmas and Damian means one thing at the head of a medical treatise, something else in Bibliothèque nationale MS lat. 10861, an Anglo-Saxon passionary.

What can be said about specific texts and their various meanings is also true of groups of texts. Poulin, Goodich, Vauchez, and others look for ideals of sanctity at different epochs by examining texts produced during the periods that they study. But an examination of the manuscript traditions within which these texts are embedded as

33. E. Wickersheimer, "Une vie des saints Côme et Damien dans un manuscrit médical du IXe siècle suivie d'une recette de collyre attribuée à la mère des deux saints," *Centaurus* 1 (1950): 38–42.

34. Célestin Charlier, "Les manuscrits personnels de Florus de Lyon et son activité littéraire," *Mélanges E. Podechard* (Lyons, 1945), 71–84, esp. 83.

35. For example, Paris, BN MS lat. 13760, composed of various ninth- and tenth-century manuscripts, including one containing a *Translatio S. Vincentii* divided into twelve readings.

well as the process of copying, reordering, and revising texts suggests that to appreciate the ideals of an epoch, we must take all the hagiographic texts of the time into account. When meaning changes with context, the difference between author and copyist disappears; for copying, excerpting, and rearranging old texts is just as significant as composing new ones. Poulin's study of the ideal of sanctity in Carolingian Aquitaine should perhaps have examined not only the lives of saints written in Aquitaine by Aquitainians during this period but also those recopied, abridged, organized into lectionaries and passionaries, and inserted into martyrologies. Is it fair to consider Michael Goodich's list of 518 "thirteenth-century saints" as reflective of the ideal of sanctity of that century when the *Golden Legend* of Jacques de Voraigne, by far the most popular hagiographic text of the late thirteenth and fourteenth centuries, contains only the lives of four of these saints? Can we study the changing spiritual values of the later Middle Ages through the processes of canonization in the manner of André Vauchez if the *Golden Legend* includes only 6 percent of the saints canonized between 993 and its redaction around 1265? I think not. Such studies are not really of the values of "their contemporaries" (Bynum), or "their societies" (Poulin), or "their age" (Goodich), and still less of the "medieval mind" (Heffernan). If such abstractions exist at all, they can be approached only through the total production and consumption of the hagiography of their day, not through an artificially designated "creation." The author of original texts has no privileged position as interpreter of the values of his or her age. The notion, dear to Mikhail Bakhtin and Aaron Gurevich, that somehow the ideals of the audience, the listener, are invisibly present "in the utterance itself,"[36] can be asserted but not demonstrated. As Roger Chartier has argued, Bakhtin's world can be turned upside down because listener or reader can take fragments (in our case, texts) and give them new meaning by embedding them in other systems of meaning.[37]

What then are the images presented in such selective bodies of hagiography? Although scholars may organize them according to

---

36. Mikhail Bakhtin, "Problema teksta," *Voprosy literatury* 10 (1976): 122–51, cited by Aaron Gurevich in *Medieval Popular Culture: Problems of Belief and Perception* (Cambridge, 1988), 35.

37. Roger Chartier, "Intellectual History and the History of Mentalités: A Dual Reevaluation," in his *Cultural History* (Ithaca, N.Y., 1988), 39–40.

modern criteria, such as texts written in a particular period or lives of
saints who lived within certain chronological boundaries, they are, as
Graus reminded us a quarter of a century ago, propaganda: they are
not simply reflective but programmatic. The production of hagiography, that is, not only the authoring of texts but also their copying and
dissemination, was intentional action, even if its consequences, the
uses to which these texts were put, were not intended by the producers. Nor was this intention essentially, or sometimes even inciden-
tally, "designed to teach the faithful to imitate actions which the
community had decided were paradigmatic," as Heffernan has suggested.[38] *Imitatio* is not a constant goal of hagiography, and the example of a life in conformity with that of Christ is not necessarily the
message of the hagiographer. As Chiara Frugoni reminds us, for
Bonaventura, even Saint Francis was to be venerated, not imitated.[39]
This purpose is especially true of much early medieval hagiography
and of the lives selected for insertion into the popular edifices of later
medieval legendaries such as the *Golden Legend*. The saint begins
perfect, his or her perfection inherited from a saintly family, as is
often the case in Merovingian hagiography, or predestined, in Carolingian.[40] Thus the virtues of the saint appear even before birth, and
difficulties, temptations, and conflicts serve not to perfect but only to
manifest perfection already present. These are not lives to be emu-
lated but rather to be admired. They glorify God; they do not provide
models for mortals.

A better sense of the intentionality behind hagiographic production can be gained by examining, instead of the "ideals of a society,"
the particular situation in which the producers—meaning authors,
copyists, and compilers—functioned. In a sense, the answer to the
question Why did they write? is simple: they sought to glorify God.
But in glorifying God, they also glorify the individual saint, the place
he or she lived or was buried, the community where God chose to be
glorified through his saints. Glorification is one of the major pro-
pagandist roles of hagiographic production, and it too can be seen
both in the writing of hagiographic texts and in their dissemination as
evidenced by the codicological tradition.

38. Heffernan, 5.
39. Chiara Frugoni, "Saint Francis: A Saint in Progress," in *Sancta, Sanctus: Studies in
    Hagiography*, ed. Sandro Sticca (Binghamton, N.Y., in press).
40. On inheritance and predestination see Poulin, 101–102, nn. 8 and 9.

Hagiography was always occasional literature. The production of *vitae, translationes,* and the like was always precipitated by some specific need external to the life of the saint or the simple continuation of his or her cult, a need external to the intertextuality of the work itself but which would render the text comprehensible. These occasions varied enormously. As Brown has suggested in the case of Merovingian *passiones,* composition might be necessitated by challenges to the importance of particular saints.[41] In the Carolingian period, veneration of saints lacking *vitae* or *passiones* was condemned by regional councils; and of course, as papal involvement in canonization grew, official recognition of cults demanded appropriate dossiers. But other factors also influenced hagiographic production and provided occasions for hagiographic writing, occasions that affected the text itself. To understand a hagiographic work, we must consider the hagiographic tradition within which it was produced; the other texts copied, adapted, read, or composed by the hagiographer; and the specific circumstances that brought him or her to focus this tradition on a particular work. The text stands at a threefold intersection of genre, total textual production, and historical circumstance. Without any one of the three it is not fully comprehensible.

The hagiographic production of Otloh of Saint Emmeram illustrates this intersection. One of the most remarkable monastic figures of the eleventh century, Otloh was born in the area of Freising and educated in Tegernsee but spent most of his life at Saint Emmeram in Regensburg, a career interrupted by a dispute that led him to Fulda for some years.[42] Through his long career he was constantly involved in writing, pausing, as he says, but rarely, only on feast days or at other appropriate times. In his autobiographical *Liber de tentationibus suis et scriptis* he discusses his writings, using the same verb, *scribere,* to describe both composing and copying.[43] The distinctions among com-

41. Peter Brown, *The Cult of the Saints: Its Rise and Function in Latin Christianity* (Chicago, 1981), 82.

42. On Otloh see Bernhard Bischoff, "Otloh," in *Die Deutsche Literatur des Mittelalters: Verfasserlexikon,* ed. Karl Langosch, 3 (Berlin, 1943), cols. 658–670, and "Literarisches und künstlerisches Leben in St. Emmeram," *Studien und Mitteilungen zur Geschichte des Benediktiner-ordens* 51 (1933): 102–142, reprinted in his *Mittelalterliche Studien: Ausgewählte Aufsätze zur Schriftkunde und Literaturgeschichte* (Stuttgart, 1981), 2:77–115; and Helga Schauwecker, *Otloh von Sankt Emmeram: Ein Beitrag zur Bildungs- und Frömmigkeitsgeschichte des 11. Jahrhunderts* (Munich, 1964).

43. Although he does speak of three separate activities, which took all of his time: "legere, scribere, aut dictare."

posing (*dictare*), revising (*emendare*), and copying, although clear, are
not radical. He lists not only his compositions but also the most
important books he has copied through his life time: one less than
twenty missals, three Gospel books, two lectionaries, and four *matuti-
nales*. His writings include sermons, a book on visions, a guide to the
spiritual understanding of the material world, a sort of personal
autobiography, and at least five *vitae* and a *translatio*. While listing his
writings, he states explicitly when and why he wrote many of them.[44]
The lives of saints Nicholas and Wolfgang he wrote at the request of
brothers of Saint Emmeram before his departure. During this same
period he wrote a life of Saint Alto as well as various poems dedicated
to this saint. At Fulda, he reworked the life of Saint Boniface at the
request of his hosts. Back at Saint Emmeram, he was encouraged by a
member of his community and also by Adalham, a monk of the
monastery of Saint Magnus, to write a life of Saint Magnus.

   Otloh's *Vita S. Altonis*, described by Max Manitius as "in itself entirely worthless" and "devoid of content."[45] illustrates the relationship
between such occasional writing and the main stream of the producer's thought. Alto was thought to have been an Irish monk who
established his monastery at Altenmünster early in the eighth century. Aside from a tradition that Pepin the Short granted him the land
on which the monastery was built and that Saint Boniface had been
present at the consecration, nothing was known of him or the history
of his monastery. The *vita* was presumably written at the request of
the nuns of Altenmünster to defend their right to draw water from a
well at the monastery which, according to tradition, Boniface had
insisted should only be used by men. A fundamental issue was probably a dispute over continuing rights to the monastery claimed by the
monks of the Welf monastery at Wingarten. By insisting that the nuns
were not allowed to draw water, the monks perpetuated their own
claims to possession of the monastery.

   Otloh's *vita* presents Alto as an archetypal monastic founder on the

---

44. *PL* 146: 55d–56a. He does not claim authorship of the most famous hagiographic
   text attributed to him, the "Translatio S. Dionysii Areopagitae"; see Andreas
   Kraus, *Die Translatio S. Dionysii Areopagitae von St. Emmeram in Regensburg* (Munich,
   1972).
45. Max Manitius, *Geschichte der lateinischen Literatur des Mittelalters* 2 (Munich, 1928),
   101.

model of Columbanus, Gallus, Pirmin, and others. Boniface, apprised of the foundation by a vision, rushed to participate in the consecration and, requested by Alto not to exclude women altogether from the site, forbade them to visit or draw water from the well.[46] Later, after the monastery had fallen into decay, Alto appeared to a venerable layman demanding that he tell Count Welf II (d. 1030) to reestablish the monastery. This was done, but later Irminda, the count's widow, replaced the community of men with one of women.[47] In 1056 the nuns petitioned for permission to use the well, and the culmination of the *vita* is an argument in their favor addressed directly to the nuns. Boniface had intended the prohibition so that monks and women would not mingle. Now that there were no men present, the prohibition should be understood differently. In scripture, *vir* applied not only to men but to all who practiced "virile virtue." Thus, for example, the psalmist speaks to all humans when he says, "Act manfully (*viriliter agite*) and your heart will be comforted, all you who hope in the Lord."

Here we see, first, a hagiographic tradition, that of the Irish monastic founder. Second, the account of Boniface's being admonished to hurry to the consecration of the monastery is echoed in Otloh's own life of Boniface, where Boniface is told by a vision of Saint Michael to proceed to the consecration of the monastery of Ordorf in Thuringia. The two texts thus reflect each other in the consistent manner in which the one common figure, Boniface, is presented. Third, the vision by which Welf is instructed to rededicate the monastery parallels Otloh's interest in visions elsewhere in his writings, particularly in his *Liber visionum*.[48] This collection in turn reflects back to both the *Vita Bonifacii* and the *Vita Altonis* by including Boniface's letter to Eadburga with its description of a vision seen by a monk of Wenlock.[49] The inclusion of Boniface's letter in the *Liber visionum* reflects Otloh's use of his letters in the saint's life; for there he stated that one finds no

46. *MGH SS* 15.2:843–846.
47. The actual origins of the monastery and the role of the Welf family are unclear; see Karl Schmid, "Welfisches Selbstverständnis," in his *Gebetsgedenken und adliges Selbstverständnis im Mittelalter: Ausgewählte Beiträge* (Sigmaringen, 1983), 430, for the competing tradition of the transfer of the monks.
48. *PL* 146. 343–388.
49. Ibid., 375–380.

greater "*auctoritas*" of the saint than in the letters written or received by him,"[50] and his primary addition to the life of Boniface was the inclusion of such letters. Finally, the solution to how the saint's prohibition was to be understood directly reflects Otloh's writings on the interpretation of scripture, for example, his *Liber de cursu spirituali*. The psalmist's injunction to "act manfully" appears among the texts Otloh singles out in his *Liber proverbiorum*.[51] All of these traditions are thus brought to bear on the occasion of a defense of the rights of Altenmünster, an occasion without which the text would not merely lose much of its meaning but never have existed at all.

Thus far, this analysis connects only the hagiographic texts composed by Otloh, but the connections are far from complete. To understand Otloh's hagiographic horizons we must look at the other saints who formed part of his cultic world in Regensburg. The first set appear in an Old High German prayer, attributed to Otloh, which appeals to fifty-five saints, beginning with Mary, the archangel Michael, and then listing apostles, martyrs, confessors, and virgins.[52] Among these we find most but not all of the saints whose lives he had written, the Roman martyrs, the patrons of Saint Emmeram, and saints associated with Bavaria. The second set is the saints venerated at Saint Emmeram, who appear in the monastery's martyrology, today Augsburg Codex 1.2.2°.[53] Here we find those saints whose feasts marked the course of the monks' year, a combination, like that of the

---

50. See Wilhelm Wattenbach and Robert Holtzmann, *Deutschlands Geschichtsquellen im Mittelalter: Die Zeit der Sachsen und Salier*, pt. 1, rev. Franz-Josef Schmale (Darmstadt, 1967), 273. This is not the place to discuss the problem of Otloh's apparent forgery of some letters of Boniface.

51. *PL* 146. 335: "Viriliter agite, et confortetur cor vestrum omnes qui speratis in Domino."

52. Ibid., 428: Mary, Saint Michael, John the Baptist; the apostles Peter, Paul, Andrew, James, John; the holy innocents; the martyrs Stephan, Laurence, Vitus, Pancratius, Georgius, Mauritius, Dionysius, Gereonis, Kylianus, Bonifacius and Januarius, Hippolytus, Cyriacus, Sixtus; the confessors Emmerammus, Sebastianus, Fabianus, Quirinus, Vincentius, Castulus, Blasius, Albanus, Antoninus, Sylvestrus, Martinus, Remigius, Gregorius, Nicolaus, Benedictus, Basilius, Patricius, Antonius, Hilarion, Ambrosius, Augustinus, Hieronymus, Wolfkangus, Zenon, Simeon, Bardus, Udalricus, Leo; the virgins Petronella, Caecilia, Scholastica, Margareta. On this prayer see Eckhard Friese, "Kalendarische und annalistische Grundformen der Memoria," in *Memoria: Der geschichtliche Zeugniswert des liturgischen Gedenkens im Mittelalter*, ed. Karl Schmid and Joachim Wollasch (Munich, 1984), 469–470, and for the literature, nn. 125–127.

53. Reproduced as *MGH Libri memoriales et necrologia*, new ser. 3.

prayer, of Roman martyrs and Bavarian saints. As in the prayer, Saint Alto is conspicuously absent. This circle of sanctity, rather than some abstraction such as eleventh-century saints or those particular saints for whom occasions presented themselves for him to write their *vitae*, must be seen as the matrix within which to understand the ideal of sanctity for Otloh. Finally, we must go one step further and place this group of saints within the communal network of Otloh's monastery. This is possible by comparing the saints of his prayer to the martyrology of Saint Emmeram, in the preparation of which Otloh was personally involved.[54] Thus we finally determine the horizons of sanctity that formed part of the daily liturgical and spiritual world of the Regensburg monk.

New Solutions

Otloh's case is but one small example of how we might better approach the relationship between hagiographic production and society. We must rediscover the meaning of hagiographic texts to their producers, the interrelationships among modes of hagiographic production, the contexts of production and distribution, and the uses of the texts, and this is being done. If one were to point to where saints, scholars, and society are heading, one might single out two scholars whose approaches exemplify the best of the new hagiography. Thomas Head, in his work on the saints of the Orléanais, begins with Bishop Walter of Orléans's 871 definition of the patrons of the region and follows the interactions between these saints and the mortals in the diocese from the ninth through the twelfth centuries.[55] By making the hagiographic and liturgical production of the diocese as well as what is known of its churches and altars the focus of his investigation, Head is able to avoid the anachronistic selection of texts, misunderstanding of authorship, and invention of a public which have plagued other scholars. The second scholar is Sharon Farmer, who, like Head, focuses on a specific region and its hagiography.[56] She takes a single saint, Saint Martin of Tours, and in what she terms a

54. Ibid., 255–289.
55. Thomas Head, *Hagiography and the Cult of the Saints in the Diocese of Orléans, 800–1200* (Cambridge, 1990).
56. Sharon Farmer, *Communities of Saint Martin: Legend and Ritual in Medieval Tours* (Ithaca, N.Y., 1991).

"carefully contextualized local study" examines his function and utility in the different religious communities of the Tours area between
the eleventh and thirteenth centuries. Saint Martin meant different
things to each community: the bishop and cathedral chapter, the
monks of Marmoutier, and the canons of the Basilica of Saint Martin.
Drawing on a tradition of early modern scholarship particularly associated with Richard Trexler's work on Florence,[57] she concentrates
not simply on the language of monastic piety and spirituality or on
the saint as "ideal type" but on the particular historical contexts in
which liturgical and hagiographic practices developed as these communities turned to Martin for very particular purposes. Her analysis
extends beyond the internal life of the religious communities and
examines the relationships among these communities and between
them and lay society.

Both these scholars recognize and confront the problems outlined
above. By concentrating on a specific locale, by examining the codicological tradition, by going beyond classic hagiographic texts to look
at liturgy, miracle collections, devotional literature, and even the
evidence of archives, they avoid artificial constructs of author and
ideal. By remaining sensitive to the context in which hagiographic
production took place, they are able to understand for whom, and
often against whom, these texts were produced. Finally, in their close
readings of their texts, they find not a "medieval mind" but a variety
of minds, a spectrum of people reacting to the living tradition of the
saints in their midst.

And yet, even while recognizing the importance of these two fine
books, I realize that something is lost. First, we have narrowed our
scope to the point that the broader meaning of medieval hagiography
cannot be answered until we have dozens of such microstudies. Second, while our texts have become valuable tools for understanding
local ecclesiastical politics and monastic history, we are less well informed about the relationship between ordinary laity and their local
saints. Third, we have learned little about the models of comportment
and ideals of human existence that saints seem to offer. Finally, the

57. E.g., Richard Trexler, "Florentine Religious Experience: The Sacred Image,"
    Studies in the Renaissance 19 (1972): 7–41, "Ritual in Florence: Adolescence and
    Salvation in the Renaissance," in The Pursuit of Holiness in Late Medieval and Renais-
    sance Religion, ed. Charles Trinkaus and H. A. Oberman (Leiden, 1974), 200–264,
    and Public Life in Renaissance Florence (New York, 1980).

saints themselves have disappeared. We have no better understanding of Martin, Lifardus, Maximinus, or Evurtius. These losses are perhaps necessary. And yet it is difficult not to feel some regret that the work of scholars since 1965 has not brought us a more perfect union of saints and their society.

2 The Uses of Archaeological Sources
for Religious and Cultural History

ЮС

Historians of early medieval religion, both those who work primarily with texts and those who work mostly with archaeological materials, face major conceptual and methodological problems as they attempt to reconstruct medieval religious culture.[1] Both groups of scholars are making major revisions in the image the past research has formed of religion in early medieval Europe. Nineteenth- and early twentieth-century archaeology saw a tendency to read religious significance into every aspect of early medieval excavations, particularly burial sites. Physical positions and orientations of bodies in burials, so-called sacred earth from far distant sites placed in graves, "ritual fires" identified in tombs, all were considered part of elaborate religious rites, some traced to millennia-old traditions. Likewise grave goods and ornaments were interpreted as evidence of a grossly materialistic belief in an afterlife in which weapons and utensils were necessary to maintain the status and comfort of the dead. The iconography of ornaments and engravings on weapons was "read" as evidence of tribal totems or elaborate mythologies from Eddic and saga literature. All these elements were combined in an attempt to reconstitute an image of the "religion" of the peoples studied, an image that could then be compared with that of a separate sys-

1. This chapter was first delivered as a lecture to members of the Institut für österreichische Geschichtsforschung and of the Institut fur Ur- und Frühgeschichte of the University of Vienna. I am grateful to Heinrich Fichtenau and Herwig Friesinger for the opportunity to discuss common issues of history and archaeology with them and their colleagues and students. I am especially indebted to Falko Daim and Bailey K. Young for their advice and suggestions.

tem—Christianity, thought to be responsible for the disappearance of "pagan" practices. When these same elements were found in burials from later periods, they were viewed as pagan survivals, of interest only to folklorists and polemicists against the superstition of the medieval church.[2]

More recent archaeology has seen the beginnings of a progressive demystification of archaeological finds.[3] In part this has resulted from a more scientific methodology: careful attention to stratigraphic relationships, to problems posed by possible tomb disturbances or intrusive material, and to accurate distinction between organic decomposition and actual fires lit in graves. Thus many notions about sacred earth and fires, positions of bodies, and the like have been modified or discarded. Likewise archaeologists hesitate to label such observed patterns as orientations of graves, grave goods, shells found in Germanic graves, and vessels that may have contained food or water as "rituals," realizing they may simply result from half-understood habits. Unusual physical conditions such as seated burials are now plausibly explained as results of rigor mortis rather than as survivals of prehistoric burial rites. Grave goods have been explained in terms of legal rights to uninheritable property (*Herrengeräte*) or simply symbols of status rather than in terms of a belief in their utility in an afterlife. Perhaps most important, improved chronology of Germanic burials in Western Europe has resulted in the indisputable constatation that the process of "Christianization," at least in the Frankish world, is at variance with the chronology of the disappearance of such so-called pagan burial customs as north-south orientation, furnished graves, burials with coins, and so on. Christians buried in the crypts of Frankish churches continued to be furnished with weapons, jewelry, tools, and even food well into the seventh century at, for example, Cologne and Morken. Likewise row cemeteries (*Reihengräberfelder*) continued to be used even later. One must begin to ask if it is really appropriate to speak of "Christian" or "pagan" burials at all. In general, then, archaeologists are increasingly reluctant to read into

2. Edouard Salin, *La civilisation mérovingienne d'après les sépultures, les textes et le laboratoire*, 4, *Les croyances* (Paris, 1959).
3. Bailey Young, "Merovingian Funeral Rites and the Evolution of Christianity: A Study in the Historical Interpretation of Archaeological Material" (Diss., University of Pennsylvania, 1975), and "Paganisme, christianisation et rites funéraires mérovingiens," *Archéologie médiévale* 7 (1977): 5–81.

archaeological artifacts or burial customs evidence of specific religious beliefs that can be characterized as pagan or Christian, much
less to attempt reconstructions of the content of Germanic belief
systems from such materials.

Historians who work exclusively with written sources have experienced a similar retreat from clear, unified visions of early medieval
religion. Medieval Christianity appears less and less as the monolithic,
articulated belief system one finds in religious texts. Following the
lead of anthropologists who study traditional non-European cultures,
historians are realizing that the distinctions between doctrine or nor-
mative guides and religion-as-cultural-system are enormous.[4] If
archaeology cannot provide a comprehensive image of Germanic
religion, written texts cannot provide an adequate image of lived
Christianity. On the level of "everyday religion" or "popular religion,"
textual historians are not even in agreement on the meaning of
medieval religion. The traditional view of the religion lived by the
majority of laity as a vulgarization of the model imposed by the clergy
is increasingly under attack.[5] This older approach to popular religion
emphasized a two-stage process of Christianization. In the first stage,
missionaries, by destroying pagan cult objects and replacing them
with relics of saints, by baptizing pagans, and by introducing Christian ritual, were thought to have imposed Christian forms on a population that remained largely pagan. In the second stage, through the
introduction of creed and Christian morality, later ecclesiastics were
assumed to have effected an internal conversion of semipagan Europe. In this view of popular religion, so-called pagan elements survived as magic or superstition on the margins of Christianity or under
a veneer of Christianity, such as for example popular pre-Christian
festivals transformed into saints' feasts.[6]

4. For an excellent introduction to the French and Anglo-American traditions of
   cultural anthropology, see R. Girtler, *Kulturanthropologie: Entwicklungslinien, Para-
   digmata, Methoden* (Munich, 1979).
5. For useful general summary of the traditional view of popular religion, see R. Manselli, *La réligion populaire au Moyen Age* (Montreal, 1975). To understand the revi-
   sionist criticism of this approach, see the extremely sharp review of Manselli by
   Richard C. Trexler, *Speculum* 52 (1977): 1019–1022.
6. On the stages of conversion the best summary is Arnaldo Momigliano, ed., *The
   Conflict between Paganism and Christianity in the Fourth Century* (Oxford, 1963). Since
   then the study of conversion within and without the empire has moved in other
   significant directions; see Judith Herrin, *The Formation of Christendom* (Princeton,
   N.J., 1987).

Increasingly, historical anthropologists are seeing popular religion not as a vulgarization of official Christianity but as an integral aspect of a cultural system uniting a society.[7] The elements of the cultural system are shared, but each group—elites and masses, lay and clerical—articulates the system in its own way depending on the its social, political, and intellectual circumstances. Of course the articulated beliefs of intellectual elites, whether Christian theology, Germanic sagas, or Celtic oral traditions, do not always appear among the masses merely as vulgarized forms. To judge from rare but important evidence from later periods, European peasants were capable of complex speculation through which a wide variety of intellectual traditions could be united into an original, unified structure.[8] But in the culture of the early Middle Ages, and hence in those aspects of it which we somewhat arbitrarily term "religious," physical reality, action, and tradition take precedence over belief and explicit intellectual elaboration. In this cultural system, distinctions between religion and law; family and politics; habit and ritual are largely anachronistic and arbitrary. Similarly, the identification of pagan versus Christian elements is futile. Instead of attaching labels, scholars must attempt to understand how various elements—actions, objects, practices, articulations—form a unity or, conversely, coexist in a state of dissonance. Meaning must be sought neither in the popular articulations of inherited high-culture beliefs nor in relation to a pagan past but in the structure of relationships uniting these elements. This is the sense of Eoin MacWhite's "patterns of significance," which is in reality but the application to history and archaeology of Ludwig Wittgenstein's definition of meaning as use.[9] The most important meanings of human

---

7. *Anthropologie historique* is a term used by a group of French historians for their approach to studying medieval mentalities and culture. Fundamental early works include Jacques Le Goff, *Pour un autre Moyen Age* (Paris, 1977), and Jean-Claude Schmitt, *The Holy Greyhound: Guinefort, Healer of Children since the Thirteenth Century* (Cambridge, 1983). See too the more recent introduction to Schmitt's collected essays, *Religione, folklore e società nell'Occidente medievale* (Bari, 1988), 1–25.

8. See, e.g., Carlo Ginzburg, *The Cheese and the Worms: The Cosmos of a Sixteenth-Century Miller* (Baltimore, 1980).

9. Eoin MacWhite, "On the Interpretation of Archaeological Evidence in Historical and Sociological Terms," in *Man's Imprint from the Past: Readings in the Methods of Archaeology*, ed. J. Deetz (Boston, 1971), 229–231; Ludwig Wittgenstein, "Die Bedeutung eines Wortes ist sein Gebrauch in der Sprache," *Philosophische Untersuchungen* (Oxford, 1953), sec. 43; Garth Hallett, *Wittgenstein's Definition of Meaning as Use* (New York, 1967).

actions are not those explicitly stated but those that emerge from the
way society organizes its physical, social, and cultural forces to accom-
plish its goals.

Thus a new methodology must take into consideration a series of
different "meanings" that appear both explicitly and implicitly in the
structure of a society. Expressed beliefs and articulations of elite
culture present one sort of meaning. A second, deeper sort must be
found in the matrix of relationships combining objects, gestures,
rituals, and articulations—in short, in the totality of reflected and
nonreflected behavior and creation. We must not expect to find total
unity and accord; for real contradictions and oppositions must exist
to account for the "historical slippage," the process of change, in a
religious culture that is dynamic and not static. But unity and dissonance can only be perceived within relationships among all parts of
the system, not in individual elements. Any attempt to proceed from
the examination of objects in isolation from the religious system in
which they had a meaning is invalid, be the object an Avar vessel, a
Christian church, or a theological treatise.

A privileged area for the elaboration of such a model is the study of
saints' relics, particularly when they are examined not to study hagiography or saints' cults as such but to understand the roles of saints'
remains in society. From the perspective of social rather than religious
or intellectual history, this subject allows for a progression from the
study of texts, objects, and gestures, to an examination of the underlying structures uniting them, to an understanding of their place in the
structure of early medieval society. Specifically, one finds in the uses
of saints' relics an image of their role in society often at variance with
the stated explicit meanings of these objects. For example, in Chapter
5, I examine a ritual of dispute settlement first discussed by Heinrich
Fichtenau,[10] the humiliation of saints' relics to obtain justice. This
practice is one of several means by which ecclesiastical institutions
managed to bring about arbitration and dispute settlement, so it
should be seen in relation to excommunication, malediction, and
interdict.[11] Religious communities often placed their most important
reliquaries on the floor of the church, covered them with thorns or

10. Heinrich Fichtenau, "Zum Reliquienwesen des früheren Mittelalters," *Beiträge zur
Mediävistik* 1 (Stuttgart, 1975), 108–144.
11. Lester K. Little, "La morphologie des malédictions monastiques," *Annales: ESC* 34
(1979): 43–60.

sackcloth, suspended their usual services, and addressed a *clamor* to God for redress of their grievances. Analyzing the verbal and physical elements of this rite, I found a contradiction in its implicit and explicit significances. Explicitly, the monks or canons were demonstrating physically the position of undeserving humility in which the saints had been placed by their prideful enemies. The monks prostrated themselves along with the prostrate relics and addressed a prayer to God, based largely on the language of the psalms, in which they asked the Lord to strike down the proud and to raise up his saints and their ministers to their proper place. Simultaneously with this explicitly orthodox if unconventional liturgy, I found an implicit punishment of the saints for not having protected their churches as they should. The treatment of the saints, the descriptions of the cases in which the ritual was actually used, and the manner in which the successful results were described, all indicated that the saints were held responsible for the honor of the community and that when that honor was harmed, the saint was coerced through the humiliation to restore it. While the articulated interpretation of the ritual was in the orthodox Christian tradition, the implicit meaning was similar to that of widely observed popular abuses of sacred objects to obtain desired results. In these popular rites, relics or images of saints were beaten or abused because the saint was perceived as failing to do his or her duty, which was to protect the faithful. Humiliation of relics was a physical punishment of the saint for failing to protect his or her community and also a means to coerce the saint to carry out his or her responsibilities.

These results can provide a model for interpreting and juxtaposing written and archaeological sources. One must carefully distinguish the actual physical and gestural system presented by archaeological and written sources from the articulated explanations of them provided by a clerical elite that is both the bearer and, in a certain sense, the captive of a written, intellectual tradition only imperfectly assimilated to the actions not only of the masses but often of this elite as well. This apparent contradiction is discernable in two archaeological-historical problems: first, the supposed effects of conversion on the relationship between living and dead; and second, the continuity of burial practices from a civilization characterized by row burials (*Reihengräberzivilisation*) to one with medieval saint cults.

The relationship between the living and dead members of their clan has long been seen as an essential one in early medieval society. The dead constituted an age class that continued to have a role and to exercise rights in society. Archaeologists have suggested that the rich grave goods in burials of the late fifth and the sixth centuries were evidence of this importance in *Reihengräberzivilization*, in which ancestors played the role of intermediaries between the clans and tribes (*Stämme*) and the gods. Kurt Böhner and others have thus suggested that Christianity, which greatly lessens the role of the dead, must have had a fundamental impact on the place of the dead in Merovingian society: "The profound change that Christianity brought with it is shown most clearly in relationships with the dead. Although these were once the ancestors of many clans and tribes in which they lived on and enjoyed divine or quasi-divine veneration, they now entered the eternality of Christ."[12] As evidence of this essential transformation in the relationship between the living and their ancestors, Böhner cites the famous passage from the *Vita S. Vulframni* in which the Frisian duke Radbod, about to be baptized, asked Wulfram, the bishop of Sens, whether there were many Frisian kings and princes in heaven or in hell. Wulfram answered that, since these *praedecessores* had not been baptized, they were surely in hell.[13] Hearing this pronouncement, the duke determined not to be baptized, saying that he could not do without the company of his predecessors. This text, whose importance for historical ethnography Herwig Wolfram has emphasized,[14] seems however to contradict other archaeological evidence which, as we shall see, places in doubt Böhner's interpretation both of the process of Christianization and of the account in the *Vita Vulframni.*

Radbod died in 719 and, it can be assumed, joined his damned ancestors. Around the same time or shortly before in the Rhineland near Alzey, Frankish nobles were founding a funerary chapel that served to preserve the memory of their pagan ancestors and, in a

---

12. Kurt Böhner, "Rheinische Grabmäler der Merowingerzeit als Zeugnisse frühen fränkischen Christentums," in *Das erste Jahrtausend,* ed. V. Elbern, 2 (Düsseldorf, 1964), 676: "Die tiefe Veränderung, die das Christentum mit sich brachte, zeigt sich uns am deutlichsten in dem Verhältnis zu den Toten: Waren diese einst die Ahnen der vielen Sippen und Stämme, in denen sie weiterlebten und göttliche oder götterliche Verehrung genossen, so gingen sie jetzt in die unendliche Ewigkeit Christi ein."
13. *Vita Vulframmi, MGH SSRM* 5:668.
14. Herwig Wolfram, *Geschichte der Goten* (Munich, 1979), 457 n. 43.

functional sense, to Christianize them retroactively. The church in question was Flonheim, and the careful archaeological study of the site by Hermann Ament suggests that the theological response to Radbod's question presents only part of the eighth-century reality.[15]

On December 29, 1876, the parish church of Flonheim was destroyed by fire. During reconstruction between 1883 and 1885 it was discovered that the church stood on the foundations of a much older building, within which were found ten Frankish burials. The oldest portion of the church was a tower, the upper part of which was Gothic; the lower, Romanesque of ca. 1100. The foundations of the Romanesque portions of the tower, a crypt, were older still; and directly under this oldest portion of the old church, was a particularly rich Frankish burial. Ament's examination of the grave goods and his reexamination of the nineteenth-century report of the excavations, demonstrated that the graves were part of a larger row cemetery, traces of which had been found in the 1950s elsewhere in the village. Moreover, the ten graves appear to be those of members of a wealthy clan. That in the Merovingian period a family would erect a mortuary chapel in which to bury its members would hardly be remarkable; examples are common, particularly even earlier ones in the more Romanized areas of Europe. What is remarkable, however, is that Ament's dating of the burials, particularly of grave 5, the one directly under the tower, is so early that the burials must predate the erection of the church (first mentioned in 764/767) and, in the case of grave 5, the conversion of Clovis. Ament compares this grave—in its depth (greater than the others at Flonheim), in its furnishings, and in its relation to the other graves—to grave 319 at Lavoye.[16] The rich furnishings of grave 5 include a famous gold-handled sword and other weapons and ornaments which both in their forms and variety argue conclusively for a date contemporary with the tomb of Childeric (481). Ament sees grave 5 as a founder's burial, like that at Lavoye. Around it, in the sixth and early seventh centuries, other clan members were buried. When the chapel was built, the importance of this founder's burial was still recalled, and the builders included the other clan graves within the confines of its walls. The erection of a

15. Hermann Ament, "Fränkische Adelsgräber von Flonheim in Rheinhessen," *Germanische Denkmäler der Völkerwanderungszeit* 5 (Berlin, 1970), 157.
16. Réné Joffroy, *Le cimetière de Lavoye: Nécropole mérovingienne* (Paris, 1974); on grave 319, see 95–100.

chapel over the graves of a clan and the particular position given to the clearly pre-Christian burial both strongly suggest that the continuity between pre-Christian and Christian clan members was not broken by baptism. In fact, on a physical, structural level, the founder was given a burial *infra ecclesia* after the fact, thus including him in the new Christianized clan tradition. Ament has compared the situation at Flonheim to those at Arlon, Speiz-Einigen, Morken, and Beckum and suggests that these other Merovingian churches containing Frankish burials may well be similar to Flonheim; for the chapels also appear to postdate the earliest burials.

The American archaeologist Bailey Young has compared these apparently ex post facto Christianizations to the observations of Detler Ellmers on early Swedish cemeteries and suggests that the practice of assimilating pre-Christian ancestors into the Christian cult of the dead may be detected there as well.[17] In Sweden, with the coming of Christianity, churches were generally built near the preexisting sepulchers of prominent families, and the last furnished burials are therefore older than the actual cemeteries. Elsewhere, pagan remains were moved into Christian burial spaces. The most famous Christian reburial in the North is that of the Dane Harold Bluetooth's pagan parents Gorm and Thyre at Jelling. Harold first buried his parents in a wooden chamber covered by a large mound surrounded by standing stones in the outline of a ship, giving them a traditional pagan burial. After his conversion around 960, he had his parents' remains removed to a church. Excavations of the present stone church (ca. 1100) indicate three previous wooden churches and a large, centrally placed grave containing the disjointed remains of a man and a woman obviously reburied there after the disarticulation of the skeletons. Harold's runestone explicitly announces that the monuments he created were dedicated "to his father Gorm and his mother Thyre," although it goes on to say that Harold "made the Danes Christian."[18]

In both the Frankish and Scandinavian situations, the archaeologi-

17. Detler Ellmers, "Monuments du début de christianisme en Suède," in his *L'or des Vikings* (Bordeaux, 1969), 54; Young, "Paganisme," 55.
18. Ejnar Dyggve, "The Royal Barrows at Jelling," *Antiquity* 22 (1948): 190–197, and "Gorm's Temple and Harold's Stave-Church at Jelling," *Acta Archaeologica* 25 (1954): 221–239; discussed in the context of the transition from paganism to Christianity by Else Roesdahl in *The Northern World: The History and Heritage of Northern Europe, AD 400–1100*, ed. David M. Wilson (New York, 1980), 157–158.

cal evidence seems to contradict the explicit statement of Wulfram. How is the historian to resolve this contradiction? I would suggest that it arises from two sources. The first is the difference noted above between the intellectualized articulation of belief by a clerical elite and actual societal practice, lay and clerical. The second is the way the specific circumstances of Radbod's aborted conversion color both the question and the response, making them part of a discussion of salvation in modern Christian terms, when the real issue is ethnicity and hegemony in eighth century Frankish terms.

In the case of Flonheim and similar burials, the meaning of the construction of a Christian church over a pagan tomb is implicit: the ancestors have been conjoined in the new cult as they were in the old. Conversion is not an individual, but a collective, act that involves the entire clan and people, a fact long recognized about two groups of Franks—those of Clovis's generation and their descendants. The collective nature of conversion implicitly applies to a third group of Franks as well, their ancestors. Although Gallo-Roman authors like Gregory of Tours have emphasized Clovis's conversion, that does not mean the Franks had lost respect for or interest in their pre-Christian ancestry. Witness the literature of Merovingian Frankish genealogy, the *Liber historiae Francorum*,[19] among others. Retroactive conversion is not articulated; indeed, it would be difficult to reconcile with orthodox Christianity.[20] But in the symbolic and ritual structure that solidified and expressed the values of Frankish-Christian civilization, a place was found for these ancestors. Here, as in the example of the ritual humiliation of saints I mentioned earlier, the physical juxtapositions present a meaning in a Wittgensteinian sense which was apparently accepted by the lay founders of the church at Flonheim as well as by its clerics. Perhaps, although we cannot be sure of how much they knew of its origins, even the monks of Lorsch, to whom the church was given in the 760s, perceived this meaning.

Thus the Franks of Flonheim, pagan and Christian, could keep each other company in the next life but not, apparently, Radbod and his pagan ancestors. It is tempting to cast this distinction in terms of the supposed two stages of conversion, the first represented by a

19. *MGH SSRM* 2:241–248.
20. Yet in the later Middle Ages, Plato and the emperor Trajan would be said to have been converted and redeemed after their deaths.

maximum accommodation to pagan tradition; the second (and this
would be the case of Radbod), an insistence on an inner meaning of
Christianity. In fact, this approach will hardly suffice. Frisia was, in the
early eighth century, hardly into a second phase of conversion; it was
at the first stages of a process that would take generations. Rather we
should consider the specific context of the efforts to convert Radbod
and his Frisians. Wulfram's contact with the duke was part of the
Frankish effort to subjugate the Frisians, an effort in which conversion was specifically conversion to Frankish Christianity. After Pepin
II defeated Radbod in 694, he sent Willibrord to convert Radbod and
his people. Wulfram's efforts were part of this mission.[21] Pepin's
intention was specifically to establish a Frankish political and cultural
basis in order to pacify the region. Conversion and baptism at the
hand of a Frankish bishop would have meant, then, the acceptance of
a specifically Frankish ethnic identity and the rejection of Frisian
autonomous traditions, political and cultural. Radbod would really
have cut himself off from his ancestors, but not merely by being
assured of heaven while they languished in hell; for he would have
become, in a real sense, a Frank. A similar break with their ancestors
was demanded of the Saxons during the eighth century. It is hardly
happenstance that the earliest condemnations of traditional Germanic burial sites in favor of church cemeteries was specifically directed at Saxon Christians: "We order that the bodies of Christian
Saxons be taken to the church cemeteries and not to the burial
mounds of the pagans."[22] Likewise the famous *Indiculus superstitionum*
was directed specifically at those "sacrileges at the tombs of the dead"
performed by the Saxons.[23] In the case of both the Frisians and of the
Saxons, the bonds uniting the conquered people to their independent
ancestry had to be broken because they were a source of anti-Frankish
ethnic and political identity, not simply because they were pagan in a
narrow religious sense. In the entirely Frankish contexts of Flonheim,
Arlon, Spiez-Einigen, and Morken, though, conversion did not mean

---

21. Bede *Historia ecclesiastica* 5.10; Letter of Boniface to Pope Stephen II, *Epistolae Merowingici et Karolini aevi* 1, 109, *MGH Ep* 3:395–396; Michael Tangl, ed., *Die Briefe der heiligen Bonifatius und Lullus (S. Bonifatii et Lulli epistolae), MGH Ep. selectae* no. 235; *Vita Willibrordi auctore Alcuino, MGH SSRM* 7:121; *Annales Xantenses, MGH SS* 2:220.

22. *MGH Capit.* 1.26.22:69: "Iubemus ut corpora christianorum Saxanorum ad cimiteria ecclesiae deferantur et non ad tumulus paganorum."

23. Ibid., 1.108:222–223.

the rejection of a cultural and political tradition. It meant instead the confirmation of tradition through the acceptance of a new and more powerful victory-giver, Christ. The benefits of such a conversion could be shared with the past as well as with the future.

Burial in row cemeteries was never condemned for Franks, nor did any ecclesiastical or lay legislation seek seriously to control burial rites, which, like those of marriage, remained essentially a private, familial affair. Nonetheless, these rural cemeteries, where they did not acquire a mortuary chapel and thus evolve into a churchyard, fell into disuse in the early eighth century in favor of burials under the church and, increasingly, in favor of the consecrated burial long sought in the Roman world. This desire to be buried next to the remains of saints raises a second problem in which archaeological and literary sources seem at variance: the origins and extraordinary importance of relics in medieval Western culture.

Western Christendom, indeed all Christendom, has no monopoly on relics. Corporeal remains are important in such diverse cultures as Islam, Buddhism, and Soviet Leninism, but a comparison of traditions reveals their far greater importance in Western Christianity than in any other culture. Moreover, this importance seems limited to Western Europe itself, not to the regions it colonized. Even those parts of the New World Christianized by the West have failed to develop the same reverence for corporeal remains in their forms of Christianity. Mexico, whose religious culture has been carefully studied by anthropologist Victor Turner, provides the most striking example.[24] Despite strong missionary efforts by the Spanish in the sixteenth century and despite the significance of saints in Mexican religion, no major pilgrimage is inspired by the physical remains of a saint. The small figures and images that became the focus of pilgrimages are physically in direct continuity with pre-Columbian traditions rather than with European traditions of body cults.

This singular importance of corporeal relics in the Western Church is even more striking given that its origins are impossible to discern with precision. Hagiologic studies of the origins of cults of martyrs and heroes in Jewish, Roman, and Hellenistic tradition do not explain why this devotion should in the West have become exclusively cen-

24. Victor Turner and Edith Turner, *Image and Pilgrimage in Christian Culture: Anthropological Perspectives* (New York, 1978).

tered on relics, whereas in Eastern Christianity it had as its objects not
only corporeal remains but *brandia* (relics that had been in close
contact with saints) and, most important, images. Furthermore, aside
from a possible head cult, suggested by archaeological finds at En-
tremont, no evidence has ever been presented for a comparable role
for physical remains in Germanic or Celtic religion. How then are we
to explain the extraordinary importance of physical remains to all
levels of medieval society? Obviously no single explanation suffices,
and a search for a formal cause is as inappropriate here as in any
historical problem. The cultural differences between the urban East
and the rural West; the political importance of icons in Byzantium,
which was unknown in the West; and the Eastern neoplatonic tradition that made possible the participation of the saint in his image
must all be considered in understanding the different place of relics in
the East and the West.[25] We must also, however, look behind the
articulated doctrine of the saints' cult (which is, in fact, remarkably
small in theology and law given the importance of saints) and consider relics from the perspective of acts, uses, and rituals in society
generally. Given the myriad roles of relics, they naturally served a
wide variety of social functions. They were sources of great personal
power for good or ill; contact with them, when properly achieved,
could bring cures, protection, and help of all sorts. Improper or
careless contact could result in serious injury or death.[26] Relics were
property owners, receiving donations and recognized as the proprie-
tors of the churches in which they were buried. They headed the
family of their religious institutions and were held responsible for
looking after the interests of that community. In return, their *familia*
owed them veneration, offerings, and continued cult service.[27]

Remarkable similarities emerge from a comparison of the treatment of relics (which were, after all, bodies of the dead) with that
generally accorded the dead in the *Reihengräberzivilisation*. In the
latter we find indications of a sense of perseverance of the personality

25. On these differences see Ernst Kitzinger, "The Cult of Images in the Age before
Iconoclasm," *Dumbarton Oaks Papers* 8 (1954)· 83–150; Jaroslav Pelikan, *Imago Dei:
The Byzantine Apologia for Icons* (Princeton, N.J., 1990); and Herrin, 295–343.
26. Pierre-André Sigal, "Un aspect du culte des saints: Le châtiment divin au XIᵉ et
XIIᵉ siècles d'après la littérature hagiographique du midi de la France," in *La
religion populaire en Languedoc du XIIIᵉ siècle à la moitie du XIVᵉ siècle*, Cahiers de
Fanjeaux 11 (Toulouse, 1976), 39–59.
27. Geary, *Furta Sacra*, 28–43.

of the dead that seems to have been centered on the grave. Likewise, we find the rights of the dead to own property, as indicated by grave objects buried with them, and also signs of some continued cult at the grave. These practices, including grave objects, food offerings, sacredness and inviolability of the tomb, respect for bodies, prefigure essential elements of the treatment to be accorded in the medieval period to one particular category of the dead: saints (a category that in the early Middle Ages was to include virtually all high ecclesiastics, bishops, and abbots, who were to benefit from a particular cult in their communities).[28] They alone will continue to be buried with the dress and insignia of their office and position. Their tombs, like earlier founders' graves, will become centers around which others will seek burial. They will participate in the important decisions of their families—the religious communities—through dreams and miraculous interventions. Finally, the period during which the transfer and relocation of corporeal relics became common in the West, the eighth century, is also the period that saw the final abandonment of most traditional row cemeteries.

This comparison of the two traditions suggests that the cult of relics carries on, through ritual gestures and actions, not a system of beliefs about the dead but an acknowledgment of the dead's place in society not very removed from the civilization of row burials tradition. Thus the place of noble saints in important Merovingian families, which has been of particular interest to Friedrich Prinz,[29] should be seen not so much as an innovation or a manipulation of adopted Roman Christian forms for political advantage as a prolongation and evolution of the roles played by such burials as graves 5 at Flonheim and 319 at Lavoye. Granted, the explicit meaning of these saints' tombs and of the intermediary role of saints in Christian tradition was

28. See Young's dissertation and his forthcoming work on episcopal burials in the early Middle Ages. See, specifically on Northern Italian bishops, Jean-Charles Picard, *Le souvenir des évêques: Sépultures, listes épiscopales et culte des évêques en Italie du Nord des origines au Xᵉ siècle* (Rome, 1988); and more generally, Y. Duval and Picard, eds., *L'inhumation privilegiée du IVᵉ au VIIIᵉ siècle en Occident: Actes du colloque tenu à Creteil les 16–18 mars 1984* (Paris, 1986). See also Otto Gerhard Oexle, "Memorialüberlieferung und Gebetsgedächtnis in Fulda von 8. bis zum 11. Jahrhundert," in *Die Klostergemeinschaft von Fulda im früheren Mittelalter,* ed. Karl Schmid, 1 (Munich, 1978), 136–177, esp. 161–164 and 174–177.
29. Friedrich Prinz, *Frühes Mönchtum im Frankenreich: Kultur und Gesellschaft in Gallien, den Rheinlanden und Bayern am Beispiel der monastischen Entwicklung, 4.–8. Jahrhundert* (Munich, 1965), 493–495.

certainly not the same in the eighth century as it had been for important burials in the fifth. Many practices of the later period, such as the
division and transfer of relics and the particular form taken by their
cult, had greatly evolved under the influence of Romano-Christian
traditions. Likewise the explicit meaning of episcopal burial with
insignia was hardly that of Frankish furnished burials. Unlike early
Franks, whose tombs were intended to be inviolate, bishops might
well be exhumed at the time of an official elevation and establishment
of a cult, and their insignia could attest their status for future generations. But evolution is essential for a tradition to remain vibrant.
Strong similarities between the periods should neither be attributed
to folkloric or magical elements in medieval Christianity nor considered chance occurrences just because their explicit meanings differ.
They are evidence of cultural continuity in the role of the dead as
members of a separate but still important segment of society.

   In conclusion, archaeologists and literary historians must recognize
that any study of religion in the early Middle Ages must be grounded
in the actions of early medieval societies rather than in the inherited
and poorly assimilated belief tradition of doctors of the Church or in
the equally complex and elite Germanic oral literary tradition. To
borrow an expression anthropologists have used to contrast contemporary non-western religions with postreform and counterreform
Christianity, medieval religion was not believed but danced. To understand the "steps" of this dance, the archaeologist must distinguish
the essential structures unifying his material and establish, as it were,
a model of a system of functional and representational interdepen-
dences among his sources. The textual historian must do the same.
Then the two models must be juxtaposed and combined and only
then compared with the articulated reflections of elite cultural traditions.

   This sort of juxtaposition of implicit and explicit meaning is always
difficult and subtle. An adequate examination must provide what
anthropologist Clifford Geertz calls "thick description," as complete a
reproduction of the social and cultural context as possible.[30] It must
follow the function of elements, not in the functionalist-reductionist
sense of early twentieth-century English cultural anthropologists but
as parts of the larger system of social meaning and process.

30. Clifford Geertz, *Interpretation of Cultures* (New York, 1973).

Despite the daunting limitations and problems, this sort of cultural-social history is the type most likely to benefit from close interdisciplinary cooperation between archaeologists and textual historians. Historians have usually looked to archaeologists for exactly the sort of answers they are least prepared to provide: specific corroboration of political narrative-historical hypotheses. Rudolf Moosbrugger-Leu's objection that "archaeology has primarily the ethnic aspects of life before its eyes, history has rather the political"[31] is less and less true. More and more, historians look at structures, long-term processes, and other issues previously the domain of ethnography and anthropology. As a result, we are increasingly aware of the limits of our written sources and also that, for much of our work, archaeology is indispensable. The time has come when we can and must work together.

31. Rudolf Moosbrugger-Leu, *Die Schweiz zur Merowingerzeit: Die Hinterlassenschaften der Romanen, Burgunder und Alemannen* 2 (Bern, 1971), 14: "Der Archäologe hat in erster Linie das Ethnikum vor Augen, der Historiker eher das Politikum."

Representing

❧

3 Germanic Tradition and Royal Ideology in the Ninth Century: The *Visio Karoli Magni*

ﻹﻉﻝ

*At illi dixerunt: Domine, ecce duo
gladii hic. At ille dixit eis: Satis est.*

On October 25, 1806, Napoleon entered the tomb of Frederick II, the Prussian king who had died twenty years before, and took the sword that lay at his side.[1] This action was a symbolic revenge for French defeats at the hands of the Prussians in the previous century. The sword, still displayed at the Musée de l'armée, became a symbol of France's victory over Prussia and of Napoleon's superiority to the great Prussian king. More than one thousand years earlier, according to Paulus Diaconus, Giselpert, the duke of Verona, entered the tomb of Alboin, the great Lombard king who had led his people into Italy some years before his murder in 572, and took the sword he found there. Paulus Diaconus went on to explain that, because of this act, Giselpert was wont to boast to ignorant people that he "had seen Alboin."[2]

---

1. I thank in particular Ernst A. Ebbinghaus, Dieter Geuenich, Richard Landes, Claude Lecouteux, Jacques Le Goff, Robert E. Lerner, Daniel Popp, and Jean-Claude Schmitt for their generous assistance.
2. *Pauli historia Langobardorum* 2.28, *MGH SSRL* 88–89: "Huius [Alboin] tumulum nostris in diebus Giselpert, qui dux Veronensium fuerat, aperiens, spatham eius et si quid in ornatu ipsius inventum fuerat abstulit. Qui se ob hanc causam vanitate solita aput indoctos homines Alboin vidisse iactabat." Although the date of this event is unknown, Duke Giselpert witnessed the foundation charter of the monastery of Santa Maria in Verona in 743; see Luigi Schiaparelli, ed., *Codice Diplomatico Longobardo* 1 (Rome, 1929), no. 83, 248.

These two deeply symbolic actions demonstrate the enduring significance of the complex topics of this chapter: first, the relationships
between this world and the next, particularly between the living and
the dead in the eighth and ninth centuries; second, the symbolic
importance of the sword in the warrior society of the early Middle
Ages, especially as a symbol of legitimacy; and third, the role of oral
tradition in early medieval propaganda, specifically, the incorpora-
tion of Germanic traditions into the Carolingian propaganda of the
later ninth century.

Visio Karoli Magni: Text and Transmission

The text that is central to my analysis is the *Visio Karoli Magni*,[3] a most
unusual vision, which has escaped the attention of scholars examining medieval visionary literature.[4] Indeed, the text fits but poorly into
the general typology of medieval visionary literature.[5] The anony-

---

3. The *visio* is found in two manuscripts: Frankfort on the Main, Stadt- und Universitätsbibliothek MS Barth. 67, fols. 131r–132r, and Paris, BN MS lat. 5016, fols.
159v–160v. Both are of the twelfth century. The text was edited from the two
manuscripts by Philipp Jaffé, *Bibliotheca rerum Germanicarum* 4 (Berlin, 1867), 700–
704. A new edition is provided in the appendix to this chapter.

4. This may be because the *visio* is not a vision of the otherworld and hence was not
discussed by Wilhelm Levison in his "Die Politik in den Jenseitsvisionen des fruhen
Mittelalters," *Aus rheinischer und fränkischer Frühzeit* (Düsseldorf, 1948), 229–246. It
is ignored by Michel Aubrun in his "Caractères et portée religieuse et sociale des
'Visiones' en Occident du VIᵉ au XIᵉ siècle," *Cahiers de civilisation médiévale* 23
(1980): 109–130; by Hans Joachim Kamphausen, *Traum und Vision in der lateinischen Poesie der Karolingerzeit*, Lateinische Sprache und Literatur des Mittelalters 4 (Frankfort, 1975); and by Peter Dinzelbacher, *Vision und Visionsliteratur im
Mittelalter*, Monographien zur Geschichte des Mittelalters 23 (Stuttgart, 1981). On
the tradition uniting visions and commemoration of the dead, see Franz Neiske,
"Vision und Totengedenken," *Fruhmittelalterliche Studien* 20 (1986): 137–185. One
of the few twentieth-century scholars to note the vision is Heinrich Fichtenau, who
made excellent use of the text in his *Das karolingische Imperium: Soziale und geistige
Problematik eines Großreiches* (Zurich, 1949), 185–186. Following Fichtenau, Andrew W. Lewis, in his *Royal Succession in Capetian France: Studies on Familial Order
and the State* (Cambridge, Mass., 1981), 5, mentions the *visio* as an early expression
of the fear that the Carolingian dynasty might end.

5. On medieval visions, in addition to the works cited above, see the still extremely
useful Francis X. Newman, "Somnium: Medieval Theories of Dreaming and the
Form of Vision Poetry" (Diss., Princeton University, 1962), and Constance B.
Hieatt, *The Realism of Dream Visions: The Poetic Exploitation of the Dream-Experience in
Chaucer and His Contemporaries* (The Hague, 1967). Although the latter deals
primarily with late medieval poetic visions, the first two chapters, 14–33, provide a
general introduction to medieval dream form and to the tradition of dream interpretation.

mous author explains that the emperor Charles always kept lamps and writing tablets next to his bed so that he could write down whatever he saw in his dreams that was worthy of memory. One night as he was going to sleep he saw a certain *persona* approach him holding a sword. The emperor asked this specter's identity and was told, "Receive this sword sent from God to protect yourself, and read and remember what is written on it because it will be fulfilled in time." Charles examined the sword and found four words written on its blade: near the hilt was RAHT; then came RADOLEIBA; then NASG; then, near the point, ENTI. On awakening, he wrote the words on his tablet.

The next morning he recounted the dream to his advisers and asked them what meaning it might have. None could tell him, and Einhard, "the one who was said to be wiser than the others," responded, "He who had transmitted the sword to you will also reveal to you its meaning." Accepting this advice, Charles proceeded to explain the meaning of the dream himself. The sword itself signified the power he had received from God and with which he had been able to subjugate so many enemies by his arms. RAHT signified the abundance of all things Charles enjoyed even above that which his parents had had. RADOLEIBA indicated that in the time of his sons some of the peoples who had been subjugated would be lost, and the sons would not enjoy the abundance of riches that he had. NASG foretold the time of their sons: they would raise tolls out of greed and would oppress travelers and the Church, despoiling them in order to reward their own followers. The last word, ENTI, indicated the end, which could be understood as either the end of the world or the end of Charles's lineage.

The author explains that this story was told by Einhard to Rabanus Maurus, who, after becoming archbishop of Mainz, was wont to tell it to many people, among whom was the author himself. He goes on to explain that the prophecies have been fulfilled: In the time of Louis the Pious, the Bretons and Slavs revolted and the kingdom was impoverished. After Louis's death, his sons Lothair, Pepin, and Louis the German began to spread NASG throughout the kingdom, as Pepin despoiled monasteries in Aquitaine and Lothair did the same in Italy. The bishops of the entire Roman church, he explains, had written a letter to Louis asking through Bishop Witgar how the Church might have peace. This letter, he says, is still to be found in the archives of the Church of Saint Martin.

The origins and circulation of this remarkable account remained

closely associated with the kingdom of Louis the German and in
particular with Mainz. The Church of Saint Martin mentioned in the
text is Saint Martin's built in Mainz around the end of the sixth
century and razed in 978 by Archbishop Willigis, who began construction of the present cathedral on its site.[6] Presumably the author
was a cleric of that church and the manuscript, which contains the
visio as well as the works of Jonas of Orléans, was copied in Mainz.
The Paris manuscript, which contains in addition to the *visio* the
chronicle of Regino of Prüm and the *Visio cuiusdam pauperculae
mulieris,* probably came from the monastery of Saint Afra in Augsburg, although its provenance is contested.[7] It may be that the vision
was believed to have been seen at Nieder-Ingelheim, a favorite palace
of Charles's in the Maingau located nine kilometers from Mainz.
By the fourteenth century, Nieder-Ingelheim was claiming to be
Charles's birthplace, and a charter of Charles IV from 1354 mentions
that there Charles the Great had received a sword from an angel.[8]
Thus the tradition of the vision seems to have remained alive in the
region in which it was formed.

The composition of the text can be dated approximately. It seems
to have been written during the reign of Louis II, the German (840–
876), as it presents him as the only son of Louis the Pious, to whom
the Church could turn for protection. The bishop Witgar was apparently bishop of Augsburg from 858 to 887. The letter (presumably a
synodal petition no longer extant) would then have been produced
between 858 and 876. The negative view of the ecclesiastical policies
of Lothair in Italy and more particularly of Pepin in Aquitaine suggests that the text may well have been written during the episcopacy
of Archbishop Charles of Mainz, the son of Pepin I of Aquitaine.
Charles fled to the kingdom of Louis in 854 and was archbishop from
856 until his death ten years later.[9] Since the author of the *visio* says

6. Eugen Ewig, "Die ältesten Mainzer Patrozinien und die Fruhgeschichte des
   Bistums Mainz," in *Spätantikes und fränkisches Gallien: Gesammelte Schriften, 1952–
   1973,* 2, ed. Hartmut Atsma, Beihefte der Francia 3/2 (Munich, 1979), 154–181,
   esp. 154–157.
7. See Wolf-Rüdiger Schleidgen, "Die Überlieferungsgeschichte der Chronik des
   Regino von Prüm," in *Quellen und Abhandlungen zur mittelrheinischen Kirchenge-
   schichte* 31 (Mainz, 1977), 35.
8. H. Falk, "Verschiedene Addenda," *Neues Archiv* 11 (1886): 617.
9. Theodor Schieffer, "Karl von Aquitanien," in *Festschrift Albert Stohr* (Mainz, 1960),
   2:42ff.; Karl Ferdinand Werner, "Die Nachkommen Karls des Großen," in *Karl der*

that the letter is "still" in the archives of Saint Martin, some time must have passed. This would place the composition of the vision around the middle of the 860s.

Such a date for a propaganda pamphlet, composed in Louis's kingdom with Germanic words incorporated, would coincide extremely well with the image of the cultivation of the theodisca lingua during Louis's reign as presented by Dieter Geuenich.[10] Contrary to the venerable tradition in Germanic philology that credits Charles the Great with having fostered the formation of a conscious Germanic political culture by encouraging the development of a "Christian literature in Germanic language"[11] and even with seeking to establish Germanic language as the basis for political unity,[12] Geuenich sees no evidence of any such linguistic program. He points out that the multiplicity of languages within Charles's empire, and particularly the numerous Germanic dialects in the eastern portions, would have doomed such a program from the start. Moreover, no evidence—aside from two famous but poorly understood statements in Einhard's *Vita Karoli* to the effect that Charles began a grammar of his maternal language and that he had collected "the ancient and barbarous songs of the acts and wars of the old kings"[13]—suggests that Charles made any attempt to create a standard Germanic language or introduce it throughout his empire, any more than he attempted to replace the various legal traditions with a unified legal system.

Große: Lebenswerk und Nachleben, 4, *Das Nachleben*, ed. Wolfgang Braunfels and Percy Ernst Schramm (Düsseldorf, 1967), 450.

10. Dieter Geuenich, "Die volkssprachige Überlieferung der Karolingerzeit aus der Sicht des Historikers," *Deutsches Archiv* 39 (1983): 104–130.

11. Helmut de Boor, *Die deutsche Literatur von Karl dem Großen bis zum Beginn der höfischen Dichtung, 770–1170: Geschichte der deutschen Literatur von den Anfangen bis zur Gegenwart* 1 (Munich, 1964), 7; cited by Geuenich, 113.

12. Geuenich, 112–113.

13. *Einhardi Vita Karoli Magni* 29, *Quellen zur karolingischen Reichsgeschichte* 1, ed. Reinhold Rau (Darmstadt, 1974), 200: "Item barbara et antiquissima carmina, quibus veterum regum actus et bella canebantur, scripsit memoriaeque mandavit. Inchoavit et grammaticam patrii sermonis." Geuenich points out that the only evidence of this grammar Einhard presents—the month and wind names Charles is supposed to have introduced—did not survive in any cultural tradition, if indeed they were introduced at all and if the statement is not simply a reflection of Julius Caesar's and Claudius's grammatical works as described in Suetonius. The *antiquissima carmina*, which philologists have long attempted to identify as texts like the Hildebrandslied, are, according to Geuenich, more likely to have been songs in praise of earlier kings of the type of the later Ludwigslied.

But while Geuenich effectively demolishes the image of Charlemagne as the father of a conscious Germanic-language tradition, he
finds exactly such a linguistic tradition in the kingdom of his grand-
son Louis the German.[14] Here, in the middle of the ninth century,
Geuenich finds abundant evidence for a self-conscious positive assess-
ment of Germanic language in liturgy, catechetics, and law. In particular he points to the gospel book of Otfrid of Weißenburg, which
was dedicated to Louis and which speaks of a Frankish people and a
Frankish land (*Frankono thiet, Frankono lant*),[15] as well as to such texts
as the old Saxon gospel book of the so-called Heliand and the gospel
harmony of Tatian, both probably produced under Louis's patronage. These and other texts indicate that in the East, after the Treaty of
Verdun, a conscious and positive appreciation of Germanic language
and tradition developed in court and ecclesiastical circles. In this
atmosphere, the elaboration of a vision text highly critical of the other
successors of Louis the Pious and incorporating Old High German
elements is entirely understandable.

If the *visio* was written during the reign of Louis the German, it was
not made up of whole cloth. What might be called the "prehistory" of
the *visio*, both that presented in the text and that which can be
surmised from its narrative elements, indicates a long and rich tradition.

The author is careful to place himself at three removes from the
story: Charles told it to Einhard, Einhard to Rabanus Maurus, and
Rabanus to the author. One could not imagine a more appropriate
series of intermediators for such a vision. Einhard, himself from
Maingau and educated at Fulda, was the primary author, who assigned to Charles the Great a lively interest in Frankish traditions. As
Geuenich rightly observes, this interest in the vernacular language
may well be a backward projection of Einhard's concerns during the
mid-820s, the period when he apparently wrote the *Vita Karoli
Magni*.[16] Karl Brunner's study of opposition to Carolingian lordship
suggests exactly what these concerns were.[17] Einhard belonged to a

14. Geuenich, 121–130.
15. Ibid., 127–128.
16. Ibid., 126. On the composition of the *vita* see Heinz Löwe, "Die Entstehungszeit
    der Vita Karoli Einhards," *Deutsches Archiv* 39 (1983): 85–103. Löwe suggests the
    most likely date of composition was 825/826.
17. Karl Brunner, *Oppositionelle Gruppen im Karolingerreich* (Vienna, 1979), esp. 66–95.
    Nikolaus Staubach, in his examination of the *vita*, "'Cultus divinus' und karo-

group of east Frankish aristocrats who had held considerable power during the last years of Charles's reign but who had, almost without exception, fallen from grace under Louis the Pious. The *vita* was an attempt to present the reconciliation of Louis's father with the old Frankish aristocracy, which had been so important to the Carolingian family's rise to power, as a model for Louis's own dealings with this group. Brunner sees Einhard's mention of Charles's supposed interest in the *barbara et antiquissima carmina* of the Franks as evidence of this old East Frankish aristocracy's identity.[18] Whether or not Einhard had actually reported the vision to Rabanus Maurus, the likelihood that he would have been interested in such a story is therefore great.

The connection with Einhard is even stronger when one considers the way in which the story complements Einhard's famous description of Charles's efforts to write. The *Vita* records that "he was accustomed to keep writing tablets and notebooks in bed under his pillows, so that when he had free time he could train his hand at forming letters."[19] As it stands, this passage makes the emperor look rather ridiculous, as though he expected to have the gift of writing arrive in the middle of the night. If, however, one compares this description to that of the *visio*, it makes much more sense: the tradition of keeping writing materials by one's bed to record dreams had been common since antiquity, and as Heinrich Fichtenau points out, even if Charles was not able to write Latin, he could certainly have recorded four Old High German words.[20] Thus the description in the *visio* not only accords with, but perhaps even clarifies, an otherwise obscure passage of the *vita*.

Einhard is said to have told the story to Rabanus Maurus, another member of an East Frankish aristocratic family from the region of

---

lingische Reform," *Fruhmittelalterliche Studien* 18 (1984): 547–581, esp. 562–571, concentrates on the significance of Charles's religious program for his *administratio regni*. Although his analysis of the text is appropriate to his subject.he focuses on Charles without considering the text's significance in the time Einhard composed it.

18. Karl Brunner, 95. Lowe's redating of the composition of the *vita* does not invalidate the essence of Brunner's argument establishing political context because, as Löwe himself points out (102), the implicit criticism of Louis is as appropriate for the mid-820s as for the early 830s.

19. *Einhardi Vita Karoli* 25, 196: " . . . tabulasque et codicellos . . . in lecto sub cervicalibus circumferre solebat, ut, cum vacuum tempus esset, manum litteris effingendis adsuesceret."

20. Fichtenau, 185–186.

Fulda and Mainz.[21] It was at Fulda during the abbacy of Rabanus that Tatian's gospel harmony was translated.[22] Later, as archbishop of Mainz during the reign of Louis the German, Rabanus was in a position to play a leading role in the formation of an East Frankish political culture. Thus Rabanus Maurus, like Einhard, was exactly the sort of person likely to have transmitted a story such as that of the *visio* in order to credit Charlemagne with an interest in Germanic language and tradition.

To summarize, I have suggested that the *Visio Karoli Magni* belongs to the propaganda literature of the kingdom of Louis the German and that it was probably transmitted orally by leading members of the East Frankish aristocracy through the ninth century in the region of Mainz before being written down in its present form in the 860s. Its purpose is clear: to glorify the role of Louis the German as defender of the Church at the expense of his Carolingian relatives to the south and west, and it does so in a way particularly appropriate in a kingdom rapidly developing a self-conscious pride in its Germanic tradition. But while this purpose clearly explains the form of the *visio* as it now exists, embedded in the text are elements indicating that before it received its final form, it had satisfied other purposes. An analysis of the prehistory of the tradition through what might be called "textual archeology" suggests that before serving as East Frankish political propaganda, the vision had at least two quite different meanings, both related to very ancient classical and Germanic visionary traditions.

But what precisely are the Germanic traditions on which it is based? Most of the visionary literature of the Carolingian period follows a fairly conservative Christian form presented by Gregory the Great in his *Dialogues* and modeled closely on the visionary tradition in the Old Testament. Someone is taken up into the otherworld and sees the rewards of the blessed and the torments of the damned,[23] or souls of

---

21. On the Otakar family of Rabanus Maurus, see Reinhard Wenskus, *Sächsischer Stammesadel und fränkischer Reichsadel* (Göttingen, 1976), 137–138; Karl Brunner, 84–85; Eckhard Freise, "Studien zum Einzugbereich der Klostergemeinschaft von Fulda," *Die Klostergemeinschaft von Fulda im früheren Mittelalter* 2 (Munich, 1978): 1032–1034; Raymund Kottje and Harald Zimmermann, eds., *Hrabanus Maurus, Lehrer, Abt und Bischof* (Mainz, 1982).
22. Geuenich, 118 and bibliog. in n. 64.
23. On the typology of such visions see Levison; Dinzelbacher, esp. 90–117; and Kamphausen.

those suffering purgation return to ask prayers or to warn former friends to mend their ways.[24] Kings have been frequent recipients of dreams and visions ever since the pharaoh of Genesis 41, and the image of Charles receiving divine communications through dreams anticipates not only the Charlemagne of the *Chanson de Roland* but Louis the German himself, who in 874 had a vision of his father, Louis the Pious.[25] Such kings do not normally explain their own visions, however, nor do the visions include such elements as swords with Germanic inscriptions. The *Visio Karoli Magni* clearly includes not only four Germanic words but also elements of a cultural tradition alien to that of Christian visionary literature—a tradition that, as we shall see, the author himself either did not understand or attempted to disguise.

The Classical and Germanic Traditions in the *Visio Karoli Magni*

To understand the *visio*, we must consider its constituent elements as they appear in classical, Christian, and Germanic dream theory and tradition. To do this, we must first separate the vision itself from its introduction and interpretation. In the *visio* the dream proper begins with the description of the moment of the vision, that is, just as Charles began to fall asleep.[26] The text then describes the vision of the *persona* approaching the emperor,[27] and Charles's fearful question-

24. On the return of the dead in visions in late antiquity and the early Middle Ages, see Jacques Le Goff, *La naissance du Purgatoire* (Paris, 1981), 111–114 and 123–131, for a discussion of Gregory the Great's *Dialogi* 4, the locus classicus for such returns. In the eleventh and twelfth century, the instances of individual dead or groups of the dead returning in visions increased to such an extent that Jean-Claude Schmitt can speak of "l'invasion des revenants" in his "Les revenants dans la société féodale," *Le temps de la réflection* 3 (1982): 287.
25. *Annales Fuldenses*, a. 874, *MGH SSRG* 7:82. On the close relationship between visionary traditions and monastic *memoria*, see Karl Schmid, "Bemerkungen zur Anlage des Reichenauer Verbrüderungsbuches: Zugleich ein Beitrag zum Verständnis der 'Visio Wettini,'" in *Landesgeschichte und Geistesgeschichte: Festschrift für Otto Herding zum 65. Geburtstag*, ed. Kaspar Elm, Eberhard Gönner, and Eugen Hillenbrand (Stuttgart, 1977), 24–41, reprinted in Karl Schmid, *Gebetsgedenken und adliges Selbstverständnis im Mittelalter: Ausgewählte Beiträge* (Sigmaringen, 1983), 514–531. On the vision of Louis the German, see 529–531. See below, note 37.
26. All quotations from the *visio* are to the edition given in this chapter's appendix: "Quadam uero nocte, cum membra ad quiescendum in lectulo collocasset ac se sopori dedisset."
27. ". . . uidit quandam personam ad se uenientem, euaginatum gladium in manu tenentem."

ing, and the specter's response.[28] It concludes with the four words and where they were inscribed on the blade.[29] Let us consider each of these elements in turn.

The moment of Charles's dream, as he was just beginning to sleep, was recognized in classical and Christian tradition as a moment of frequent dreams but not usually of true, divinely inspired visions. Normally, the visionary is keeping a vigil or has fallen ill and may even appear dead when a divinely inspired vision takes place. The early part of sleep is, on the contrary, the most likely time for demons to visit men to torment them.[30]

If true Christian visions do not usually arrive in light sleep, we may perhaps understand in part Charles's fear upon seeing a vision: its timing might suggest a diabolic origin. But in Germanic tradition, and particularly in saga literature, it is exactly this moment when one is most likely to experience true visions.[31] Thus the moment of the vision suggests that in its setting the tradition is perhaps closer to Germanic than to classical oneirology. This hypothesis is strengthened by an analysis of the vision itself.

Charles sees a *persona* approaching him. Certainly one is tempted to

28. "Quem cum metuens interrogasset quis esset uel unde uenisset, audiuit ab eo in responsione huiuscemodi uerba: 'Accipe,' inquit, 'gladium istum pro munere tibi a Deo transmissum, et scripturam in eo digestam lege ac memoriter retine; quoniam statutis temporibus implebitur.'"
29. "Quem cum accepisset formamque illius diligenter inspexisset, uidit quatuor loca in eodem litteris exarata. In primo quidem loco iuxta capulum eiusdem mucronis erat scriptum 'RAHT' [Paris, BN mS lat. 5016: Rant], in secundo uero 'RADOLEIBA' [Paris, BN mS lat. 5016: Radeleba], in tercio 'NASG,' in quarto iuxta cuspidem eiusdem ensis 'ENTI.'"
30. Macrobius, in his *Commentarii in somnium Scipionis* 1.3, 7, ed. Jakob Willis (Leipzig, 1970), 10, terms the *visio* experienced "cum inter uigiliam et adultam quietam in quadam, ut aiunt, prima somni nebula adhuc se uigilare aestimans, qui dormire uix coepit," a phantasma unlikely to have a value in predicting the future. On the moment of Christian *visiones* see Aubrun, 112.
31. On dreams in saga literature generally see W. Henzen, *Über die Traume in der altnordischen Sagaliteratur* (Leipzig, 1890); and Georgia Dunham Kelchner, *Dreams in Old Norse Literature and Their Affinities in Folklore* (Cambridge, 1935). Kelchner provides texts and translations of the major dreams: 114, for Thorkel's vision of the dead Skefil in the *Reykdæla Saga,* as edited by V. Ásmundarson (Reykjavik, 1897), translated in Thule 11 (Jena, 1921), 19.347–349; 113–117, for that of Vilhjálmur in the *Sigurðar Saga;* 118, for the visions in the *Sturlunga Saga;* 106–108 for the *Landnámabók.* For some sagas, more modern, post-Kelchner editions are available; see *Sigurðar Saga,* ed. Agnete Loth (Copenhagen, 1963); *Sturlunga Saga,* ed. V. Guðni Jónsson (Reykjavik, 1948); and *Landnámabók* ed. Jakob Benediktsson (Reykjavik, 1968).

identify this figure as an angel; for the identification was explicitly made in the later Middle Ages, and it accords well with official Carolingian visionary tradition. As Hans Joachim Kamphausen has pointed out, in the discussion of dreams and visions in the *Libri Carolini*, composed in the late eighth century, dreams (*somnia*) are said to be caused by demons, whereas true visions are the work of angels.[32] The figure's identity is not so specified in the text, however, and the selection of vocabulary and word order suggests another interpretation. There is no compelling reason to translate *quaedam persona* as "a certain person." *Persona* would be superfluous, particularly since at Mainz the author was probably a native German speaker who would not be translating a vernacular form of *une certaine personne*, as one might expect in a Romance region. The *persona* could be understood several ways in the classical and Germanic traditions. According to Macrobius, the person who carries an *oraculum* is "a relative or some other holy and serious personage or a priest or even a god."[33] In the Christian tradition, the agent was normally an angel or possibly a saint, as in the tenth-century *Vita Oudalrici* that I examine in more detail below.[34] By the twelfth century, the person transmitting the *oraculum* was expected to be an angel or a priest. William of Conches, in the "Glosae super Macrobium," offers the possibility that messages might be transmitted "through some honest person as an angel or a priest."[35]

But whereas the later Christian tradition would ultimately reserve the role of intermediary for the Church or God's messengers, the

32. Kamphausen, 56; *Libri Carolini sive Caroli Magni capitulare de imaginibus, MGH Concilia* 2, suppl., 3.26.
33. Macrobius, 1.3, 8: " . . . parens vel alia sancta gravisve persona seu sacerdos vel etiam deus."
34. *Gerhardi vita Sancti Oudalrici episcopi, MGH SS* 4:389.
35. William of Conches, "Glosae super Macrobium," Rome, Vat. Palat. 953, fol. 84ra: "Per ammonitionem aliqui honeste persona utpote siue ipsius uel angeli uel sacerdotis Deus nobis denunciat quid sit futura"; and Rome, Vat. Urb. 1140, fol. 15: " . . . per ammonitionem siue aliquis honeste persone utpote angeli siue sacerdotes reuellant futura." This progressive transformation of the vision of the dead toward a clerical model is developed by Jean-Claude Schmitt in his "Temps, folklore, et politique au XIIᵉ siècle: A propos de deux récits de Walter Map *De Nugis Curialium* I 9 et IV 13," in *Le temps chrétien de la fin de l'Antiquité au Moyen Age, IIIᵉ–XIIIᵉ siècles*, Colloques internationaux du Centre national de la recherche scientifique 604 (Paris, 1984), 489–515; in his "Les revenants," 285–306; and in his "Les morts qui parlent: Voix et visions au XIIᵉ siècle," in S. Auroux et al., eds., *La linguistique fantastique* (Paris, 1985), 95–102, 66–72.

early medieval tradition was closer to that of Macrobius, wherein,
particularly in the case of kings, one finds that previous generations
appear to warn their descendants. Gregory of Tours knew that
the Merovingian king Childebert II had seen the dead Chilperic I
chained by three bishops and thrown into a cauldron of boiling water,
a warning to his successor.[36] Louis the German, as I have mentioned,
had himself been visited in 874 by his father, Louis the Pious, who
asked the son to have prayers said for his father's soul and warned
him not to follow the father's example of sins of commission and
omission. This vision is particularly interesting because of its familial
significance. It took place after Louis the German's visit with his father's former advisers at Seligenstadt, the monastery Einhard founded.
From the monastery he went to spent Lent in Frankfurt and there
experienced the visitation. In particular, Louis the Pious was said to
have disregarded twelve directives (*capitula*) transmitted to him by the
archangel Gabriel, who had appeared to Einhard's notary, Ratlei-
cus.[37] Once more Einhard appears in the context of Carolingian
visions, this time, a vision about a vision. Moreover, after Louis commanded that, in accord with the instruction given him by his father,
monasteries throughout the kingdom should pray for the repose of
the late emperor's soul, he met successively with his nephew Louis in
Italy and his sons Karlman and Louis in Forchheim. The vision thus
seems to have led to a family rapprochement, making it not only
political but familial.

The tradition preserved in the saga literature likewise knew of the
appearance of the dead to admonish, warn, or advise living descen-

36. *Gregorii episcopi Turonensis libri historiarum* 10, MGH SSRM 1.1, 2d ed., 329.
37. *Annales Fuldenses*, a. 874, 82: "Diebus autem quadragesimae, cum negotiis secu-
    larium rerum depositis orationi vacaret, vidit quadam nocte in somnis genitorem
    suum Hludowicum imperatorem in angustiis constitutum, qui eum hoc modo
    latino affatus est eloquio: 'Adiuro te per dominum nostrum Iesum Christum et per
    trinam maiestatem, ut me eripias ab his tormentis, in quibus detineor, ut tandem
    aliquando vitam possim habere aeternam.'" Einhard's account of Ratleicus's vision
    appears in his *Translatio et miracula Sanctorum Marcellini et Petri*, MGH SS 15.1:252–
    253. This vision clearly follows the ecclesiastical visionary tradition in form, but the
    transmission of twelve *capitula* suggests that in content it is related to the tradition
    of supernatural letters either fallen from heaven or transmitted by angels, which
    was widespread across late antiquity and the early Middle Ages. On this tradition
    see Joseph-Claude Poulin, "Entre magie et religion: Recherches sur les utilisations
    marginales de l'écrit dans la culture populaire du Haut Moyen Age," in *La culture
    populaire au Moyen Age*, ed. Pierre Boglioni (Montreal, 1979), 121–143, esp. 126–
    130.

dants. Generally, the apparitions in saga visions were of six types: fetches, that is, the inherent souls of living persons, which normally appeared to others as animals; familial spirits, usually female *hamingja*, more rarely, masculine *spamathr* (prophets); trolls or dwarfs; gods; living persons; or the dead. Of the latter the most significant was the *draugr*, or barrow-dweller,[38] the most famous example of which is in the *Hervarar Saga ok Heidreks* (although that spirit does not appear in a vision). Hervùr awakens her dead father, Angantyr, to obtain his magic sword Tyrfing, which has been buried with him. Angantýr parts with the sword only reluctantly, and he provides as well a warning: "You shall bear offspring who in after days shall wield Tyrfing and trust in his strength" and "Tyrfing, daughter, shall be ruin and end of all your family."[39]

This text bears a striking resemblance to the *visio:* a person from the otherworld transmits a sword that is the symbol of trust but that also prophecies the ultimate destruction of the family. Does *persona* in the *visio* retain something of its ancient meanings of *larva* or mask? Is it an ancestor, perhaps Charles Martel or Pepin the Short, appearing to Charles in his birthplace to warn him of impending danger to his stirps? Perhaps the text is intentionally ambiguous. But beneath the final version of the *visio* we can see an earlier, familiar tradition, one in which the past, present, and future generations of the royal stirps are brought together just as in the vision of Louis the German.

This second stratum is not the only preexisting one that can be glimpsed through the final text. A third can be uncovered by examining the sword in the visionary and propaganda tradition of barbarian society.

The Symbolism of Swords in Early Medieval Society

In both the *Hervarar Saga* and the *visio* the prophecy is intimately connected with the transmission of a sword. The long sword, termed the *spatha* or *ensis*, was a weapon of great importance in the migration period and the early Middle Ages. The techniques of manufacture and the great investment of scarce steel made the sword more than a

---

38. Kelchner, 17–53, 62–72.
39. *Hervarar Saga ok Heiðreks konungs*, trans. Christopher Tolkien (London, 1960), vv. 33 and 32, p. 16. As Kelchner points out, the *draugr* most often appears to the conscious rather than to those asleep, although both occur.

weapon: it was a symbol of status and an object of magic. Its magical character was in fact one of its essential qualities; it had not only its own name (Tyrfing in the *Hervarar Saga,* Durendal in the *Chanson de Roland*) but its own personality as well. Its forces came from the otherworld, either supernatural or subterranean, and in Germanic tradition it was frequently the handwork of dwarfs. As Edouard Salin has pointed out, the fate of the user was attached to his sword in a mysterious and fatal way, and thus anyone able to acquire the sword thereby acquired the virtues of its previous owner.[40] Small wonder then that the sword attained a privileged role as a symbol of legitimacy and continuity.

This tradition far antedated the Germanic migrations, however. In his description of the Scythians, Herodotus told of a golden battle-ax (*sagaris*), which fell from the sky along with a golden plough, a golden yoke, and a golden cup.[41] The two eldest sons of Targitaus, the first inhabitant of the region, each attempted to pick them up, but the objects caught fire at their touch. Only the youngest son, Colaxais, was able to handle the objects, and the others accepted this as a sign that he was to rule the entire kingdom.[42] Herodotus goes on to relate that the gold objects were still guarded by the king of the Scythians with the greatest care.

40. Edouard Salin, *La civilisation mérovingienne, 3, Les techniques* (Paris, 1957), 57–112, esp. 108. In the classical literature of practical handbooks of oneirology, one finds, however, no particular significance attached to swords. In the three editions of the *Somniale Danielis* edited by Lawrence T. Martin, *Somniale Danielis* (Frankfort, 1981), only one version, current in England from at least the tenth century, specifically mentions swords: "Gladium ferre et de ipso ludere: anxietatem significat," 131.

41. Herodotus *Histories* 7:64 describes the *sagaris* as the typical weapon of the Scyths: "Σάκαι δὲ οἱ Σκύθαι περὶ μὲν τῆσι κεφαλῆσι κυρβασίας ἐς ὀξὺ ἀπηγμένας ὀρθὰς εἶχον πεπηγυίας, ἀναξυρίδας δὲ ἐνεδεδύκεσαν, τόξα δὲ ἐπιχώρια καὶ ἐγχειρίδια, πρὸς δὲ καὶ ἀξίνας σαγάρις εἶχον."

42. Ibid., 4:5: "Γένεος μὲν τοιούτου δή τινος γενέσθαι τὸν Ταργίταον, τούτου δὲ γενέσθαι παῖδας τρεῖς, Λιπόξαιν καὶ Ἀρπόξαιν καὶ νεώτατον Κολάξαιν. Ἐπὶ τούτων ἀρχόντων ἐκ τοῦ οὐρανοῦ φερόμενα χρύσεα ποιήματα, ἄροτρόν τε καὶ ζυγὸν καὶ σάγαριν καὶ φιάλην, πεσεῖν ἐξ τὴν Σκυθικήν, καὶ τῶν ἰδόντα πρῶτον τὸν πρεσβύτατον ἆσσον ἰέναι βουλόμενον αὐτὰ λαβεῖν, τὸν δὲ χρυσὸν ἐπιόντος καίεσθαι. Ἀπαλλαχθέντος δὲ τούτου προσιέναι τὸν δεύτερον, καὶ τὸν αὖτις ταὐτὰ ποιέειν. Τοὺς μὲν δὴ καιόμενον τὸν χρυσὸν ἀπώσασθαι, τρίτῳ δὲ τῷ νεωτάτῳ ἐπελθόντι κατασθῆναι, καὶ μιν ἐκεῖνον κομίσαι ἐς ἑωυτοῦ· καὶ τοὺς πρεσβυτέρους ἀδελφεοὺς πρὸς ταῦτα συγγνόντας τὴν βασιληίην πᾶσαν παραδοῦναι τῷ νεωτάτῳ." Philippe Ernest Legrand, the editor of the Budé edition (Paris, 1960) 4:50 n.2, suggests that the three objects were symbols of the three classes of Iranian society: the cup that of the priests, the *sagaris* that of warriors, and the plough that of the farmers.

This tradition of a sacred weapon fallen from the sky as a symbol of legitimacy was not forgotten in the migration period. Jordanes, in his *De origine actibusque Getarum*, transmits a report of the Greek historian Priscus that Attila had acquired the sacred Scyth weapon (now called a sword, *gladius*) and considered that this sword of Mars both gave him power in war and constituted him "prince of the entire world."[43] The possession of the weapon then led him to reject the title of *strategos* or general offered by the emperor because he considered himself the equal of the latter.

The tradition of Attila's sword either continued or was revived in the eleventh century. Around 1063 the widowed Hungarian queen Anastasia sent a precious sword to Otto von Northeim, the duke of Bavaria. In time the sword passed to Luitpold of Meersburg, a close supporter of Emperor Henry IV. After Luitpold was accidentally killed by the sword in a fall, the weapon was reputed to be the sword with which Attila had attacked Christendom. Lampert of Hersfeld specifically identified this sword with the one described by Priscus.[44]

Attila's was not the only sword sought after in the early Middle Ages. The passage from Paulus Diaconus cited at the beginning of the chapter is another strong indication of the importance of the legit-

---

43. *Prisci Panitae fragmenta*, Fragmenta historicorum Graecorum 4, ed. Karl Muller (Paris, 1885), 96: "Qui [Attila] quamvis huius esset naturae, ut semper magna confideret, addebat ei tamen confidentiam gladius Martis inventus, sacer apud Scytharum reges semper habitus. Quem Priscus historicus tali refert occasione detectum. Quum pastor, inquiens, quidem gregis unam buculam conspiceret claudicatem, nec causam tanti vulneris inveniret, sollicitus, vestigia cruoris, insequitur: tandemque venit ad gladium, quem depascens herbas bucula incauate calcaverat, effossumque protinus, ad Attilam defert. Quo ille munere gratulatus, ut erat magnanimus, arbitratur se totius mundi principem constitutum, et per Martis gladium potestatem sibi concessam esse bellorum."

44. *Lamperti monachi Hersfeldensis opera*, MGH SSRG 38:130: "Notatum autem est hunc ipsum gladium fuisse, quo famosissimus quondam rex Hunorum Attila in necem christianorum atque in excidium Galliarum hostiliter debachatus fuerat. . . . Legitur autem de hoc gladio in Gestis Getarum, qui et Gothi dicuntur, quod Martis quondam fuerit, quem bellandi presidem et militarium armorum primum repertorem gentiles mentiebantur, eumque post multa tempora pastor quidam in terra leviter absconsum deprehenderit ex sanguine bovis, cuius pedem, dum in gramine pasceretur, vulneraverat, isque eum Attilae regi detulerit, divinatumque illi fuerit omnium tunc temporis aruspicum responsis, quod gladius idem ad interitum orbis terrarum atque ad perniciem multarum gentium fatalis esset." Percy Ernst Schramm, in *Herrschaftszeichen und Staatssymbolik*, Schriften der Monumenta Germaniae historica 13.2 (Stuttgart, 1955), 485–491, discounts the possibility that the Hungarian saber in the Vienna Schatzkammer, which dates from the late tenth or early eleventh century, was necessarily the sword described by Lampert.

imacy and continuity expressed by a hero's weapon. Alboin had been the leader of the Lombards who had conquered Italy in the sixth century. The account of his death indicated that Paulus was clearly utilizing Lombard oral epic tradition still very much alive in the eighth century: Alboin had been allied with Cunimund, king of the Gepids, who broke his treaty with the Lombards and began a war against them. Alboin killed Cunimund in battle, beheaded his fallen enemy, and made a drinking cup, or *scala*, from his skull.[45] Alboin married Cunimund's daughter Rosimund shortly after and, during a feast, made the fatal mistake of inviting his wife "to drink with her father" from his cup.[46] Unable to bear this affront, Rosimund decided to kill her husband. She tricked a servant into sleeping with her and then told him that if he did not kill the king, she would tell her husband of the deed. The servant complied and Alboin was slain.

The continuing importance of the great Lombard conqueror was certainly not lost on Duke Giselpert of Verona. By opening the tomb and removing the king's sword and other grave goods, he was by no means despoiling a grave: he was entering the otherworld, meeting with the dead king, and returning to this world as his successor. Thus Paulus's disparaging comment, "For this reason he was accustomed in his vanity to tell the ignorant people that he had seen Alboin,"[47] should be understood quite literally. Giselpert was not claiming to have looked upon the *body* of the king but to have met and perhaps contended with the king himself. The ignorant people, *indoctos*

45. *Pauli Historia Langobardorum* 1.27, p. 69: "In eo proelio Alboin Cunimundum occidit, caputque illius sublatum, ad bibendum ex eo poculum fecit. Quod genus poculi apud eos 'scala' dicitur, lingua vero Latina patera vocitatur."
46. Ibid., 2.28, p. 87: "Cum in convivio ultra quam oportuerat apud Veronam laetus resederet, cum poculo quod de capite Cunimundi regis sui soceris fecerat reginae ad bibendum vinum dari praecepit atque eam ut cum patre suo laetanter biberet invitavit."
47. Ibid., 88–89. This act may have been a form of the grave violation, or *crapworfin*, strongly condemned in the *Edictum Rothari*, col. 15, *MGH Edictus ceteraeque Langobardorum leges*, 16: "De crapuuorfin. Si quis sepulturam hominis mortui ruperit, et corpus expoliauerit aut foris iactauerit, nongentos soledos sit culpauelis parentibus sepulti. Et si parentis proximi non fuerint, tunc gastaldius regis aut sculdahis requirat culpa ipsa, et ad curte regis exegat." *Crapworfin* seems much more an affront to the dead and to his kindred than the act described by Paulus; yet the heavy penalty (900 solidi) for violation of graves recorded in Lombard and other barbarian laws seems to reflect in part the recognition that such actions were not merely motivated by a desire to obtain material wealth but had a supernatural meaning. See Heinrich Brunner, *Deutsche Rechtsgeschichte* 2, ed. Claudius Freiherr von Schwerin (Munich, 1928), 880.

homines, meant not the common people, or the *vulgus,* but rather those still attached to the traditional understanding of such grave-entering. By emerging with Alboin's sword he claimed the right to lead the Lombard people in the serious period of crisis that would culminate in the Frankish conquest of the kingdom of Pavia. Duke Giselpert was acting in a tradition common both to the classical and Germanic worlds. Suetonius, in his life of Augustus, describes how in Alexandria the emperor had the tomb of Alexander the Great opened and the mummy brought to him. After gazing on its features for a long time, he crowned its head with a golden diadem and strewed flowers on the body. When asked if he also wanted to see the tomb of the Ptolemaic kings, he replied that he had wanted to see a king, not corpses.[48] Caligula was said to have worn the breastplate he had removed from Alexander's tomb.[49] These classical precedents were no doubt behind Otto III's opening of the tomb of Charlemagne in 1000, which, as Helmut Beumann has pointed out, was undertaken for secular, not religious, motives.[50]

Such accounts of entering tombs to claim swords appear frequently in saga literature, and though chronologically and geographically distant from Carolingian Europe, they create parallels so great as to suggest a common culture.[51] In some instances, the sword seems to have been acquired as a gift, or at least without a fight. One such barrow raid was accomplished by the hero Skeggi in the Þorðar Saga Hreðu.[52] The saga mentions in passing that once Skeggi had come to the ancient royal Danish capital of Lejre and had broken into the burial mound of King Hrolf Krakis. From the mound he took the king's sword, Sköfnung, "the best sword that came to Iceland."[53]

48. Suetonius *Augustus* 18.
49. Suetonius *Caligula* 52.
50. Helmut Beumann, "Grab und Thron Karls des Grossen zu Aachen," in Braunfels and Schramm, 9–38. On the *Annals of Hildesheim,* which term the action *ammirationis causa* and contrast it with Otto's visit to the tomb of Adalbert of Prag (*causa orationis*), see 34.
51. For swords in barrows or received from the otherworld, see Inger M. Boberg, *Motif Index of Early Icelandic Literature,* Bibliotheca arnamagnaeana 27 (Hafniae, 1966). See Kelchner, 67–68, on breaking into barrows.
52. *Þórðar Saga Hreðu,* ed. V. Ásmundarson (Reykjavik, 1900), col. 3, trans. Walter H. Vogt, *Die Geschichte von Thord und seinem Ziehsohn,* Thule 10 (Jena, 1900), 213–214.
53. In *Hrólf Saga Kraka,* ed. Finnur Jónsson (Copenhagen 1904), trans. Paul Herrmann, *Die Geschichte von Hrolf Kraki,* Thule 21 (Jena, 1923), 306. After the king's death in battle, "over King Hrolf a mound was thrown up and his sword Sköfnung was laid by his side."

In the *Reykdæla Saga ok Viga-Skuta*,[54] Thorkel, who had removed a sword from the burial mound of Skefil, thought to return it. But the previous owner appeared to Thorkel in a vision and told him that, though it was good that he wished to return the weapon, he, Skefil, would give it to him. Another direct gift of a sword is reported in the late *Sigurdar Saga Thogla*.[55] Two brothers, Halfdan and Vilhjalmr, were recovering from battle on a remote shore when Halfdan saw a dwarf's child.[56] He threw a rock at it, breaking its jaw. That night he had a dream in which a gigantic dwarf warned him of future misfortunes and then struck him with a staff. He awakened with a severe headache. Vilhjalmr then walked to the same place, saw the dwarf's child, and gave it a gold ring. That night he too had a dream, but in it the giant praised him for his kindness, promised that his brother would recover, and gave him a sword, Gunnlogi (Battle-flame) and a prophecy that using it he would never be defeated in duel or battle.

Generally, the otherworld owner of the sword did not part with it willingly. The *Hervarar Saga*, mentioned above, is one such example.[57] Hervùr had to force her dead father, Angantýr, to part with Tyrfing, and even then he did so with a prophecy that was very like a curse. In the *Grettis Saga*, Grettir, while staying on an island with Thorfinn, son of Kar the Elder, saw a light coming from a barrow, a sure sign of buried treasure.[58] He learned that the barrow was the tomb of Kar. He dug until he struck wood, and then, because he wanted to see "who lives there," he entered and bumped against a chair in which sat a man, his feet on a mound of gold and silver. Grettir took the treasure and tried to leave, but someone drew him back. He drew his sword Jùkulsnaut and cut off the head of the barrow dweller, then left and went to Thorfinn's farm. Among the treasures he took with him was a short, wide sword. When Thorfinn saw it he was furious and refused to allow Grettir to keep it until he accomplished a great deed of valor.

54. *Reykdæla Saga ok Viga-Skuta*, trans. Walter H. Vogt, *Die Geschichte von den Leuten aus dem Rauchtal*, Thule 11 (Jena, 1921), 19.347–349.
55. *Sigurdar Saga Thogla* 7.113–117. This text was missed by Kelchner.
56. A dwarf or troll in Germanic tradition was a form changer and could be either a giant or a small creature; see Kelchner, 40–45.
57. See above at note 39.
58. *Grettis Saga Ásmundarsonar*, ed. R. C. Boer (Halle, 1900), trans. Paul Herrmann, *Die Geschichte von dem starken Grettir, dem Geachteten*, Thule 5 (Jena, 1913), 47–51. Grettir was a historical personage, born Bjarg, Northern Iceland, in 996, died 1031.

The most famous such struggle, at least to English readers, is that between Beowulf and Grendel's mother, which reads very much like the fight between Grettir and Kar the Elder.[59] In the den of Grendel's mother, which is described as like a subterranean barrow, Beowulf finds a sword, with which he finally kills the monster. Though the sword melts from the heat of her blood, it is described as the principal treasure taken from her lair.

These similar historical and literary texts indicate the continuity and homogeneity of sword traditions in Germanic oral tradition. Swords come from the otherworld; they have magical names and powers; they are either given by or taken from the dead or otherworldly beings; their possession indicates the prowess, and hence authority, of their wielder. The sword in the *visio*, bearing as it does four mysterious Germanic words, seems to belong to this tradition. Analysis of the words and their possible meanings only strengthens this hypothesis.

Charles the Great and the Saxons: The Old High German Words

During the Carolingian period the techniques of sword production developed to the point that the engraving of words or symbols on blades became somewhat common.[60] From the seventh and eighth centuries a few such swords are known, some with runic inscriptions such as the one on the Saebù sword: "Thormud possesses me."[61] Slightly later swords of Frankish manufacture, such as the so-called Ulfberht group, contain inscriptions that run the center of one side of the blade in clear Roman capitals. The name on these swords, as on the later *Ingelred fit* (for *fecit*) swords, presumably indicates the armorer.[62] No extant swords from this period carry the name of their owner on the blade, and none carries as long a text as that reported in

---

59. *Beowulf and the Fight at Finnsburg*, ed. Frederick Klaeber, 3d ed. (Boston, 1950), lines 1492–1590, 56–59.
60. Rudolf Wegeli, "Inschriften auf mittelalterlichen Schwertklingen," *Zeitschrift für historische Waffenkunde* 3 (1902–1905): 177–183, 218–225, 261–268, 290–300. See Michael Müller-Wille, "Zwei karolingische Schwerter aus Mittelnorwegen," *Studien zur Sachsenforschung* 3 (1982): 101–168, cited in Karl Hauck, "Text und Bild in einer oralen Kultur: Antworten auf die zeugniskritische Frage nach der Erreichbarkeit mündlicher Überlieferung im frühen Mittelalter," *Frühmittelalterliche Studien* 17 (1983): 510–599, 530.
61. Wegeli, 181.
62. Ibid., 183.

the *visio*. The idea of such a sword, particularly a legendary one, was certainly conceivable, however, such as the sword Hrunting, which Unferth lent Beowulf, the name of which was inscribed at the hilt,[63] and the "wave-scrolled" sword with which Beowulf killed Grendel's mother.[64] The "wave-scrolling" might indicate the pattern-welding technique by which the blade was frequently made.[65]

The author of the *visio* explains the meaning of the four words in a manner that is congruent with the propaganda message for which the *visio* is intended and which has been accepted without question (although not without difficulty) by modern philologists. RAHT he explains as divine help, and the word has been seen as the Old High German *Rât*, "concilium," "Rat," by Eberhard Graff and as "copia," "facultas," "opes" by Karl Müllenhoff, whose philological advice Phillipp Jaffé followed in his edition. RADOLEIBA has presented more trouble. The author explained it only indirectly: "in omni re que cito deficiet," an explanation accepted by Graff, who derived the word from *rado*, "schnell," "fast," and "Leibe, Überbleibsel, zu leibu wër-dan."[66] Müllenhoff, however, recognized the word as Old Saxon and suggested that it was the word *radelêve*, "hereditas utensilium."[67] NASG is not well explained by the author, who refers only indirectly to its meaning: "When however they [the sons of Charles the Great] die and their sons begin to reign after them it will be what was written in the third place, *Nasg*. They will increase the tolls out of a twisted desire for gain, and they will oppress foreigners and travelers with their power."[68] Graff was uncertain about the meaning of the word.[69] Müllenhoff translated it as "abliguritio," "to waste away," and related

63. *Beowulf*, line 1457.
64. Ibid., line 1666.
65. Salin, 3:58–69.
66. Although Eberhard Gottlieb Graff, *Althochdeutscher Sprachschatz* 2 (Berlin, 1836), App., col. 49, adds "cf. niederd. radeleve, *reliquiae utensilium* oder gehört dieses zu rat?"
67. Jaffé, 4:703 n. 2: "Neque vero verbum illud quidquam nisi vetus Saxonicum 'radelêve' esse ideoque proprie idem quod 'hereditas utensilium' valere videtur."
68. Ibid.: "Cum autem et illi obierint et filii eorum post eos regnare ceperint, erit, quod tertio loco scriptum erat, 'Nasg.' [Paris, BN MS lat. 5016 could be read as Hasg] Augebunt enim theloneum turpis lucri gratia, et advenas et peregrinos obpriment per potentiam."
69. Graff, 2:1105: "Sollte hiemit nastahit (s. eid) zusammen-hàngen?" For *Nasteid*, see ibid., 1:152: "Ist dieses Wort in dem nastahit (al. nasthait; in Db. als nasthaiet aufgeführet) der 1. alam, 56 zu finden? S. Grimms *Deutsche Rechtsaltertümer*, p. 906. Dürfte nast aus nesan, *servari* zu erklären seyn; durch den Schwur des nastahit rettete die kinderlose Wittwe ihre Morgengabe."

it to the modern German "naschen." ENTI is understood by the author as "end," and both Graff and Müllenhoff accepted this without question.

These explanations and hypotheses leave room for considerable doubt, both because of the uncertainty as to the actual words and because such unrelated words are hardly what one would expect to find on a sword, even a supernatural one. Considering the parallels between this vision and the texts from Germanic tradition discussed above, one might hypothesize that the vision originally had a close connection to the Germanic visions of swords as symbols of authority and legitimacy received from the otherworld. The words might thus have had quite a different meaning, one either no longer understood by the author (who by his own admission is telling it at third hand) or intentionally suppressed to serve the purposes of ecclesiastical propaganda. One must therefore search for the words' meaning apart from that provided by the *visio* author, relying instead on philological examination of the words themselves to arrive at alternative meanings.

Following this hypothesis, Claude Lecouteux proposes a radically different reading of the text, one that makes much more sense in terms of Germanic traditions such as those apparently cultivated in the kingdom of Louis the German.[70] First, he suggests that the words be considered as a phrase and that we look for a grammatical link among them. Second, he assumes that the author may have improperly divided the five syllables into words, either out of ignorance or by design. He suggests restoring the text as follows:

The first word, RAHT, cannot be Old High German *rât* because the *h* would have to be a sign of length, impossible at this period when it is a fricative whose graphic is *h* or *ch*. The final *t* suggests either a substantive of the type *naht* or *reht* or the third person singular of a verb. The hypothesis that the words form a phrase argues for the last possibility because a noun would have no syntactic link with the other terms. If the word is not a noun such as *râhha* or *rah/ra(h)ha*, and if the verb *rehhan* is excluded because its preterit form is *ruoch*, the word must be the preterit of *re(c)chen*, a verb with "Rückumlaut," that is, *rahta*, with the apocope *a* for metrical reasons. Its meaning: "(He) brandished or was brandishing."

RADOLEIBA he argues is certainly a proper name, the Old Saxon

70. Personal communication.

Radeleif, in which *leif* signifies son or daughter as in the Norse *leifr* in proper names. Its feminine ending is not unusual, especially in myth. It is the subject of the verb *rah(a).*[71]

NASCGENTI is the present participle of the verb *nerien,* Gothic *nasjan.* The $g = j$ as in old Germanic *ner an* (being a sonoral spirant and guttural "i" or occlusive "k"). That this present participle presents the graphic variant $g = j$ indicates that the author or scribe was influenced by an earlier stage of the language. The preservation of an archaic form would suggest that the word is a proper name, and in this case, the name of the sword, Savior.[72]

Lecouteux concludes that the text on the blade originally read "Radoleiba brandished Savior." This reconstruction is of course a mere hypothesis, and one with which many philologists take exception. The suggestion that the words on the sword should be connected grammatically is reasonable, however, and his particular interpretation of them makes sense in terms of the probable original meaning of the tradition: a sword from the otherworld had been brought to Charles by a superior being as a symbol of his legitimacy as successor of a past hero and as the elect of the gods or of God.

But who was the hero Radoleiba to whom Charles was successor? The Saxon form suggests a Saxon hero, and in the region in which this vision was reported, such an identification would have been entirely conceivable. The Saxon wars were the longest and most frustrating conquests in which Charles engaged, and his need to establish the legitimacy of the Franks, their religion, and their king in Saxony was a constant preoccupation. Possibly the original content and significance of the vision was in relation to the Saxon pacification. Further research may be able to further identify the hero Radoleiba whose successor Charles was to be. Or the meaning may have originated quite apart from Charles and the other vision traditions. It may

71. Dieter Geuenich has kindly referred me to the appearance of this name in various forms in several early medieval sources: *Ratleip* and *Ratleif* in the Reichenauer Verbrüderungsbuch, 108.D3 and 144.C1; *Ratleib* four times in charters of Lorsch (in the years 788 and 815); *Ratliub* in a Fulda charter in 837; possibly in the form *Radleuba* in a Saint Gall charter; and *Ratlob,* a monk of the Fulda dependency of Hünfeld in 904.

72. In a personal communication, Geuenich has suggested alternative meanings such as "Rettung bringend" and "Schutz gewährend" and thus that the name might mean something akin to "protector," a similar and equally appropriate name for a sword.

have been grafted onto the latter only at a fairly late date in the kingdom of Louis the German, where, as we have seen, Germanic tradition was being cultivated.

Whether or not this specific interpretation of the Old High German words is correct, it is appropriate to conclude that the third stratum recognizable in the *visio* is that of a legitimacy-conferring tradition. The sword transmitted from the otherworld signified the right of its bearer to be the successor of its previous owner.

The Sword Vision in Later Imperial Propaganda

Charles was not the first king to receive confirmation of his legitimacy through the transmission of an otherworldly sword, and he would not be the last. In the ninth century the transmission of a sword was an established means of designating a successor. For example, on his deathbed Charles the Bald charged his wife Richilde to transmit to his son Louis the Stammerer "the sword called of Saint Peter, through which he invested him with the kingdom,"[73] and Louis in turn transmitted the "sword and the rest of the regalia" to his son Louis III at the end of his life.[74] In the next century, Gerhard, the hagiographer who composed the first life of Bishop Udalrich of Augsburg, would again turn to this tradition, but the differences between the ninth- and tenth-century versions indicate the integration of the sword vision into the general tradition of Christian visionary literature.[75]

Gerhard relates how one night, when Bishop Udalrich had fallen asleep, Saint Afra, the patroness of the cathedral of Augsburg, appeared and ordered him to follow her. She led him to the Lechfeld (where, a few years later, thanks largely to the heroic efforts of Udalrich, Otto I would be able to destroy the Magyars). There he saw

---

73. *Annales Bertiniani*, a. 877, *MGH SSRG* 5:138: "Richildis Compendium ad Hlodowicum veniens . . . attulit ei praeceptum, per quod pater suus illi regnum ante mortem suam tradiderat, et spatam quae vocatur sancti Petri, per quam eum de regno revestiret, sed et regium vestimentum et coronam ac fustem ex auro et gemmis."

74. Ibid., a. 879, 148: " . . . coronam et spatam ac reliquum regium apparatum filio suo Hludowico misit."

75. *Gerhardi vita Sancti: Oudalrici*, col. 3, 388–390. On the tradition of the two swords as it developed in medieval propaganda literature, see in particular Wilhelm Levison, "Die mittelalterliche Lehre von den beiden Schwertern: Ein Vortrag," *Deutsches Archiv* 9 (1951): 14–42.

Saint Peter and many bishops and saints holding a synod to condemn
the Bavarian duke Arnulf because of the latter's destruction of many
monasteries whose lands he had distributed to his lay vassals. Saint
Afra showed Udalrich two excellent swords (*enses duos valde heriles*),
one with a hilt, the other without. She then said, "Tell King Henry
that this sword without a hilt signifies one who holds the governance
of the kingdom with divine blessing."[76]

The mise-en-scène, *cum corpus lectulo ad dormiendum collocasset;* the
accusation against Arnulf[77] of destroying monasteries and the im-
plication that for this reason he would not be king; the two swords
that are a message for Henry—all suggest not just similarity to, but
familiarity with, the Carolingian *visio.* The fact that Udalrich was
bishop of Augsburg, the likely provenance of the Bibliothèque nationale manuscript of the *visio,* makes this connection even more
likely.

There are some interesting differences in the two visions, however.
Most notable is that the king no longer dreams himself—a church-
man dreams for him—which is typical of most Carolingian and post-
Carolingian otherworld visions and represents the attempt to introduce the Church as mediator between the two worlds.[78] Second, the
persona of the Carolingian vision is now clearly a saint, the patroness
of the cathedral. And third, though this figure appears to Udalrich in

76. Ibid.: " . . . quia quadam nocte cum corpus lectulo ad dormiendum collocasset,
    vidit sanctam Afram in magna formositate, pulcra tunica indutam atque suc-
    cinctam, stantem ante ipsum dicentemque sibi: 'Surge et sequere me.' Et haec
    dicens, eduxit eum in campum, quem Lehcfeld vulgo dicunt. Ibi enim s. Petrum,
    principem apostolorum invenit cum multitudine magna episcoporum et aliorum
    sanctorum, et eorum quos ille ante non videbat, et tamen nutu Dei bene cog-
    noscebat synodale colloquium cum eis facientem et magna et innumerabilia dis-
    ponentem, Arnolfumque, ducem Bawariorum, adhuc viventem de destructione
    multorum monasteriorum, quae in beneficia laicorum divisit, de multis sanctis ac-
    cusatum legaliter iudicantem, et enses duos valde heriles, unum cum capulo et
    alterum sine capulo, sibi ostendentem, et sic loquentem: 'Dic Regi Heinrico, ille
    ensis qui est sine capulo significat regem qui sine benedictione pontificali regnum
    tenebit; capulatus autem, qui benedictione divina regni tenebit gubernacula.'"
77. Arnulf of Bavaria had been raised by the Bavarians as king *in regno Teutonicorum.*
    He would be the greatest and most persistent opponent of Henry I and would
    outlive him.
78. Compare in particular the *Visio Otcharii,* ed. Wilhelm Wattenbach, *Anzeiger fur
    Kunde der deutschen Vorzeit,* new ser., 22 (1875): 72–74, with the *Visio Eucherii, MGH
    Capit* 2:432–433. On the latter see Ulrich Nonn, "Das Bild Karl Martells in den
    lateinischen Quellen vornehmlich des 8. und 9. Jahrhunderts," *Frühmittelalterliche
    Studien* 4 (1970): 70–137, esp. 106–114.

his sleep, she leads him away to another place rather than bringing the swords to him; this too is typical of the "orthodox" vision tradition. Finally, as swords have been, at least since the ninth century, part of the regalia, the two visions are obviously closely related to traditions of legitimacy as old as Herodotus. What has happened is that the Church has interposed itself, in the persons of its saints and bishops, as the guarantor of this legitimacy and of the communication between the two worlds. The sword (or swords) that symbolize this legitimacy are clearly identified in the conflict between emperor and pope in the next century. Perhaps, then, it is no accident that just when the vision of the sword transmission has been completely transformed into a vehicle of ecclesiastical rather than imperial propaganda, we begin to hear more of the *sacra lancea*, first mentioned by Liudprand of Cremona,[79] which progressively supplants the sword as the sacred weapon of the imperial office.

In conclusion, the *Visio Karoli Magni* reflects but a moment in a long, complex, and constantly changing visionary tradition. Although modified and codified for propaganda purposes in the 860s, it contains internal evidence of much older and more complex stages and forms. First, it contains elements of the tradition of familial visions through which obligations uniting present, past, and future generations of the royal stirps are articulated.[80] Second, it belongs to an ancient tradition of legitimization visions in which a magical barbarian weapon, the sword, is transmitted to a powerful leader from a predecessor in the otherworld as a sign of his right of succession. Finally, the tradition does not end with the ninth century: in the next century this central object of the royal regalia, like the vision tradition itself, was increasingly appropriated by the Church. The sword, already termed the "sword of Saint Peter" in the ninth century, had become by the tenth an unambiguously ecclesiastical symbol of divine approval transmitted and interpreted for kings by angels and bish-

79. *Antapodosis* 4.24, in Joseph Becker, ed., *Liudprandi episcopi Cremonensis opera omnia*, MGH SSRG 41:118–119. See Schramm, 492–537, esp. 501.
80. The connection between the extinction of the royal stirps and the end of the world may anticipate the mid-tenth-century treatise of Adso of Montier-en-Der, "De ortu et tempore Antichristi necnon et tractatus qui ab eo dependunt," in which Adso argued that the end of the world could not come as long as the Frankish kings remained; see D. Verhelst, "Adso van Montier-en-Der en de Angst voor het jaar Duizend," *Tijdschrift voor Geschiedenis* 90 (1977): 1–10.

ops. Although the sword as symbol of royal authority and justice would never disappear, another weapon, equally rich in tradition but less directly appropriated by the Church, the lance, would take the place of the sword as the central martial symbol of the emperor's legitimacy.

Appendix

ఌఞ

The *Visio Karoli Magni* has been edited four times, the first in an extremely limited edition by J. F. Gadan using the Paris manuscript;[81] then by Graff,[82] who used only the Frankfurt manuscript; by Jaffé from both manuscripts;[83] and finally by Heinrich Gengler.[84] The following edition is based on Frankfort on Main, Stadt- und Universitätsbibliothek, MS Barth. 67, fols. 131r–132r (manuscript A),[85] with alternate readings (see Notes) from Paris, Bibliothèque nationale, MS lat. 5016, fols. 159v–160v (manuscript B).[86]

Incipit Visio Domni Karoli Regis Francorvm[a)]

Karolus imperator quondam Francorum diuersarumque gentium, ubicumque noctu manebat siue domi[b)] siue in expeditione, lucernas et tabulas sibi[c)] contiguas habere solitus erat; et quicquid uidit in somnis memoria dignum litteris tradere curauit, ne[d)] a memoria labi potuisset. Quadam uero nocte, cum membra ad quiescendum in lectulo collocasset ac se sopori dedisset, uidit quandam personam ad se uenientem, euaginatum gladium in manu tenentem[e)]. Quem cum metuens interrogasset[f] quis esset uel unde uenisset, audiuit ab eo in responsione huiuscemodi uerba: "Accipe," inquit, "gladium istum

81. J. F. Gadan, *Collection du bibliophile troyen* (Troyes, 1821).
82. Graff, 3 (1837), 853–856.
83. Jaffé, 4:700–704.
84. Heinrich Gottfried Gengler, *Germanische Rechtsdenkmaler* (Erlangen, 1875), 237–240.
85. For a full description of the manuscript, see Gerhardt Powitz and Herbert Buck, *Die Handschriften des Bartholomaeusstifts und des Karmeliterklosters in Frankfurt am Main*, Kataloge der Stadt- und Universitätsbibliothek, Frankfort on Main 3/2, ed. Clemens Köttelwesch (Frankfort on Main, 1974), 142–143.
86. For the contents and provenance of this manuscript, see Schleidgen, 35.

pro munere tibi a Deo transmissum, et scripturam in eo digestam lege ac memoriter retine; quoniam[g] statutis temporibus[h] implebitur." Quem cum accepisset formamque illius diligenter[i] inspexisset, uidit quatuor[j] loca in eodem litteris exarata. In primo quidem loco iuxta capulum eiusdem mucronis[k] erat scriptum "RAHT[l]," in secundo uero "RADOLEIBA[m]," in tercio "NASG," in quarto iuxta cuspidem[n] eiusdem ensis "ENTI." Euigilans uero iussit sibi lucernam et tabulas afferri et eadem uerba eodem tenore conscripsit. Mane autem facto horis kanonicis[o] iuxta morem decantatis et suis[p] orationibus finitis, omnibus qui aderant optimatibus suis[q] somnium quod uiderat indicauit et solutionem eius[r] sibi ab eis exponi postulauit. Cumque omnes tacuissent, unus qui sapientior cęteris, dicebatur nomine Einhart[s], respondit, "Domine," inquiens, "imperator, ille qui uobis illum transmisit gladium etiam interpretationem scripturę in eo exaratę, nobis tacentibus, uobis reuelabit." Tunc[t] imperator:

"Si uultis," inquit, "audire prout nobis uidetur secundum possibilitatem ingenioli nostri significationem predictę insinuabimus uobis scripturę. Gladius[u] qui nobis a Deo transmissus est potestas ab illo nobis collata non inconuenienter accipi potest, quoniam auxilio illius freti, hostes plurimos armis[v] nostrę subiectos habemus ditioni. Et quod modo, sedatis hostibus, plus quam parentum nostrorum temporibus ubertas frugum esse dinoscitur, quod significat prima in mucrone scriptura "Raht,"[w] id est rerum omnium habundantia. Quod autem secundo loco exaratum erat "Radoleiba," arbitramur, nobis a seculo transeuntibus, filiorum nostrorum temporibus compleri; uidelicet quod nec tanta frugum erit habundantia et quędam gentes, modo subactę, deficiant, quod significat "Radoleiba," in omni re quę cito deficiet. Cum autem et illi obierint et filii eorum post eos regnare ceperint, erit quod tercio loco scriptum erat, "Nasg." Augebunt enim theoneum turpis lucri gratia et aduenas et peregrinos obpriment per potentiam, nullam habentes uerecundiam cum quali confusione et ignominia sibi congregent[x] diuitias. Res ęcclesiasticas quoque[y] a nobis uel a[z] progenitoribus nostris clericis et monachis ad seruitium dei traditas, siue minis siue blandimentis tollent suisque satellitibus more beneficii dabunt, quod significat "Nasg." Sed et hoc quod cuspide[aa] eiusdem ensis scriptum erat, "Enti," id est finis, duobus modis intellegi potest: Aut enim finis seculi tunc erit aut stirpis nostrę; scilicet quod nullus[bb] de progenie[cc] nostra deinceps in gente Francorum regnaturus sit."

Hęc sicut ipse somniator interpretatus est, et Einhart[dd] abbas

Rabano monacho, et idem Rabanus postea archiepiscopus multis narrare solebat, quorum[ee] unus ego sum, et[ff] litteris commendaui.

Quorum quędam prioribus, quedam modernis completa sunt temporibus, nam Ludouico imperatore post obitum KAROLI regnante, Brittones et plurimę Sclauorum gentes defecerunt et rerum penuria regnum illius in nonnullis locis afflixit. Post cuius obitum filii eius Lotharius et Pippinus[gg] et Ludouuicus[hh] per regnum sibi derelictum NASG dilatare ceperunt. Nam Pippinus[ii] quanta monasteria spoliauerit in Aquitania et res ęcclesiasticas ac[jj] utensilia clericorum et monachorum tulerit suisque satellitibus dederit, longum est enarrare. Lotharius[kk] quoque in Italia similia fecisse perhibetur. De qua re extat ępistola temporibus filii sui ab uniuersis[ll] episcopis Romanę ęcclesię Ludouuico[mm] regi Germanico destinata, sciscitandi per Witgarium ępiscopum qualem pacem haberet sancta Romana ęcclesia; quę adhuc in armario sancti Martini scripta continetur[nn], in qua ei inter cętera responsum est: "Sancta Romana ęcclesia suusque patronus et populus generaliter sauciatur, diripitur, discerpitur[oo], humiliatur, adnichilatur." Explicit V(isio) K(aroli)[pp].

Notes

[a] *Incipit . . . Francorvm* omitted in B.
[b] *siue domi* omitted in B.
[c] = *sibi. Contiguas* in B.
[d] = *nec* in B.
[e] = *habentem* in A.
[f] = *interogaret* in A.
[g] = *quia* in B.
[h] = *diebus* in B.
[i] *diligenter* omitted in B.
[j] = *IIIIor* in B.
[k] *eiusdem mucronis* omitted in B.
[l] = *RANT* in B.
[m] = *Radeleba* in B.
[n] = *capulum* in B.
[o] = *canonicis* in B.
[p] *suis* omitted in B.
[q] = *obtimatibus suis qui aderant* in B.
[r] *eius* omitted in B.
[s] = *Einart* in B.
[t] = *Tum* in B.
[u] = *gladium* in B.

[v] *armis* omitted in B.
[w] = *Rant* in B.
[x] = *congregent sibi* in B.
[y] = *quoque ęcclesiasticas* in B.
[z] *a* omitted in B.
[aa] = *quod in cuspide* in B.
[bb] *nullus* omitted in A.
[cc] = *propienie* in B.
[dd] = *Einhrt* in B.
[ee] = *ex quibus* in B.
[ff] = *qui* in B.
[gg] = *Pipinus* in B.
[hh] = *Ludoicus* in B.
[ii] = *Pipinus* in B.
[jj] *ac* omitted in B.
[kk] = *Lutharius* in B.
[ll] = *uenerabilis* in B.
[mm] = *Ludoico* in B.
[nn] = *continetur in armario sancti Martini* in B.
[oo] *discerpitur* omitted in B.
[pp] *Explicit . . . K(aroli)* omitted in A.

4 Exchange and Interaction between the Living and the Dead in Early Medieval Society

☙❧

The idea of gift exchange as a fundamental bond of early medieval society is hardly a new concept. Marcel Mauss, in his ground-breaking study of gift giving, was largely inspired by the role of gifts in German sagas.[1] Georges Duby has discussed the importance of giving and receiving in the early Middle Ages.[2] Nor is the application of the model of gift exchange to the relationship between monastic communities and secular society original: Otto Gerhard Oexle has provided us with two rich essays on the topic. He discusses prayers as spiritual gifts and also the exchange mechanism by which prayers were given in return for land.[3] This chapter is intended to expand these analyses so as to examine a different set of relationships established through gifts and countergifts: those uniting the living and the dead in secular society in the period before the year one thousand. More specifically, it explores four phenomena. The first is how the exchanges of prop-

1. Marcel Mauss, *The Gift: Forms and Functions of Exchange in Archaic Societies*, trans. Ian Cunnison (New York, 1967). This chapter is a revision of a paper presented at the annual convention of the American Historical Association in December 1980. Its present form has been improved thanks to the discussion and questions of those present at the session, in particular Gabrielle M. Spiegel. I am also grateful to Elizabeth Brown, Edward Champlin, Natalie Zemon Davis, William Jordan, Jean-Claude Schmitt, Robert Tignor, and Bailey Young for their criticisms of earlier drafts.
2. Georges Duby, "Taking, Giving and Consecrating," in his *The Early Growth of the European Economy*, trans. Howard B. Clarke (Ithaca, N.Y., 1974), 48–57.
3. Otto Gerhard Oexle, "Die Gegenwart der Toten," in *Death in the Middle Ages*, ed. Herman Braet and Werner Verbeke, Mediaevalia lovaniensia, ser. 1, Studia (Louvain, 1983), 19–77, and "Memoria und Memorialüberlieferung im frühen Mittelalter," *Frühmittelalterliche Studien* 10 (1976): 70–95.

erty, assistance, and identity between the two groups continued the relationships formed in life through and beyond death. The second is the way these exchanges themselves altered and clarified the relationships among the living. The third is the dual role of the bond with the dead. As we have seen in Chapter 2, the dead can be rightly termed an "age group" in medieval society, and thus the continuing bond served social cohesion. It also articulated an image of social stability in a society in constant structural flux.[4] Fourth is the gradual involvement of the Church as an essential third party in the exchange between the living and the dead. Finally, the chapter offers some hypotheses to explain this tendency to reserve to the Church the vital link among the past, present, and future generations.

Exchanging with the Dead

Modern studies of death in society emphasize the importance of the paradoxical need both to push the dead away, so the living can re-establish their normal activity, and to "keep them alive," to maintain social bonds in spite of death. This paradox is at the core of the system of exchanges informing the relationship of mutual dependence between the living and the dead in the early Middle Ages. The gifts the living had received from the dead were so great as to threaten the receivers unless balanced by equally worthy countergifts. The gifts of the dead included nothing less than life itself, property, and personal identity. Without suitable countergifts, the imbalance would become intolerable; for as anthropologists observe, a donor keeps eternal rights in the gift and hence in the recipient. Only by finding a suitable countergift could a recipient "revenge himself or herself" on the giver (the Latin term *talio* can mean both countergift and vengeance). Hostile or dominating intrusions by the dead in the society of the living could only be prevented by restoring balance between the parties to gift transactions. But because social bonds were based largely on these same great gifts from the dead, the dead could not be banished entirely from the society of the living; a benevolent relationship had to be established and continued.[5]

4. Natalie Zemon Davis, "Ghosts, Kin, and Progeny: Some Features of Family Life in Early Modern France," *Daedalus* 106 (1977): 92.
5. Robert Blauner, "Death and Social Structure," *Psychiatry* 29, no. 4 (1966): 378–394. I have also found particularly helpful Robert Kastenbaum and Ruth Aisen-

The first and most fundamental object of exchange was wealth. Gifts of land through inheritance and as indirect gifts to the dead through the Church united the three generations of medieval families: the living, the dead, and the future. Moreover, these donations defined, even constituted, these kin groups, designating them and establishing the relative connections among them, giving form to the fluid early medieval kin groups outlined by Karl Schmid and his school and most clearly documented in *libri memoriales*.[6] Inheritance and kinship were virtually coexistent and involved members in a series of cross-generational obligations.

The first was the obligation to exchange prayers for land. A noble Frankish woman, Dhuoda, in a manual of instructions for her young son written in 843, is quite explicit in her development of this theme. Her manual is a unique document in early medieval history: a book of advice composed by the wife of Bernard of Septimania, Louis the Pious's closest adviser, for her son William, who had just commended himself to Charles the Bald. It was written at Uzès, on the edge of the Rhône valley on the border between Provence and Septimania, where Dhuoda spent the last years of her life. Unlike the "mirrors of princes," which preceded and would follow, Dhuoda's book was intended as a practical, comprehensive guide for her older son rather than as a general treatise on the Christian prince.[7] In Book 8, Dhuoda urges William to pray and provides him with a three-part schema for ordering those for whom he should pray—the whole Christian community. The place and nature of William's kin within this schema is central to perceptions of early medieval kindred.

---

berg, *The Psychology of Death* (New York, 1976). The notion of countergift as revenge is developed in a medieval context by Jean-Claude Schmitt in "Temps, folklore et politique au XII⁴ siècle."

6. Karl Schmid's 1957 article remains the classic statement of his approach: "Zur Problematik von Familie, Sippe und Geschlecht, Haus und Dynastie beim mittelalterlichen Adel: Vorfragen zum Thema 'Adel und Herrschaft im Mittelalter,'" *Zeitschrift fur die Geschichte des Oberrheins* 105 (1957): 1–62, reprinted in his *Gebetsgedenken*, 183–244.

7. Dhuoda *Manuel pour mon fils*, ed. Pierre Riché, Sources Chrétiennes 225 (Paris, 1975). On the family of Bernard of Septimania as it appears in the *Manuel*, one should consult Riché's introduction and, most particularly, Joachim Wollasch, "Eine adlige Familie des frühen Mittelalters: Ihr Selbstverstandnis und ihre Wirklichkeit," *Archiv für Kulturgeschichte* 39, no. 2 (1957): 150–188. On mirrors of princes see H. H. Anton, *Fürstenspiegel und Herrscherethos in der Karolingerzeit* (Bonn, 1968).

The first division is hierarchical. William should pray for ecclesiastics, for kings and magnates, for his lord (Charles the Bald), for his father, and finally for all the people of God. The second division is eschatological. Dhuoda urges him to pray for the dead and the living. Both groups, whether good, indifferent, or bad, should be prayed for alike in the hope of resurrection. The distinction between the two is minimal: the living should be seen as those who are going to die; the dead, as those who will live again. The third division is domestic. Dhuoda distinguishes between the *extraneis* (outsiders) and *domesticis* (kin) and divides the latter into the *proximi* (close) and *propinqui* (very close) kin. William should pray particularly for these *domestici:* "I who am going to die admonish you to pray for all the dead, but especially for those from whom you have received your origin in the world."[8]

The next advice is crucial for understanding gift exchange in early medieval kinship. Dhuoda exhorts William to pray for his father's relatives, those "who have left their property in legitimate inheritance." This is the inheritance that Bernard was enjoying and in which one day William might participate. The names of these *parentes* she included at the end of the manual. This list of eight names, which she calls a "genealogia," should be augmented, she explains, when other members of William's stirps, such as his uncle Aribert (who had been blinded in 830 on the orders of Lothair I) and Dhuoda herself, die.[9] This list is not a genealogy in any modern or even high-medieval sense. The names, as she makes clear, are of those who have transmitted property to William's father. Hence the list is based not on biologic proximity but on transmission of property. After William has received his portion, his own "genealogy" will no doubt be different, depending on the origins of his possessions.

Not only is the kin group defined exclusively by inheritance, but the relationship between William and each member is determined by the amount of property each has left to Bernard: "To the same extent that they have bequeathed, pray for the possessor."[10] Thus there is a

---

8. Dhuoda, 8.13.318: "Orandum est pro omnibus, maxime pro his qui fidem Christi acceperunt; et non solum pro extraneis, uerum etiam pro domesticis, hoc est proximis et propinquis parentum nostrorum, maxime crebrius orare debemus. Hoc itaque dico ut ad id perueniam quod desidero. Admoneo te, licet moritura, ut pro omnibus defunctis ores, maxime autem pro his ex quibus tu originem trahis in saeculo."

9. Ibid., 10.5.354.

10. Ibid., 8.14.320: "In tantum quod illi remanserunt, ora pro possidentes."

proportional reciprocity within this kin group, and as potential future heir William must return prayers for property. His particular devotion toward his godfather and uncle Theoderic is based on this principle. Theoderic had left with Bernard all his goods so that William might some day benefit from them in their entirety. This bequest obligated William to a particular attention in prayers for his uncle.

William's kin, living and dead, were therefore coextensive with his real and potential benefactors and were defined both in extent and degree by his property. In a society in which inheritance was spread among all children male and female and in which everyone was free to divide her or his estate by testament, the resulting image of kinship was extremely fluid. In William's case, tentative identification of those considered kin (both the dead in the genealogia and the living) in the manual include, besides his mother and father, his grandfather William, William's first wife (William II's grandmother?), William's second wife (?), William's paternal aunt, three of his paternal uncles, and possibly a maternal uncle and maternal aunt. Not mentioned are William's younger brother Bernard or his cousin Charles the Bald.[11] Neither are related to William by property, although William is tied to both, the former by the responsibilities of guidance and education, the latter as his lord. In such a strict sense of kin, each person, as beneficiary of a particular set of bequests, had his or her own personal list of kindred; this kin group changed in each generation; and it also could change during a person's life as he or she was included in or excluded from the estates of potential benefactors.

The reciprocal obligation Dhuoda outlined is confirmed in hundreds of charters of donation I have studied from the Rhône valley.[12] Each act records, in a sense, the formation of a new inheritance kin because it establishes prayers, hence, formal articulation of a group related in a new way through the donation. The group is composed of three parts: the person or persons in possession of the property at the time of the donation; those from whom they had received it; those who might have inherited it had it not passed to the Church. The

11. On the tentative identifications of persons in the list, see Riché's notes, 354–355, and Wollasch.
12. I surveyed cartularies and collections of charters from Arles, Saint-André-le-Bas, Saint Victor-de-Marseille, Gellone, Nantua, Romans, Aniane, Ainy, Montmajour, Lérins, Psalmodi, Conques, Saint-Marcel-de-Châlon, Apt, Cluny, and Avignon. For those institutions outside of the Rhône valley–Provence area, I considered only charters pertaining to these regions.

three cannot always be separated simply into present, past, and future (potential) possessors of the property, but in general they are present as follows: the donor (present) cedes the property for the souls of specifically enumerated persons including the donor but also frequently those from whom the property was obtained (past) and obtains the assent in the form of subscriptions from those who have a potential claim on the property as the donor's heirs (future). These charters are of course formulaic, but the choice of formulas, particularly the choice of those for whom one is making the donation, resulted from consultation between scribe and donor. The various expressions used in my sample cover nineteen different kin or connections in such a wide variety of combinations that they could only have been constructed cooperatively with particular donors. The most frequently mentioned relatives are of course fathers (thirty-five) and mothers (thirty-one). This is hardly surprising given that inheritance from parents was the most common form of land transfer and that children usually made arrangements for the burial of their parents if the latter had not already done so themselves. Even if they had, the children would be most likely to execute the previously determined arrangements. Of course mentions of donations for the souls of the father and mother are very frequently accompanied by the intention to include the soul of the donor and in general all the donor's relatives, as in the donation made to Psalmody in 1004 "for our souls and the soul of our lord and father Anno from whom by hereditary law these and other goods came to us, and for the souls of our other relatives living and dead."[13] This exchange looked not only to fulfill the obligation of returning to the dead what had been received from the dead (keeping the dead alive) but also to benefit the living by securing divine favor for the donors both in this life and in the next.

After donations for the souls of fathers and mothers, the specific mentions of kin in the *pro animis* formulas become much less frequent but more telling. In frequency they follow roughly the pattern of probable inheritance or acquisition of land from others: brothers, wives, sons, lords, sisters, uncles, nephews, husbands, cousins, grandparents. Moreover, whenever it is possible to determine the origin of property donated for the soul of one of these relatives, it appears to

13. Nîmes, Archiv. dép. du Gard, MS. H 106, fols. 18v–19r.

have been received by the donor from that person. For example, one Agilbertus gave property to the Church of Apt in 977 "for the salvation of my soul and for the soul of my uncle Agilbernus who left me possession of this same inheritance."[14] Similarly, when a feudal lord is mentioned, it is always because the land was feudal and not allodial. The donor was obligated not only to obtain the lord's permission to alienate the land in the first place but also to share with his lord the spiritual benefits that accrue from the gift: Genirius and his wife donated to Montmajour in 961 a parcel of land "for my lord Boso and his late wife who had given me this land."[15]

Aiding the Living and the Dead

Property exchanges were the fundamental form of living–dead interaction. They united past and present and met the obligation of countergift while limiting the amount of property owed in return, thus freeing the remainder for the living and for future generations. Almost as important, however, were the more dynamic functional exchanges of assistance between dead and living. The dead did continue to be involved in the society of the living, even though this involvement is difficult to see outside of the ecclesiastical tradition. It can be seen in Germanic sagas, in which the dead regularly return to inflict punishment, share meals, exact revenge, give advice, teach, or give gifts; and it appears in vision literature, in which the dead offer advice or—more often, through mute suffering, warnings—to repent.[16] The classic saga account of such an exchange is that between

14. Noël Didier, Henri Dubled, and Jean Barruol, eds., *Cartulaire de l'église d'Apt, 833–1130?* (Paris, 1967), no. 27.
15. Paris, BN MS lat. 13915, fol. 28r.
16. Vision literature and dreams in Western medieval society are only beginning to receive the attention they merit. The political aspects of early medieval visionary literature have been studied by Wilhelm Levison, "Die Politik in den Jenseitsvisionen." The learned tradition of dreams and dreaming has been studied in the excellent unpublished dissertation of Francis X. Newman, "Somnium," and by Peter Dinzelbacher, *Vision und Visionsliteratur.* Attention has since been directed to medieval handbooks for the interpretation of dreams: Lawrence T. Martin, "The Earliest Versions of the Latin *Somniale Danielis," Manuscripta* 23 (1979): 131–141; Kamphausen, *Traum und Vision;* Alf Önnerfors, "Über die alphabetischen Traumbücher ("Somnalia Danielis") des Mittelalters," *Mediaevalia: Abhandlungen und Aufsätze,* Lateinische Sprache und Literatur des Mittelalters 6 (Frankfort, 1977). I am grateful to Lawrence Martin for allowing me to examine portions of his disserta-

the warrior woman Hervùr and her father Angantýr in the *Hervarar Saga.*[17] This violent young woman visited the island where, in fiery barrows, were buried the dead and approached the barrow where the berserks, including her uncles and her father, lay with their weapons. She boldly called for Angantýr to awaken and to give her Tyrfing, the sword forged by the dwarf Dvalin which, once drawn, could not be resheathed without tasting blood. Angantýr was reluctant to be called from the dead and still more reluctant to give her the sword, but, unable to refuse, relinquished it, with the prophecy, twice announced, that "Tyrfing, daughter shall be ruin and end of all your family." The rest of the saga bears out the dead father's prophecy.

To this text about a society chronologically and geographically distant from the one that is my main focus here, let me juxtapose two others, one in which a person likewise receives a sword and a prophecy and one in which a dead person appears to warn his descendants. The first is the *Visio Karoli Magni* recounted at the beginning of Chapter 3. The second text is the report of another vision, but this time the visionary was not a king but a bishop. Hincmar of Reims reported to the Council of Quierzy in 858 a vision that Bishop Eucherius of Orléans had seen during the reign of King Pepin III over a century before. While at prayer, Eucherius had been taken up and shown, among other things, the sufferings of those in hell, among whom he saw Charles Martel. When the vision ended, he called Boniface and Fulrad, abbot of Saint-Denis, and sent them to see whether Charles was in his tomb. When the two opened the tomb a dragon rushed out, and they found the tomb's interior blackened as though burned. These two signs were taken as evidence that the vision had been accurate and that Charles had been condemned to hell for his despoliation of Church property.[18]

---

tion, *Somniale Danielis: An Edition of a Medieval Latin Dream Interpretation Handbook,* which appeared as volume 10 in the series Lateinische Sprache und Literatur des Mittelalters (Frankfort, 1981). In spite of the suggestion by Jacques Le Goff in "Les rêves dans la culture et la psychologie collective de l'Occident médiéval," in *Pour un autre Moyen Age,* 299–306, that dreams should be studied as an important part of medieval culture, social historians have not, however, given them the attention they deserve. More progress has been made on the role of dreams in Islamic society; see G. E. von Gruenbaum and R. Callois, eds., *The Dream and Human Societies* (Berkeley, Calif., 1966).

17. *Hervarar Saga,* vv. 22–43.

18. *MGH Capit.* 2:432–433. The most complete examination of the *visio Eucherii* is that of Ulrich Nonn, "Das Bild Karl Martells."

Sufficient similarities exist among these three texts and other Germanic materials to suggest that although the visions of Charles and of Eucherius were largely propaganda pieces, their origins were not entirely divorced from the Germanic culture that surrounded the Carolingians. Runic inscriptions on swords were of course common, as were stories of swords received from the dead or from the other world.[19] Fires in burials and dragons guarding them were likewise common in Germanic literature.[20] In fact, one must imagine that, as Jacques Le Goff has pointed out in studying the legend of Saint Marcel of Paris, a dragon emerging from a tomb might have been a sufficiently ambivalent event to suggest meanings other than the damnation of the occupant. While ecclesiastical tradition attempted to equate the dragon or serpent with the devil, a strong secular tradition continued to see the dragon as a military symbol of material abundance. Either or both would have been appropriate to Charles Martel.[21] Finally, the dead frequently gave warnings and prophecies to the living, both in Germanic tradition and in the tradition of the dialogues of Gregory the Great.[22]

The differences, however, between the meeting of Angantýr and Hervùr on the one hand and the experiences in the other two visions on the other are greater and more fundamental than are their similarities. Charles received a sword, but from whom it is not said. Was this *persona* an ancestor, an angel, or something else? Moreover, the sword and its prophecy came from God through the messenger, not from its owner, as did Tyrfing. The vision of Charles Martel's damnation is even further removed from the saga. Although the vision was directed as a warning to Pepin III to restore ecclesiastical property, both the visionary and the interpreters were ecclesiastics. Indeed, in

19. In particular, see Inger M. Boberg, *Motif-Index*, E300–399, "Friendly return from the dead."
20. One need think only of the "wyrm" in *Beowulf*, line 2287. For Icelandic examples, see Boberg. On the ambiguous evidence concerning ritual fires in Merovingian graves, see Edouard Salin, *La civilisation mérovingienne*, 2, 202–212; Bailey Young, "Paganisme," 30–36.
21. Jacques Le Goff, "Culture ecclésiastique et culture folklorique au Moyen Age: Saint Marcel de Paris et le dragon," in *Pour un autre Moyen Age*, 236–279.
22. Boberg, E366, "Return from the dead to give counsel"; and E367, "Return from dead to preach repentance." Gregory's fourth book of dialogues was the major Christian source for descriptions of post mortem communications and wonders. One could cite in particular chap. 40, the vision of the torments of Paschasius; chap. 47, visions of the monks Antonius, Verulus, and Ioannes; etc. See Levison, 232.

royal visionary literature recorded from the ninth century, visions, if
not actually experienced by churchmen, were usually reported to
kings and princes by ecclesiastics acting as intermediaries between
dead kings and their living successors.[23] This role of middleman
parallels the ecclesiastical role in the exchange of property, a parallel
to which I return shortly.

If the continued communication and exchange between living and
dead laity is only dimly perceived through vision literature, it is
abundantly obvious in the ecclesiastical tradition of the cult of saints
and patrons. Oexle explores this activity in detail in his article entitled
"Die Gegenwart der Toten" [The presence of the dead].[24] He shows
that the forms of preparation for death and the types of commemoration of the dead in monastic communities all point to the supposition
that death will be a transformation but not a fundamental break in the
relationship between the dead person and his or her community. This
relationship, not reserved exclusively to saints, was understood to
require the dead to continue to support the community both in its
dealings with the saeculum, in which the dead were abundantly active, and also before God.

In this period during which, it has been argued, the idea of purga-
tory was only beginning to be formed, when the possible involvement
of the dead in the world of the living was not yet fixed, even those
dead able to intervene for the living could benefit, nonetheless, from
the intervention of the living. Thus the ritual of death as it evolved in

23. Among these visions one should cite the vision reported by Gregory of Tours in his
Historia Francorum 8.5; the visio Baronti; the visio Fursei; the visio Rotcharii; the visio
Wettini; the visio pauperculae mulieris; and the visio Bernoldi. See Levison, "Die Politik
in den Jenseitsvisionen," 233–243. Somewhat apart are the visio Karoli 3, which
purports to be the account of a vision seen by Charles himself, and the vision of
Louis the German, in which he saw the torments of his father Louis the Pious
(Annales Fuldenses a.874). One must note that the third-party intervention in the
communication between living and dead need not in itself be attributable to the
growing role of the Church in these exchanges. It may be part of the structure of a
particular type of vision in which the third person (interpreter or visionary) serves
as witness or intermediary. This is frequently the case in the visions reported by
Peter the Venerable which pertain to the twelfth century, a period with a social
structure much different from that of the early Middle Ages (PL 189. 851–954). In
the Carolingian examples, the increasing role of the Church appears rather in the
frequency with which this third person is an ecclesiastic.

24. On the saints as a particular group of the dead who continue to be involved with
the living, see Peter Brown, The Cult of the Saints, esp. chap. 4, "The Very Special
Dead," 69–85.

the early Middle Ages, particularly in the Roman rite, emphasized the unity of the living and the dead and expressed continuity in terms, common as well to other cultures, of the dying as a traveler.[25] In the sacramentary of Gellone (eighth century), for example, the soul of the dying is urged to "go forth, soul, from this world"; then follows the prayer "Receive, Lord, your servant."[26] With the expansion of the Roman liturgy from the eighth century across the Carolingian empire, the liturgy evolved to specify prayers before, during, and after death, thus minimizing the degree to which death separated the living and the dead. A similar sense of the unity of the living and the dead was noted above in Dhuoda's urging that her son pray for the living as those who would die and the dead as those who would live again.[27]

Names

Besides wealth, besides assistance, another bond united generations: the preservation of personal identity through names. The commemoration of names in liturgy, the preservation of them in necrologies and memorial books, and the recollection of the deeds of past generations all allowed the dead to live on in the society of the living. As Oexle has pointed out, the pronunciation of the name of the dead was more than simply recollection: it was the means by which the dead were made present.[28] This observation, valid for names not only of the dead but of the living as well, as in the use of names in cursing and blessing, gives particular significance to the role of libri vitae which Oexle and his colleagues in Münster and Freiburg have published and studied.[29] In the lower Rhône valley, ninth- and tenth-century sacramentaries from Lyons and Arles which I have studied are explicit in their evocation of benefactors' names. The prayer over the

25. Damien Sicard, La liturgie de la mort dans l'église latine des origines à la réforme carolingienne, Liturgiewissenschaftliche Quellen und Forschungen, 63 (Münster, 1978), 403.
26. Paris, BN MS lat. 12048, fol. 246v. On the liturgy of the dead in the early Middle Ages, see Frederick S. Paxton, Christianizing Death: The Creation of a Ritual Process in Early Medieval Europe (Ithaca, N.Y., 1990). On the Gellone sacramentary and its commendatio animae, see Paxton, 116–119.
27. Dhuoda, 8.13.
28. Oexle, "Memoria," 84.
29. Ibid., passim.

offerings from the oldest sacramentary from the diocese of Lyons
shows the evolution in the liturgy from the earlier Roman version:
"Be pleased to accept, we ask you Lord, the soul of your servant N. for
whom we offer to you the sacrificial host" continues further, "and for
the souls of all the orthodox Catholic faithful whose names are seen to
be written before your altar."[30] Similarly, the ninth-century sacramentary of Arles asks, in the Mass for the living and the dying, mercy for
those "whose bodies lie in this monastery and whose names are seen
written before your altar." In the tenth century, this general recognition was no longer sufficient; names of individuals were written into
the margin at that point in the liturgy so that these persons might be
made present each time the sacramentary was used.[31]

The importance of the bonds formed by names extends quite
beyond their role in liturgy. By reusing certain name elements or
entire names from generation to generation, families or individuals
were consciously preserving their own names and those of their ancestors. Names were a form of immaterial inheritance, and with them
might well go the possibility or likelihood of other inheritance—thus
the so-called *Grafenbar* (of such social status that they might be made
counts) carriers of particularly significant names in aristocratic Frankish families or the "ecclesiastical" names transmitted to sons destined
for the clergy. When Charles the Great advised Paulus Diaconus that
he had "named his first [legitimate] son with the name of his father
and great grandfather," and his second likewise for "his [illegitimate
half-] brother and grandfather," this choice should be seen as be-
queathing to these boys the destiny and expectations of the family.[32]
Bernard Vernier has studied a similar phenomenon in the contemporary society on the island of Karpathos. He finds there a society like
that of the early Middle Ages, in which membership in a family is fluid
in terms of biologic continuity. The practice is to give the eldest
daughter the name of her maternal grandmother and the eldest son
the name of his paternal grandfather, and this naming serves two

30. Lyons, BM MS. 537, fol. 102v. For similar texts in other sacramentaries see Oexle,
    "Memoria," 77 and n. 46.
31. Paris, BN MS lat. 2812, fol. 136v.
32. Paulus Diaconus *Gesta episcoporum Metensium, PL* 95. 719. On the significance of
    this text for understanding Charles's own perception of his family, see Michel Sot,
    "Historiographie épiscopale et modèle familial en Occident au IXᵉ siècle," *Annales*
    33 (1978): 433–449.

functions: to make *anastassi*—that is, to resuscitate—the ancestor, and to add these symbolic goods to the patrimony received in other ways.[33] The pattern in early medieval society was hardly as clear-cut as it is in present-day Karpathos; for it implied, in the words of Karl Ferdinand Werner, not a set of laws but a limit of choices.[34] Nevertheless, the gift of a name was a means of preserving one's name and hence one's self beyond the grave. Nor was this tendency limited to royalty and great aristocrats. Ninth-century polyptiques show that Germanic naming patterns were continued even among the *mancipia* of great monastic estates,[35] and by the late tenth century a minor landholder near Vienne could donate a vineyard with the following explanation: "I give this vineyard to St. Maximus because my wife had no son but only daughters, and she walked before St. Maximus and prayed to the Lord and to St. Maximus and he heard her [that is, she bore a son] and I gave him my name and he was called Artaldus."[36]

What was expected in return for this name gift? Obviously, the preservation of the name, hence of the person, through deeds that would enhance an *illustre nomen;* through the recollection of the deeds of the person in oral tradition; and through the offering of prayers by the name carrier and his agent, the Church.

The Church's Role

In each of these forms of obligatory gifts and countergifts, property for property, aid for aid, name for name, we have seen that the act of giving continued and articulated bonds created during life. Moreover, it not only reaffirmed relationships beyond death but made them more explicit, thus redefining the place of the living and the dead in the lives of their kindred. Finally, we have seen that lay society

33. Bernard Vernier, "La circulation des biens, de la main-d'oeuvre, et des prénoms à Karpathos: Du bon usage des parents et de la parenté," *Actes de la recherche en sciences sociales* 31 (1980): 63–87.
34. Karl Ferdinand Werner, "Liens de parenté et noms de personne," in *Famille et parenté dans l'Occident médiéval,* ed. Georges Duby and Jacques Le Goff (Paris, 1977), 25.
35. For example, in the polyptique of Saint Victor of Marseille, in B. Guérard, ed., *Cartulaire de l'abbaye de Saint Victor de Marseille* 2 (Paris, 1857), 644, the children of "Astrebertus mancipium" are Austrildis, Astremundus, Austremares, and Austreberga.
36. U. Chevalier, ed., *Cartulaire de l'abbaye de Saint-André-le-Bas de Vienne,* Collection de Cartulaires dauphinois 1 (Lyons, 1869), no. 181, 130–131.

had at its disposal means by which to effect these exchanges directly, without benefit of clergy. The dead left property and names to the living and counseled and admonished them through apparitions and dreams. The living preserved the dead through the continuation of names, oral tradition of illustrious deeds, and spiritual gifts returned for material ones through prayer. In every case, however, the Church came in time to dominate the exchange if not to reserve exclusively to itself the role of middle man. How is this intervention to be interpreted? We must reject a conspiracy theory of ecclesiastical culture wrenching from the laity the major role in dealing with ancestors and suggest instead that the Church was given the role primarily because ecclesiastical institutions were better at maintaining and using these channels than were any secular institutions.[37]

The purpose of establishing the place of the dead may be, as sociologists tell us, the preservation of order and stability in a social system, but the social system of the early Middle Ages was particularly fluid. The scholarship of the Schmid-Tellenbach school has shown that the early medieval family was constantly changing, loose in structure, and ever threatened, not with extinction, but with transmutation.[38] Preservation of identity, if left to the family itself, might not be possible beyond three generations; and even then, competing allegiances to agnatic and cognatic sides, the relative freedom with which land might be dispersed among potential heirs, and the propensity of members of the Frankish aristocracy in particular to move about with the expansion and contraction of the empire all made preservation even less likely. The only institutions with continuity both of place and over time were ecclesiastical foundations, which increasingly enjoyed the favor of the dying seeking consecrated burials. By involving the Church in the communications between the living and the dead, some stability could be assured: gifts of property to the dead through

37. Such a conspiracy theory is implicit in many studies of the relationship between kindred and church, e.g., Jack Goody's *The Development of the Family and Marriage in Europe* (Cambridge, 1983), esp. 103–156. Such interpretations underestimate the interrelationship and indeed interpenetration of laity and Church. For a more appropriate understanding of these relationships, see the pathbreaking study of Barbara H. Rosenwein, *To Be the Neighbor of Saint Peter: The Social Meaning of Cluny's Property, 909–1049* (Ithaca, N.Y., 1989).

38. Schmid, "Zur Problematik," 4 and 20. This threat is also a major theme in Barbara H. Rosenwein's *Rhinoceros Bound: Cluny in the Tenth Century* (Philadelphia, 1982).

the Church could assure perpetual prayers for the departed; entrusting the clergy with the *memoria* of the dead assured that names of the deceased and hence the deceased themselves would be present at the sacrifice of the Mass even if their biologic descendants should disappear. Thus a priest from Vienne, lacking descendants, could make a donation to Saint Maurice, "for the salvation of my soul and the commemoration of my name."[39] The Church possessed the body of the dead, often the bodies of a large part of the kindred.[40] It maintained a continuous cult in which the dead might be included. It held bodies of certain dead, the saints, who continued to benefit the living. Finally, it was a master of the written word, which could, in a charter of donation, present the structure of a family as articulated at the death of a member and preserve it into the future more surely than could oral tradition. For all of these reasons, the Church made an ideal component in family strategy for overcoming death.

Once incorporated into the family strategy, however, the Church in turn molded and gradually increased its role in these relationships. We can examine this role by returning to the vision literature of the ninth century, where we see the dead still guiding the living, but only through the mouth of the Church. In the vision Hincmar reported, Charles Martel does not appear to his son, Pepin the Short, and warn him directly not to do what he himself had done; the warning is provided by a bishop, Eucherius, who sees Charles for Pepin. Moreover, the message is no longer simply between ancestor and descendant—it is from God and may pass through the ancestor. In contrast, the bearer of Charlemagne's sword in the *Visio Karoli* is only a messenger.[41] Like the saints, that special group of dead through whom God acts, the dead are servants subordinated to the heavenly king. If

---

39. Chevalier, no. 108*, no. 12*.
40. Ibid., e.g., a donation to Saint-André-le-Bas for the souls of various family members and "for all of my kin who here repose," no. 182, 130–131.
41. The identity of this messenger is impossible to determine, although the choice of the word *persona* suggests a tantalizing hypothesis. *Persona* means of course not simply "person" but, originally, "mask." A synonym for *persona* in this sense is *larva*, which could mean both "mask" and "ghost," or "specter." The use of the term *persona* may hence be evidence of an earlier version of the story in which the messenger was indeed a *larva* or ghost, probably of one of Charles's ancestors. This hypothesis is strengthened by the emphasis, in the interpretation of the vision proposed by Charles, on his family, both in the past (parentum nostrorum temporibus) and future (filiorum nostrorum temporibus). See above, Chap. 3.

they are abroad, for good or for ill, it is at his pleasure. Finally, the Church is also the arbiter that decides how and in what quantity the gifts of the dead are to be repaid. On the advice of Boniface and Fulrad, who had confirmed Eucherius's vision, Pepin restores the Church property confiscated by Charles Martel; the monks of Cluny determine that the countergift appropriate for a deceased relative is one manse.[42] But these are perhaps small prices to pay in return for stability in the relationship between living and dead, a stability that extends through the entire family structure, providing, before the reforms of the eleventh century, a core around which to organize continuity between past and future generations.

42. Georges Duby, *La société aux XIᵉ et XIIᵉ siècles dans la région mâconnaise*, 2d ed. (Paris, 1971), 222, n. 18.

Negotiating

5 Humiliation of Saints

ကလ

Monastic communities performed two religious functions vital to medieval society at large.[1] First, clerics prayed for the salvation and well-being of the local population, particularly their benefactors and supporters. Inclusion in the prayers of the religious during one's lifetime and after one's death was a vital concern to a population obsessed with the insecurity of this life and the uncertainty of the next. Second, through the divine office, the Mass, and the cult of the saints whose relics were honored in the community's church, the regular clergy fulfilled the ritual actions necessary to keep the spiritual powers benevolently disposed toward human society. The relationship between saints in particular and the communities in which their bodies or relics lay was perceived as reciprocal: the saint was the protector and patron of the human community that responded to this protection, and in fact earned the right to it, through the veneration it accorded the saint.

Unlike the secular clergy, monks and regular canons had no means of forcing lay cooperation or fair dealing through excommunication or interdict, and they frequently lacked effective political or military force. Thus they naturally turned to the two services I have just described for their leverage over the rest of society. Specifically, they manipulated their "salvific" function by ceasing to pray for their opponents and, in an inversion of the normal course of their prayers,

1. I am grateful to the departments of History and Religion and to the Social Science Committee of the University of Washington, with whose members I discussed a preliminary draft of this chapter, and to John Bossy and Karl F. Morrison for their advice.

by cursing them. As Lester Little has shown, curses were solemn
rituals performed by monastic communities to ensure that a malefac-
tor was damned rather than saved.[2] The ceremony closely resembled
that of excommunication, but as the monks did not have the power,
which was reserved to the bishop, of casting an offender out of the
Church, they could only associate themselves as closely as possible
with this power and invoke biblical curse traditions while praying that
the offender be damned. The second religious function, that of continuing the proper cult of Christ and the saints, the monks manipulated in a more subtle and varied way through the ritual of the clamor
and the accompanying humiliation of relics and images.[3] These latter
measures were grounded in the physical control the religious had
over the most important sacral objects in the Christian tradition: the
body of Christ through the Eucharist and the bodies of the saints.
Again, unlike bishops, the religious could not legally suspend the
Christian cult as retaliation against an opponent, but they could
mistreat cult objects and prevent popular access to them, thus disturbing the proper relationships between the human and supernatural orders, with consequences not only for the alleged opponent
but for all of society dependent on these powers.

The clamor and the humiliation were thus an important part of the
spiritual arsenal religious communities could command in disputes
with their neighbors. Moreover, these two mechanisms, in their vary-
ing forms, made possible an escalation of force not attainable through
curses. A curse called on God to damn a person, and damnation was
an absolute act, not one of degree; whereas clamor and humiliation
could be performed in several ways, depending on the gravity of the
situation. The clamor could be made alone, or it could be accom-

2. Lester K. Little, "Formules monastiques de malédiction aux IXe et Xe siècles,"
Revue Mabillon 58 (1975): 377–399.
3. Most discussions of humiliation of relics in recent years have been based on the
collection of examples of this practice published by Charles Du Cange in his article
"Reliquiae," *Glossarium Mediae et Infimae Latinitatis* 7 (Paris, 1886), 112–113. The
brief discussion of the subject in Nicole Herrmann-Mascard's *Les reliques des saints:
Formation, coutumière d'un droit* (Paris, 1975), 226–228, does not go beyond Du
Cange. Henri Platelle has written an excellent article in which he presents the
humiliation of saints in the context of monastic reform and judicial procedures:
"Crime et châtiment à Marchiennes: Etude sur la conception et le fonctionnement
de la justice d'après les miracles de Sainte Rictrude, XIIe s.," *Sacris erudiri* 24 (1980):
155–202. More generally on the liturgical clamor see Lester K. Little, *Benedictine
Maledictions: Liturgical Cursing in Romanesque France* (Ithaca, N.Y., 1993).

panied by a temporary humiliation of the church's relics and sacred images lasting until the completion of the clamor, or in extreme cases the humiliation could continue beyond the completion of the clamor until the dispute had been settled. The rites of clamor and humiliation are extremely rich in fundamental symbolic juxtapositions and gestures that clearly illuminate the monastic preoccupation with *humilitas* (humility) and *superbia* (pride) so well described by Little in another article.[4] They are worthy of study not simply to illustrate monastic symbolics but also to illuminate those relationships between religious and secular communities which were determined by each group's attitude toward these sacred objects. Moreover, although these rituals are rich in verbal articulations of Christian traditional prayers in time of affliction and are quite orthodox in their stated theology, they simultaneously incorporate systems of multivalent symbolic gestures that cause them to resemble in structure other purely popular rites designed to coerce saints into aiding their *famuli*, or "servants." The ways in which these two sets of rites, monastic and popular, were used in specific historical circumstances, and the contemporary descriptions of their effectiveness, demonstrate the fundamental unity of religious perception and experience which, in the eleventh and twelfth centuries, cut across categories of lay or clerical, illiterate or literate, popular or elite.

The Liturgy of Humiliation

The clamor and the humiliation are closely related and appear in various combinations in liturgical manuscripts from the tenth until the thirteenth century. Although specific references to the humiliation are rare, the rite's inclusion in the *Liber tramitis*, the Cluniac customary written for the monastery of Farfa sometime between 1030 and 1040, strongly suggests that in the eleventh and twelfth centuries the practice was known in Cluniac houses throughout Europe.[5] Most

---

4. Lester K. Little, "Pride Goes before Avarice: Social Change and the Vices in Latin Christendom," *American Historical Review* 76 (1971): 16–49.

5. Peter Dinter, ed., *Liber tramitis aevi Odilonis abbatis*, Corpus consuetudinum monasticarum 10, ed. Kassius Hallinger (Siegburg, 1980), 244–247. The origin of these consuetudinaries was first demonstrated by Ildefonse Schuster, in "L'abbaye de Farfa et sa restauration au XIᵉ siècle sous Hugues 1," *Revue Bénédictine* 24 (1907): 17–35 and 374–402, esp., 374–385. See Joachim Wollasch, "Zur Datierung des *Liber tramitis* aus Farfa anhand von Personen und Personengruppen," in

simply and frequently, the clamor was a cry to the Lord for help, made
during the Mass between the Pater Noster and the Pax Domini. At
that time, while the priest held the newly consecrated host, a prayer
was recited asking the Lord's help. The prayer could be either a short
prayer, the "lesser clamor," or the longer "greater clamor." During
the recitation of the clamor the religious might prostrate themselves
before the Eucharist as a form of humiliation.

The clamor could also be accompanied by the humiliation of relics,
images, or both. As the monks descended from their choir stalls to the
floor of the church (*ad terram*), the church's most important relics and
images could be placed on the ground before the altar to join the
monks in their humiliation. After the recitation of the clamor the
relics and images could be returned to their proper places. The most
serious form of humiliation occurred in a separate ceremony, after
which the relics remained in their humiliated circumstances until the
dispute was terminated.

The ritual of humiliation is preserved in two forms: the temporary
humiliation as a part of the clamor from the above-mentioned customary of Cluny and the liturgy for the separate humiliation as
practiced at Saint-Martin of Tours.[6] At Cluny the ritual was an expansion of the clamor and occurred at the principal mass, between the
Pater Noster and the Libera Nos Quaesumus Domine. The officiating
clergy open, on the floor before the altar, a piece of coarse cloth such
as would be used for a hair shirt. On it they place the crucifix, the
Gospel books, and the relics of the saints. All the religious then
prostrate themselves on the floor and sing Psalm 73 sotto voce. Next,
two bells are rung and the celebrant genuflects before the "newly
consecrated body and blood of the Lord and before the above-
mentioned relics" and sings, in a loud voice, six other psalms and the
clamor, the text of which I shall turn to shortly. After the clamor is
completed, the relics are returned to their places and the priest
recites, sotto voce, the collect, Libera Nos Quaesumus Domine.

At Tours, the humiliation has a ritual that takes place outside of the

Personen und Gemeinschaft im Mittelalter: Karl Schmid zum fünfundsechzigsten Geburts-
tag, ed. Gerd Althoff et al. (Sigmaringen, 1988), 237–255; and Barbara H. Rosenwein, Thomas Head, and Sharon Farmer, "Monks and Their Enemies: A Comparative Approach," *Speculum* 66 (1991): 771.
   6. Edmond Martène, ed., *De Antiquis Ecclesiae Ritibus* 3 (Rouen, 1702), 431–432; 2d
ed., 2 (Antwerp, 1737), cols 898–899.

Mass. After prime, when all the bells of the tower have been rung, the canons enter the choir. They sing seven psalms and a litany (unfortunately lost). Then the most important members of the community and the ministers place on the ground before the subdean's seat a silver crucifix and all of the reliquaries of the saints and put thorns on top of and all around the tomb of Saint Martin. In the center of the nave they place a wooden crucifix likewise covered with thorns, and they block with thorns all but one of the church doors. At dawn, matins is rung for, and the office of the day begins in a subdued tone. The canons (the clergy of Saint-Martin were regular canons, not monks) descend from their stalls and follow the office on the ground. Everything about the hours is muted; antiphons are not neumic, the choir sings In Cappa, candles are not brought up around the altar in the usual way. The mass of the day is celebrated as though it were a private mass. After the Pater Noster, the clamor is recited in much the same way as at Cluny: the deacon says the great clamor while the celebrant stands before the altar, holding the Eucharist, and the canons lie prostrate on the ground. After the clamor, all say Psalm 51, the bells of the church are rung, and the service continues in a loud voice. Thus the major humiliation differs in two significant ways from the minor: although the clamor is recited later, the physical humiliation is performed in a separate ceremony, and the ritual humiliation continues until the humiliation caused by the injustice has been ended.

The ceremony at prime is essentially private, announced to the rest of the world only by the ringing of the bells. The most important members of the community are charged with placing their most precious objects, the silver crucifix and the relics, on the ground, although they remain before the subdean's seat and hence still in the choir. Thorns are placed on Saint Martin's tomb because it could not be moved and thus had to be humbled in place. By dawn, arrangements are complete. The ceremony of the clamor is included in the Mass in much the same way as at Cluny. The divine services continue but in a reduced way. Again, the physical association of the humiliated canons and the humiliated saints is emphasized by the canons joining the relics on the floor before the Eucharist.

The prayers and psalms sung during the rite elucidate the situation and articulate the community's official interpretation of the nature of the injustice and the necessary conclusion of the affair. Essentially drawn from the rich psalm literature of cries to the Lord in times of oppression, the primary prayers are Psalms 73:1, "Utquid, Deus reppulisti"; 84:8, "Ostende nobis Domine misericordiam tuam"; 105:4, "Memento nostri, Domine"; 7:7, "Exsurge Domine"; and 101:2, "Domine, exaudi orationem meam et clamor meus ad te veniat." The theme is clear. The monks and canons cry with the psalmist to the Lord that he may deliver them from their enemies: "Remember this congregation which you gathered of old." "Aid us in this time of persecution." The enemy is characterized as acting out of pride, the vice that, as Little has shown, was seen in monastic literature as the cardinal sin: "The pride (*superbia*) of those who hate you rises" (73:23). "They have burned by fire your sanctuary, they have polluted on the earth the sanctuary of your name" (73.7). The religious call on the Lord to destroy the proud, to eradicate them from the land of the living.[7]

The clamor itself, in its longest and most complete form, is found with only slight variations across a wide geographic area from the tenth until the fifteenth centuries, although most of the manuscripts do not include rubrics for its use.[8] The prayer elaborates the same

7. The prayers of clamor, the psalms, and the collects closely resemble those that Little found in the malediction liturgy ("Formules," esp. 378–380). The collect Hostium Nostrorum appears in the Roman missal among prayers against persecutors and in time of war. P. Bruylants, *Les oraisons du missel romain*, 2, *Orationum textus et usus iuxta fontes* (Louvain, 1952), no. 628, 174.

8. V. Leroquais, in *Les sacramentaires et les missels manuscrits des bibliothèques publiques de France*, 4 vols. (Paris, 1924), lists eleven manuscripts containing clamors beginning "In spiritu humilitatis." The earliest is in a tenth-century sacramentary of Saint-Martin of Tours (Paris, BN nouv. acq. lat. 1589) and was the text Martène used in his edition. If the manuscript is from Saint-Martin, the prayer must have been copied from a manuscript of Saint-Maurice of Tours, as the saints named in the clamor are the Virgin and Maurice. Other early copies of the clamor are likewise written in at the beginning or end of earlier manuscripts, like the text on fol. 3v of the Pontifical of Langres (Dijon, BM MS. 122) added in the eleventh century. In the twelfth and thirteenth centuries, the clamor was frequently placed among prayers for protection from invasion or for the Holy Land, as in the Valenciennes BM MS. 108, a twelfth-century collectionary of Saint-Armand, fol. 50v; or it is found among excommunications, as in a thirteenth-century missal of Sainte-Courneille de Campiègne (Paris, BN MS lat. 17319, fol. 216). In the latest manuscript, a fifteenth-century missal of Riermont (Paris, BN MS lat. 14283, fol. 81r), the clamor has been included as a prayer to be said immediately after the Pax Domini. In this version, like that of Sainte-Courneille, no place is left for including the names of the malefactors, and the prayer seems more a regular part of the

themes found in the psalms in a more precise way: "In a spirit of humility and with a contrite heart, we come before your holy altar and your most sacred body and blood, Lord Jesus Redeemer of the world."[9] The opening sentence recognizes the ritual moment at which the clamor is recited: the deacon or priest reciting the prayer as well as the entire community are before the altar and before the newly consecrated bread and wine. It also establishes the spiritual disposition—a spirit of humility proper to a human community: "And we acknowledge ourselves guilty of our sins against you for which we are justly stricken."[10] They acknowledge the justice of their suffering for their sins: "To you, Lord Jesus, we come, prostrate we raise our cry to you."[11] Again, the literal and figurative prostration of the community is recalled: "Because evil and proud men and their followers rise up against us, they invade and destroy the lands of this, your house, and of the churches subject to you."[12] The enemies of the community are acting out of pride, the cardinal vice in the monastic tradition, and the crime they commit is not primarily against the religious but against the house of the Lord: "They cause your poor devotees to live in sadness and hunger and nudity, they slaughter them with torments and with swords; they steal our property from which we ought to live in your service and which the blessed in spirit gave to this place for their salvation and take them violently from us."[13] The damage to the community is presented as evil primarily because it removes those necessities of life the religious must have in order to render the divine cult: "Your church, O Lord, which you founded and raised up long

---

ordinary than a special invocation in times of difficulty. This change may be the result of condemnation of the humiliation in the later Middle Ages.

9. "In spiritu humilitatis et in animo contrito, ante sanctum altare tuum, et sacratissimum Corpus et Sanguinem tuum, Domine Jesu Redemptor mundi accedimus."

10. "Et de peccatis nostris pro quibus iuste affligimur, culpabiles contra te nos reddimus."

11. "Ad te, Domine Jesu, venimus, ad te prostrati clamamus."

12. "Quia viri iniqui et superbi suisque viribus confisi undique super nos insurgunt, terras huius sanctuarii tui ceterarumque tibi subjectarum ecclesiarum invadunt, depraedantur, vastant."

13. "Pauperes tuos cultores earum in dolore et fame atque nuditate vivere faciunt, tormentis etiam et gladiis occidunt; nostras etiam res, unde vivere debemus in tuo servitio, et quas beatae animae huic loco pro salute sua reliquerunt, diripiunt, nobis etiam violenter aufferunt."

ago to the honor of your saints [here are mentioned the patrons of the community] now lies in sadness. There is no one who might console and free it, except you, Lord."[14] The saints, whose relics lie humiliated before the altar, are mentioned but not addressed directly. Rather, they too, along with their servants, make their clamor to the Lord: "Rise up, therefore, Lord Jesus, comfort us and aid us. Defeat those who assault us [here space is left for the insertion of the opponents' names]. Break the pride of those who afflict your place and us."[15] Again, the sin of *superbia* is contrasted with the *humilitas* of the community: "You know who they are, Lord, and their names and hearts were known to you before their births."[16] This second reference to the names of the malefactors, known to the Lord since before their birth, recalls the importance attached to the ritual use of names in blessing or cursing: "Wherefore, Lord, act justly toward them in your power as you know to do, make them recognize their evil as it please you; and free us in your mercy. Do not despise us, Lord, who cry to you in affliction, but because of the glory of your name and your misericord by which you founded this place, and in honor of your saints [again are mentioned the patrons' names whose relics are being humiliated] bring us peace and free us from the present danger. Amen."[17] The final lines of the prayer repeat the plea for justice, for divine intervention that will make the evil recognize their sins, and for divine mercy on the monastery the Lord had raised up to the glory of the saints.

In conclusion, the ritual of humiliation establishes, both physically and liturgically, three interrelated constructs: status reversal in the proper human-divine hierarchy; interdiction of access to cult objects; and injury to the saints through mistreatment of their images. Both lesser and the greater humiliations ritually and physically represent

14. "Ecclesia tua haec, Domine, quam priscis temporibus fundasti et sublimasti in honore et nomine sanctorum tuorum [space for names] sedit in tristitia. Non est qui consoletur eam et liberet, nisi tu Deus noster."
15. "Exsurge igitur, Domine Jesu, in auditorium conforta nos, et auxiliare nobis. Expugna impugnantes nos [space for names]. Frange etiam superbiam illorum qui tuum locum et nos affligunt."
16. "Tu scis, Domine, qui sunt illa, et nomina eorum et corda antequam nascerentur tibi sunt cognita."
17. "Quapropter eos, Domine, sicut scis, iustifica in virtute tua, fac eos recognoscere prout tibi placet, sua malefacta; et libera nos in misericordia tua. Ne despicias nos, Domine, clamantes ad te in afflictione sed propter gloriam nominis tui et misericordiam qua locum istum fundasti, et in honore sanctorum tuorum [space for names] visita nos in pace et erus nos a presenti angustia. Amen."

the injustice done to the community. The clamor and humiliation occur just after the most solemn part of the principal, and therefore public, mass. The community has just prayed in the Pater Noster to be delivered from evil. The Eucharist is still present on the altar. Before it, the most sacred objects of the church are humiliated, as are the members of the community. The verbal clamor is preceded by the clamor of the bells, and the prayer is addressed to the Eucharist as it is held above, while the community, saints and monks alike, lie below. The saints have been humiliated by injustice; hence they are placed in a humbled position along with the monks who share in the harm done the saints.

At Tours and elsewhere, the thorns are reminiscent of the crown of thorns, the mocking humiliation of Christ. But they serve a second purpose: they prevent people from approaching the tomb, touching it, or otherwise being as close to the sacred object as was usual in the medieval devotion to saints. The wooden cross covered with thorns in the nave (probably at the position from which the Eucharist was distributed) is in close proximity to the laity, who, as will be seen, are selectively admitted into the church to witness the humiliation. Likewise, the thorns in the doorways both call attention to the plight of the community and deny access to the shrine.

The aggression against the church has inverted the proper hierarchy of human and divine relationship. The physical rite actualizes this inverted hierarchy: the crucifix, relics, and monks are on the ground, the *humus;* the church is obstructed with thorns. Likewise, the liturgy emphasizes the lowly circumstances of the monks and saints who, prostrate, cry up to the Lord: "submissa voce," "officium altum," "missa quasi privata," "in suppellicis," "in cappa," and so on. The psalms and the clamor exhort the Lord to reverse this situation— "leva manus tuas," "exsurge Domine,"—while the *superbia*, the pride of the offender, is constantly emphasized. After the conclusion of the clamor proper, the bells are rung and the service continues in a loud voice anticipating the ultimate restoration of the proper order.

The ritual also juxtaposes public and private by removing from public access the primary objects of devotion. The actual humiliation is performed in private before dawn; the clamor is done publicly at Mass. The location of the humiliated objects (see the floor plan of Saint-Martin of Tours) shows a division between those objects publicly humiliated and those privately humiliated: Saint Martin's tomb

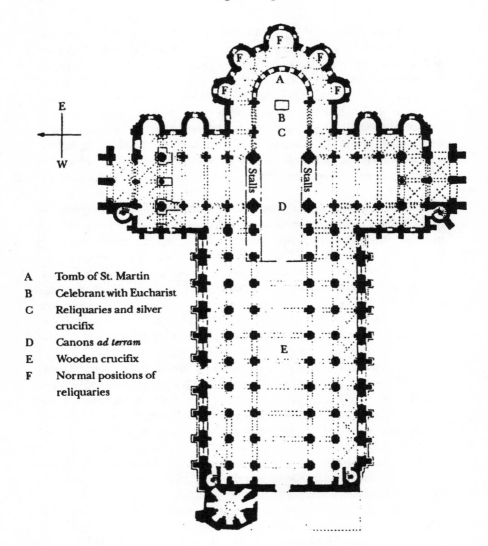

E

W

A   Tomb of St. Martin
B   Celebrant with Eucharist
C   Reliquaries and silver
     crucifix
D   Canons *ad terram*
E   Wooden crucifix
F   Normal positions of
     reliquaries

Saint-Martin of Tours, c. 1100. After Carl K. Hersey, "The Church of Saint-Martin at Tours, 903–1150," *Art Bulletin* 25(1943): 1–30.

and the wooden crucifix remain in the parts of the church open to the public, although they are surrounded and thus isolated by thorns. The other reliquaries have been removed from their normal public places in the apsidal chapels and are, along with the silver crucifix, separated from the faithful by the chancel wall.

Finally, not only are the relics and other sacred objects humiliated; they are punished. Obviously such an interpretation is not to be found in the articulated prayers of the liturgy; but ritual is always susceptible to levels of interpretation by participants and spectators alike, and the ritual of humiliation is no exception. At one level, the monks are simply dramatizing what has happened to the saints at the hands of the *superbi,* but the very dramatization of this situation involves placing the saints in situations normally associated with sinners undergoing penance. Prostration is a gesture required for a monk who has committed a serious sin at Cluny.[18] Thorns are traditionally symbolic not only of suffering but also of sin. And of course the hair shirt is a major form of penance. Perhaps even more significant, the ritual of humiliation closely resembles another common monastic ritual practiced as a form of penance: the so-called prostrate psalms sung during the season of Lent in many monasteries. These psalms are added to the divine office during the season and sung while the members of the community lie prostrate in penance for their sins.[19] Whether or not the humiliation ritual developed directly from the prostrate psalms, the similarities necessarily recalled the Lenten ritual, and since the relics and images underwent this same physical humiliation, they too appear to have been doing penance and are being punished for wrongdoing. This point will be most important when we examine the ways humiliation of relics could be interpreted and used in medieval society.

The humiliation ritual, with its physical and liturgical juxtapositions of *humus, humilitas, superbia, sublimation,* and so on, is aesthetically and dramatically well conceived. It must, however, be judged historically, not merely liturgically. In other words, we must determine how well this ritual worked in historical circumstances to protect monastic claims. We must also examine the perception of the ritual's efficacy by contemporaries. Fortunately we can investigate both these issues because we have accurate descriptions of the use of the humili-

---

18. *Liber tramitis,* 216–218.

19. As, for example, in Rabanus Maurus *De universo* 22.19, *PL* 111.518: "Spina vero est omne peccatum, quia dum trahit ad delectationem, quasi pungendo lacerat mentem." On the prostrate psalms, see, e.g., the *Decreta Lanfranci,* in David Knowles, ed., *The Monastic Constitutions of Lanfranc* (London, 1951), 19–20.

ation ritual, including, most remarkably, an instance at Tours in which the canons of Saint-Martin used precisely the ritual I have described.

Humiliation in Practice

In late 996 or early 997, Count Fulk Nerra of Anjou and Touraine entered the cloister of Saint-Martin of Tours with armed retainers and did damage to the house of one of the canons, the treasurer. This incident probably took place during Fulk's siege of the city of Tours. The canons took the attack as a gross injustice and an atrocity of the first order, in as much as the monastery was in theory immune from the count's jurisdiction. Having no other recourse against the powerful count, they decided to humiliate the relics of their saints and the crucifix on the ground, and they placed thorns on the sepulcher of the confessor Martin and around the bodies of the saints and the crucifix. They kept the doors of the church closed day and night, refusing admission to the inhabitants of the castle, opening them only to pilgrims.[20] Thus, after humiliating the relics, the canons refused the count and his men access to the church while, nonetheless, admitting outsiders, no doubt so they would witness the pitiable condition of Martin and the other saints and spread the word far and wide.

The canons were not merely blocking Fulk's access to Saint Martin. Because Fulk's ancestors and relatives including Enjeuger, the founder of the family, were buried at Saint-Martin of Tours, the canons had also cut him off from his ancestors, who for five generations had maintained a close relationship with the monastery. Eventually his attitude softened, for the account continues:

The count, regretting his actions not long after, and seeking forgiveness, by his own free will entered the cloister and went to the house of Secardus, the master of the students. From there, barefoot, he humbly entered the church with some of his followers. Stopping first before the sepulcher of Blessed Martin,

20. This chapter in its original version incorrectly identified the Fulk of the document as Fulk V, following the examination of Emile Mabille, *La pancarte noire de Saint-Martin de Tours* (Paris, 1866), 206. For the correct dating see Olivier Guillot, *Le comte d' Anjou et son entourage au XIᵉ siècle* 2 (Paris, 1972), 12, 27. The document was published by Louis Halphen in *Le comté d'Anjou au XIᵉ siècle* (1906; reprint, Geneva, 1974), 348–349. I am grateful to Bernard Bachrach for this correction. The doors of the church were closed day and night, "castrensibus etiam non introeuntibus, solis peregrinis patuere."

after giving sureties, he promised to God and to Blessed Martin through the hands of Bishop Rainald of Angers never to do such a thing again. Then he made satisfaction before the bodies of the saints and finally before the crucifix.[21]

Apparently, then the humiliation had precisely the desired results. The count, in his pride, had caused the humiliation of Martin and the other saints. To make satisfaction, he had to humiliate himself physically. Thus, barefoot, he entered the church and went in turn to each humbled sacred object, starting with the most important. When the monastery was violated and its patrons humiliated, the canons had placed themselves and their most sacred objects in the position of humility implied by the count's action. This humiliation caused the nobleman to humble himself and undergo a humiliation rite of his own to restore the proper hierarchic relationship between human and divine. Neither the humiliation of the saints nor that of the count resulted in permanent loss of status. As Lothar Bornscheuer has pointed out, the necessary result of humiliation is sublimation,[22] and so the saints are raised up in a joyful rite and returned to their proper places and the count is returned to his proper position of honor among men. The subsequent good relations between Fulk and the monastery of Saint-Martin indicate that the count had acquired the monastery as an ally in Tours.

The description of Fulk's humiliation is quite similar to one that occurred in 1152 at the monastery of Saint-Amand. A noblewoman, Gisela, and her son Stephen attempted at the death of their husband and father, Heriman, to usurp, as their inheritance rights, those things Heriman had enjoyed in fief from the monastery. The description of what followed, reported by Bishop Gerald of Tournai, emphasizes the same mechanism of hierarchic inversion we saw at Tours.

21. Halphen, 349. Note on the floor plan Fulk's progression from the periphery of the basilica to the nave to the choir. On the relationship between the counts of Anjou and Saint-Martin of Tours, see Louis Halphen and R. Poupardin, eds., *Chroniques des comtes d'Anjou et des seigneurs d'Ambroise* (Paris, 1913). On the cults of Saint Martin at Tours, see Sharon Farmer, *Communities of Saint Martin*.

22. Lothar Bornscheuer, *Miseriae Regum: Untersuchungen zum Krisen- und Todesgedanken in den herrschaftstheologischen Vorstellungen der ottonisch-salischen Zeit* (Berlin, 1968), 76–93 and esp. 194–207. On rituals of humiliation and penance see Geoffrey Koziol, *Begging Pardon and Favor: Ritual and Political Order in Early Medieval France* (Ithaca, N.Y., 1992); and Mayke de Jong, "Power and Humility in Carolingian Society: The Public Penance of Louis the Pious," *Early Medieval Europe* 1 (1992): 29–52.

The injustice had inverted the proper relationship between the monastery and the lay community, represented by Gisela and Stephen. The monks then physically represented the resulting humiliation of the saints in the humiliation ritual. They took the reliquaries "in which saints Stephen, Cyrinus, and Amand had been placed to be honored and, lowering them from the place of their lofty and honorable sanctuary, they humiliated them on the ground before the altar. The monks, their souls likewise humiliated in the dust, poured out their prayers in the sight of the highest majesty." The last sentence is an obvious reference to the clamor before the Eucharist. The two evildoers were so terrified that, like Fulk, they approached the monks to ask for mercy. Again, the final reconciliation was in the church before the humiliated relics, where Gisela and Stephen bound themselves by "a terrible oath" taken on the relics of Saint Amand. Immediately after the oath, the monks, "in a voice of exaltation and praise, raised the relics up from the ground and replaced them in their proper locations."[23] Again this final act was accompanied by a liturgy, which has not yet been rediscovered.[24]

Obviously, then, the humiliation worked, at least in the cases reported by the victorious clerics. We must ask why it did so. Were the offenders simply terrified into repentance by the solemnity of the ritual? Probably not. First, the final reconciliation often came quite a while after the humiliation, sometimes more than a year later.[25] Moreover, in spite of the monks' contentions, the actions of the nobles were frequently not as clearly evil or unjust as one might at first believe. Often the nobles seem to have acted out of a different concept of their own rights and those of the monastery, but one that corresponded to other widely held social norms.

23. Paris, BN nouv. acq. lat. 1219, fols. 170–174 (nineteenth-century copy of the cartulary of Saint-Amand, Lille, Arch. dép. du Nord, MS. 1211 1, fols. 99v–102r). A partial copy of the latter appears in Edmond Martène and Ursin Durand, eds., *Thesaurus Novus Anecdorotum* 1 (Paris, 1717), 429–433.

24. A twelfth-century manuscript from Saint-Amand (Valenciennes, BM MS. 121, fol. 89r) contains an ordo, "Quo modo fit clamor pro tribulatione," which calls for the prostration of the community and contains some of the same psalms and collects as the Tours and Cluny liturgies. No mention of the relics' humiliation appears, however. The Valenciennes BM MS. 108, a twelfth-century collectionary that contains the clamor "In spiritu hummilitatis" (fol. 50v), does not give rubrics describing its use or mentioning the humiliation.

25. As when Saint-Médard of Soissons humiliated its relics against Duke Goscelin of Lorraine for a year; see Léopold Delisle, ed., *Recueil des historiens des Gaules et de la France* 11 (Paris, 1876), 455–456.

Typical here is the case of Gisela and her son. The inheritance rights they demanded at Heriman's death were perfectly natural in a society in which offices and duties were normally hereditary. A similar case involving a disputed succession occurred around the same time at the monastery of Meung-sur-Seine.[26] A certain Erunus had held a piece of monastery land and had regularly paid the dues owed the monks. Upon his death his son Odo claimed the land as his own property. This time, the humiliation of Saint Lifard's relics did not convince Odo of the justice of the monks' cause, and he paid for his *superbia* with his life. Thus the disputes settled by humiliation of relics were often conflicts between two opposing traditions of rights: legal rights defended by the religious and customary rights claimed by the laity. Viewed from this perspective, the balance of justice is not and was not as clear as the canons and monks would have wished.

If the humiliation did not have a direct effect on the alleged wrong-doers, it did act on others, helping to shape public opinion on the issue. At Tours, for example, the bishop of Angers, probably eager to end a dispute that was causing grave difficulties not only to the principals but also to the local population, who depended on the power of Saint Martin, seems finally to have arbitrated the dispute. Similarly, Gisela and Stephen did not just give in to the monks' claims. After the humiliation they agreed to submit the case to arbitration by eight laymen and eight clerics. Likewise, at Saint-Jean-d'Angély, the humiliation of Saint Lucinius's relics against the local duke so disturbed the bishop and the count that they pressured him into a reconciliation.[27] The ritual of humiliation, while directed at the evildoer, was actually most effective, it seems, in gaining support and sympathy, or at least concern, from third parties who could put pressure on the offender to negotiate. In a sense, the monks or canons went on strike from their primary task of providing local access and proper veneration to Christ and the saints. They dramatized their work stoppage by the humiliation and thus caused enough disturbance in society at large to have their opponent forced to the bargaining table for binding arbitration.

Humiliation was, consequently, excellent propaganda for the ecclesiastics' cause. But in the context of medieval society it would be

---

26. *Acta Sanctorum ordinis S. Benedicti* (hereafter cited as *AASSOSB*) 1:161.
27. Du Cange, 7:112.

superficial and anachronistic to dismiss the rite as nothing more. Its efficacy rested on a universally shared sense of the importance of supernatural intervention in human affairs, a sense common to the monks, their opponents, and society at large. Regardless of the justice of the monks' cause, their critical role as those responsible for maintaining supernatural favor gave them an extra advantage. Whether the monks were right or wrong, an opponent and the rest of society could not forever endure the mistreatment of their defenders and patrons. Eventually, the opponent had to come to terms, not necessarily out of any sense of personal wrongdoing or guilt, but because he found himself, as in the words of Bishop Baldwin of Noyon describing the compromise agreed to by one Gerald with the monastery of Saint-Eloi of Noyon, "exceedingly terrified and advised by his wiser friends."[28]

Gerald and others in his situation quite probably were terrified of supernatural retribution. But although the liturgy of the humiliation called upon God for deliverance, all parties apparently looked not to God but to the humiliated saints for this retribution, even though, as we have seen, the saints seemed to be participants with the monks in the clamor rather than objects of it. This apparent contradiction deserves close examination.

Humiliation as Coercion

The liturgy, we saw, essentially involved placing the monks and the saints together in the same humiliated position and then raising the clamor to the Lord for help. Except for the litany, which probably included the invocation of the community's patrons, all the prayers were directed to God alone. Physically, the saints shared the floor with the monks. Moreover, they lay between the monks and the Eucharist, thus holding a proper, intermediary position between the community and the Lord. When help did come, however, it was almost always credited to the direct intervention of the saint on behalf of the community. This perception leads us to reconsider the third element of the humiliation liturgy, the punishment of the saints.

This third element of the ritual, not the cry to the Lord for help,

28. Paris, BN MS lat. 12669, fol. 109v: "his ille perterritus et ab amicis suis sapienter consultus."

is emphasized most frequently in descriptions of the humiliation. Bishop Baldwin, for example, explained that the monks "had deposited the bodies of the saints from their positions onto the ground." Orderic Vitalis, describing the humiliation of saints which took place at Le Mans in 1090, said only, "The holy images of the Lord on the crucifixes and shrines containing the relics of saints were taken down, the doors of the churches blocked up with thorns, the ringing of bells, the chanting of offices and all the accustomed rites ceased as the widowed church mourned and gave itself up to weeping."[29] These descriptions are only natural considering that, as we have seen at Saint-Martin of Tours and elsewhere, the humiliation did not end with the conclusion of the clamor but continued until the dispute had been resolved. During the clamor liturgy, the humiliation was justifiable as a physical representation of the saint joining with the monks in the cry for help to the Lord, but when the humiliation continued beyond the liturgy, it then became an act of coercion and of punishment directed against the saint himself.

Heinrich Fichtenau was the first to notice that humiliation of relics was directed not only against the perpetrator of the offense but against the saint as well, for allowing the offense to happen.[30] The monks and canons had an obligation to render their patrons proper liturgical service. In return, the saints were obliged to protect the community from harm. Thus, while the human offender was at fault for abusing the community, the saint was also at fault for allowing the abuse to have happened in the first place. The ritual humiliation therefore functioned on two levels. The first was the orthodox, verbalized clamor with and through the saints to the Lord, which physically represented the humiliation to which the saints had been subjected. Since the liturgy was developed from the psalms and perhaps from the Lenten practice of the prostrate psalms, it was natural that the prayers should all be directed to God. Simultaneously, however, in the physical act of humiliation, the saints themselves were humiliated, punished in order to force them to carry out their duties. In this second function, humiliation-as-coercion, the ritual did not differ greatly from a popular one designed to force saints to protect their followers, the ritual of beating saints' relics.

29. *The Ecclesiastical History of Orderic Vitalis,* ed. and trans. Marjorie Chibnall, 8 vols. (Oxford, 1973), 4:194–195.
30. Fichtenau, "Zum Reliquienwesen im früheren Mittelalter," 68.

Humiliation was practiced chiefly by ecclesiastics because they were the people with primary access to saints' bodies. Occasionally, however, the laity had unsupervised access to the saints and were known to practice a ritual clamor of their own characterized by physical attacks on the relics. From Saint-Calais-sur-Anille, for example, we have a fairly detailed account of such a practice. Peasants on a distant monastic property suffered silently repeated injustices at the hands of a local lord. Finally, when no relief appeared in sight, they set off for Meung, carrying gifts, to appeal directly to the saint, who, as owner of the monastery, was in a real sense their lord and hence responsible for their protection. They arrived late at night after an all-day fast and convinced the porter to allow them to enter the church alone.

Once inside the church, they began their "clamor." First, they lay before the altar praying and crying. Then two peasants rose approached the altar with their staffs, removed the altar cloths, and then began to strike the altar stone containing relics of Saint Calais, all the while crying aloud, "Why don't you defend us, most holy Lord? Why do you ignore us, sleeping so? Why don't you free us, your slaves, from our great enemy?" and so on. The porter heard the commotion and, when he saw what was going on, expelled the peasants from the church. Needless to say, the evil nobleman soon fell from his horse and broke his neck—the classic end of the sinner puffed up by pride.[31] The saint appeared to have done exactly what the peasants had told him to do.

The description need not be taken as strictly historical (no names or specific details are given); for the conclusion—"Let no one dare to disturb the possessions of the Venerable Calais or of his monastery"—clearly shows that the story is designed as a cautionary tale and not as history. Yet the detailed description of the peasants' clamor, which was neither necessary for the moral lesson of the tale nor approved of by the author, is probably not pure fiction.[32] Moreover, the story is not our only known example. The Miracles of Saint Benedict at Fleury tell of a certain Adelard who persisted in mistreating peasants on monastic lands. Once he stole something from a woman, who then

31. *Miracula S. Carilefi ad ipsius sepulcrum facta,* AASSOSB 1:650–651.
32. For an excellent general examination of the value of miracles and, more specifically, of exempla for the study of popular culture, see Jean-Claude Schmitt, "'Jeunes' et danse des chevaux de bois: Le folklore méridional dans la littérature des exempla, XIIIᵉ–XIVᵉ siècles," *Cahiers de Fanjeaux,* 11 (1976):127–58.

ran to the saint's church. There she threw back the altar cloths and
began striking the altar, crying to the saint, "Benedict, you sluggard,
you sloth, what are you doing? Why do you sleep? Why do you allow
your servant to be treated so?"[33]

Because the serfs of these monasteries were the servants of the
saints to whose monasteries they belonged, they believed the saints
were obliged to protect them. Oppression was therefore the fault of
the saints. The ritual by which they attempted to rectify the situation
was an inversion of their usual relationship to the saint, just as the
monks' ritual was an inversion of theirs. The peasants arrived and
entered the church as they normally would to pray to the saint.
Before entering into contact with the sacred object, they had prepared themselves through the journey, the fasting, and the gifts. In
the church, they prostrated themselves, but this prostration should
not be seen as the same as the monks' in their humiliation. Pride and
humility are vice and virtue of the aristocracy, lay and ecclesiastic, not
of the peasantry. The peasants' rite of coercion, even though it shared
the purposes of the clerics' rite, accordingly used a different set of
symbols. Their prostration is, rather, the incubation that, since antiquity, had been a normal means of coming into contact with the supernatural in a holy place, as is clear from the description of their actions:
"Verum illi cum orationibus diutius incubuissent. . . . "Likewise, the
physical action against the saint was one most appropriate within a
peasant culture and not a monastic one. Punishment in lay society
comes not in the form of hair shirts, thorns, or prostration but in
blows. Thus the peasants beat their saints, just as they would beat a
reluctant beast of burden, to awaken him and force him to do his job.

Allowing, then, for variations between two cultural systems with
their own sets of symbols, and omitting the intellectualization of the
monastic liturgy, we find a fundamental similarity between the two
rituals. The saint as protector of the community has not provided the
protection he is obliged to provide in return for veneration and
offerings. He therefore is punished, differently in each case, according to the norms for punishment in the cultures of the two communities. The saint is then stirred to action and begins to perform his
duty. Given that the actions of the humiliation were directed against
the saint even though the words of the liturgy were directed to the

33. E. de Certain, ed., *Les miracles de Saint Benoît* (Paris, 1858), 282–283.

Lord, it is not surprising that when help does come, the saint is credited, as Calais was believed to have intervened on behalf of his serfs. In the mid-eleventh century, for example, the monastery of Saint-Médard of Soissons humiliated its relics against Duke Goscelin of Lorraine because he had received from Henry I the village of Donchéry, claimed by the monks.[34] The relics continued to lie on the church floor for an entire year while the duke remained obstinate. Finally, according to the monks, he returned the village after experiencing a vision in which the monastery's patrons, Sebastian, Gregory, Médard, and Gilderd, were discussing in his presence what was to be done with someone who abused their property. They began to beat the duke on the head, and he awoke bleeding from his mouth and ears. After a year of humiliation, the saints had finally taken matters into their own hands. Similarly, when Odo, the son of the vassal of Meung-sur-Seine who had attempted to turn his fief into an allod, suffered a stroke after the humiliation of Saint Lifard, the monks as well as Odo's family attributed the punishment to the saint himself.

We can conclude, then, that monks, lords, and peasants in the eleventh and twelfth centuries shared one understanding of the mutual rights and responsibilities between the supernatural and the human worlds, though they expressed that understanding in different symbolic systems. Their focus, in times of crisis, was on the patron saints of their communities, with whom they had a special bond; and when one party failed to live up to his or her obligations, the other could force compliance through, respectively, miraculous intervention or beating.

The Decline of Humiliation

I began with the observation that humiliation of saints was a means by which otherwise powerless communities could obtain redress of grievances. For monks and canons as for serfs, it was a form of self-help, a way of going directly to the supernatural powers and begging or bullying them into doing their job. The popular clamor with its ritual beating was never condoned by the Church; for access to the divine was intended to be through the intermediary of the clergy. Although initially acceptable, the ecclesiastical humiliation rite fell into dis-

34. Delisle, 11:455–456.

favor as alternative means of redress appeared, means that operated through the channels of an increasingly centralized and hierarchic Church. Humiliation had often been accompanied by other forms of sanctions such as curses and appeals to bishops for excommunication. In 1049, for example, Abbot Remigius of Saint-Eloi asked Bishop Baldwin of Noyon to excommunicate the monks' opponent, against whom they had humiliated their relics. But by the thirteenth century the episcopal and papal hierarchy was becoming increasingly unhappy with the tendency of communities to humiliate their relics and images and to discontinue services without canonical grounds. The practice, particularly frequent among canons, was contrary to the increasingly legalistic organization of the Church and hence no longer acceptable. Such action, taken without formal public notification of the causes and without an attempt at adjudication, went outside the hierarchy by appealing directly to the supernatural powers. The Second Council of Lyons in 1274 condemned humiliation in the context of condemning arbitrary cessation of the liturgy—wildcat strikes, as it were.[35] Simultaneously, the church fathers seem to have reacted strongly to the mistreatment and punishment of the saints implicit in the humiliation; for they termed it a "detestable abuse of horrendous indevotion."[36] Thus, as the hierarchy was converting the Church from a ritual system to a legal one, it was also condemning the close reciprocal relationships between men and saints which had belonged to an earlier sort of Christianity, one in which both people and saints could honor or humiliate, reward or punish each other, depending on how well each performed in a mutually beneficial relationship.

35. Carl Joseph von Hefele and Henri Leclercq, *Histoire des conciles* 6 (Paris, 1914), can. 17, 195.
36. Ibid.: "Ceterum detestabilem abusum horrendae indevotionis illorum, qui crucis, beatae Virginis aliorumve sanctorum imagines, seu statutas, irreverenti ausu tractantes, eas in aggravationem cessationis huiusmodi prosternunt in terram, urticis spinisque supponunt, penitus reprobantes: aliquid tale de cetero fieri districtius prohibemus."

6 Coercion of Saints
in Medieval Religious Practice

ﻼﻼ

In an imaginative study, Pierre-André Sigal has examined the literature of divine chastisement as it appears in eleventh- and twelfth-
century hagiography.[1] Saints manifested their power not only
through beneficial miracles like working cures and finding lost objects
but also by punishing and afflicting people who had offended them.
In the collections of miracles Sigal examined, saints were credited
with having punished pillagers of monastic property, thieves who
stole church treasures, and attackers of pilgrims traveling to or from
saints' shrines. In addition, a more varied group of persons and
animals who had penetrated the sacred presence of the saints' relics
without proper preparation or respect found themselves the victims
of divine wrath: even an inadvertent glance at relics accidentally
uncovered in the course of church construction and renovation could
result in serious physical punishment. Sigal goes beyond a mere
description and classification of these punishments and examines the
psychological mechanisms by which certain misfortunes that befell
people were assigned to miraculous interventions of either divine or
saintly origin. In the majority of attacks on the saint's church or
pilgrims, the interpretation that established the causal connection
was the product of the victim, not of the one punished, or else of
other, third-party observers. In a minority of cases, the victims made
the connection, either because they recognized their guilt after the
visitation of divine wrath or because they gradually came to a consciousness of their guilt, usually through dreams in which the saint

1. Pierre-André Sigal, "Un aspect du culte des saints: Le châtiment divin."

appeared and beat them for their crimes. In any case, the perception of divine punishment rested on a shared understanding of sanctity and the nature of saints: saints were capricious, powerful, severe, jealous of their rights, and quick to reward or punish those who either trespassed or denied them.

This chapter examines the obverse of this relationship so well described by Sigal: if saints were quite capable of demanding their due and ready to strike whose who offended them, they also owed certain reciprocal obligations to their devotees, and in the eleventh and twelfth centuries neither clergy nor people hesitated to pressure, threaten and even physically abuse saints who shirked their duty.

Modern sensibilities would lead us to suppose that coercion and physical abuse of saints would have been considered improper by both religious and lay societies and that some clear limitation would have existed, if not always in practice, then at least in law. But when we look for parameters it becomes clear that this issue, like almost every other aspect of the cult of saints and their relics, was virtually ignored by canonists and theologians.[2] Devotion to saints was so universally accepted, and the cult of relics so natural a part of human life, that regulation and limitation of these phenomena was not even considered, except on an ad hoc basis when a case of abuse or fraud was so evident and so harmful to the community of the faithful that it could not be ignored. Thus the levels of force and intensity by which the faithful, lay and religious, sought to gain the favor of the saints developed naturally and increased in intensity with the urgency of the problems brought to the saints' attention.

---

2. On the slow formation of a canon law of relics, see Nicole Herrmann-Mascard, *Les reliques des saints*. A few theologians did attack aspects of the cult of relics, but they were quite exceptional; see Klaus Guth, *Guibert von Nogent und die hochmittelalter-liche Kritik an der Reliquienverehrung* (Ottobeuren, 1970). Guibert of Nogent concentrated on attacking claims to physical relics of Christ, and his objections must be seen in the context of his eucharistic theology, which must in turn be seen in the Anselmian tradition; see Jaroslav Pelikan, "A First-Generation Anselmian, Guibert of Nogent," in *Continuity and Discontinuity in Church History: Essays Presented to George Huntston Williams on the Occasion of His Sixty-fifth Birthday*, ed. F. Forrester Church and Timothy George (Leiden, 1979), 71–82; R. I. Moore, "Guibert of Nogent and His World," in *Studies in Medieval History Presented to R. H. C. Davis*, ed. Henry Mayr-Harting and R. I. Moore (London, 1985), 107–117; and Gary Macy, *The Theologies of the Eucharist in the Early Scholastic Period: A Study of the Salvific Function of the Sacrament according to the Theologians, c. 1080–1220* (Oxford, 1984), 81–82. Neither Moore nor Macy seems aware of Guth's work.

Normally, saints were honored primarily in their bodies or relics, which, in a very real, concrete sense, *were* the saints, continuing to live among their people.[3] Pilgrims from all states and stations of life sought the same sorts of aid in the same ways: the most frequent requests were for physical cures, help in finding lost property, and protection from human or natural threats. Like people of many cultures and religions encountering the holy, they prepared themselves by fasting and the ordeal of a journey, they entered the church and approached as near as possible to the saint's shrine, they attempted to touch it to insure physical contact with the sacred, and they often passed the night sleeping or keeping watch near the shrine, calling upon the name of the saint.[4]

The clergy who staffed the churches usually did little to regulate the exact nature of these phases other than to keep the pilgrims from interfering with their own official celebration of the liturgy in the monastic hours. Efforts to go beyond this minimal control and to regulate the times of contact and the sorts of popular prayers and supplications generally met with little success. At Conques, for example, pilgrims were already, in the tenth century, accustomed to passing the night in the church of Saint Foy, singing all manner of rustic songs and carrying on what the monks considered frivolous conversations. But when the community tried to exclude pilgrims from the church at night, the doors were miraculously opened and the pilgrims were found the next morning carrying on their popular invocations as usual. The monks took this miracle as a sign that God willed that the peasants be allowed unlimited access to Saint Foy and ceased closing the church doors at night.[5]

A similar tolerance was shown toward the sorts of somewhat extraordinary prayers people used to convince the saints to help them. At Chaise Dieu, for example, an old, blind beggar stood before the tomb of Saint Robert for three days, crying out incessantly the name of the saint. The man's wife finally tried to silence him by advising that a more spiritual and interior sort of invocation would be more effective: "Do you think that you will not be heard by the saint unless by

3. On saints as living members of the community, see Geary, *Furta Sacra*, chap. 6, 108–128.
4. See Jacques Paul's study, "Miracles et mentalité religieuse populaire à Marseille au début du XIVᵉ siècle," in *La religion populaire en Languedoc*, 61–90.
5. A. Bouillet, ed., *Liber miraculorum Sancte Fidis* 2.12, (Paris, 1897), 120–122.

exaggerated entreaties? Wait rather in silence and pour out your prayers in the private recesses of your heart." The man reacted to this advice with scorn, telling her to be quiet and asking, "Do you think the saint has such delicate ears that they will be injured by loud cries?" Saint Robert apparently supported the beggar's more external, physical form of invocation because he then cured him of his blindness. The monastic writer who recorded the miracle likewise thought that the man had shown greater devotion, and he compared him to the blind man who cried out to the Lord even when the disciples attempted to silence him.[6]

Thus pilgrims enjoyed great latitude in their devotion to saints, and when ordinary means failed, extreme—*improbis* in the words of the woman—measures were not only permissible but encouraged. Moreover, such means were practiced not only by the uneducated populace but by the monks themselves. To return to Conques for an example, a local lord dared to pasture his favorite horse with impunity on monastic property. Because the man could not be convinced to stop his horse from destroying the crops, the monks, in the words of Bernard of Chartres, "stirred up Saint Foy by means of excessive cries [*improbis clamoribus*], and they long exhorted her with prayers that she would turn away this plague from them." When finally the horse literally ate himself to death, rupturing his sides and falling dead in the monks' field, they interpreted his fate as Saint Foy's answer to their prayers.[7]

Improbi clamores were not necessarily limited to long and loud appeals for saintly protection. The cry could also contain a threat that if the saint should not fulfill his or her obligations, he or she would cease to be honored and might even be physically abused. Cistercian saints, in a tradition that probably dated to the earliest days of the order, when monasteries were not supposed to be pilgrimage sites, were frequently said to have been ordered by the abbots to stop working miracles.[8] After the death of Stephen of Grammont, to cite but one example, miracles worked at his tomb resulted in a pilgrimage that threatened the peace and isolation of the community. The prior approached his tomb and solemnly commanded him to cease his

---

6. *Miracula S. Roberti auctore Bertrando, AASS,* April 3, 330.
7. Bouillet, app., 229–230.
8. G. G. Coulton gives examples of this topos in his *Five Centuries of Religion* 3 (Cambridge, 1936), 98–99.

miracles, or else, he was told, his body would be disinterred and cast into the nearby river.[9] And threats did not always stop at words. Frequently in times of crisis, appeals to saintly protection were dramatized by the suspension of a cult, and the church was closed to the faithful wishing to pray or make offerings to the saints. Still more serious were the monastic rite of humiliating saints and the parallel lay practice of coercion, both described in Chapter 5.

These increasingly severe types of coercion—loud, constant entreaties; threats; abandonment; physical mistreatment; and finally, corporal punishment—appear at first to contradict the picture of the sacred, jealous, wrathful power Sigal's study presented. If saints were quick to punish even those who accidently touched them or acted irreverently in their presence, how could they tolerate such abuse? In fact, the punishment of saints by people is a reasonable extension of the punishment of people by saints and illuminates the matrix of reciprocal rights and responsibilities binding saints and men together.

Saints were vital, powerful members of society and commanded reverence, honor, respect, and devotion. They were entitled to deference, service, and an enthusiastic cult. When people purposefully or accidently failed to give them their due, either directly by acting improperly in their relics' presence or indirectly by infringing on their *honores* (their property, religious community, or devotees), they could retaliate with violence. They in turn owed, to their faithful, services that varied with the nature of the particular community. They were obliged to defend their monastic and lay families in their lives and in their property. Normally they were expected to work the miracles that formed the basis for their cult appeal and hence the usefulness of the church in lay society. In certain communities, however, such as Cistercian houses, they were instead obligated to avoid those sorts of saintly miracles that would disturb the isolation of the monks. When saints failed to fulfill their part of the bargain, they could expect to be threatened and abused until they relented, as Martin was pressured by the canons when he failed to protect Saint-Martin of Tours from Fulk Nerra, as recounted in the last chapter.

While the threats and punishments may have been extreme, they were never irreverent. Quite the opposite. Cistercian saints being threatened with exhumation and banishment were reverently ad-

9. Ibid., 99; *Vita S. Stephani Grandimontensis, PL* 204.1030.

dressed even while their options were clearly spelled out to them. Not only did humiliation of relics require an elaborate liturgy, but the actual placing of the relics on the ground had to be done by the highest ranking members of the community. Even the peasant beatings of saints were prepared for in accordance with the tradition for encountering the sacred under more normal circumstances: the peasants fasted, journeyed, and lay before the saint in respectful preparation for his chastisement.

The choice of punishments, too, was not capricious; those chosen were the same ones inflicted on people by saints. The most frequent divine punishment of disrespectful or evil nobles was casting them down from their horses, the traditional punishment for pride.[10] Humiliation of saints was exactly the same punishment: the saint was taken down from his lofty place of honor and placed on the ground. Sigal notes that saints often appeared to men in their dreams and beat them with staffs; the peasants of Saint-Calais and elsewhere simply did the same thing to the saint. Not surprisingly, in fact, the punishment of the saint could lead to the punishment of a man by the punished saint. About 1036, Henry I alienated a property of the monastery of Saint-Médard of Soissons and gave it to Duke Gozelon of Lorraine. The monks, who claimed the property by a donation from Charles the Bald or Charles the Great, were unable to recover it by appeals, either to the king or the duke. In desperation they humiliated the bodies of their principal saints. A year passed during which time the relics remained dishonored and services were suspended, but the duke remained obstinate. Finally, while attending services during Holy Week at the monastery of saints Marie and Servat at Troyes, the duke fell asleep and dreamed that he saw the patrons of Saint-Médard, Pope Gregory the Great, Sebastian, Médard, and Gildard, discussing what should be done to someone who had agreed to hold property of the Church unjustly. At the order of Gregory, Sebastian took a staff and began to beat the duke on the head. He awoke to find blood pouring from his mouth and ears and, mending his ways, returned the land to the monastery.[11] In this example, quite similar to those examined by Sigal, we see the gradual recognition of guilt, experienced as punishment by the offended saint, and resulting from punishment of the saint.

10. See Lester K. Little, "Pride Goes before Avarice.
11. Léopold Delisle, *Recueil des historiens des Gaules et de la France,* 455–456.

Chastisement of saints resembled that of people not only in the varieties of punishment but also in the effects on society at large. The full significance of divine or saintly chastisement made its greatest impression, we have seen, not on the individual being punished but rather on the rest of society, which, by the violent and unusual occurrence, came to see the connection between the initial offense and the event being interpreted as supernatural punishment. Likewise, the larger community was involved in the coercion of saints and came to understand the significance both of the punishment and of the events that led up to it. *Improbi clamores,* threats, isolation, humiliation, and beatings are all highly visible actions that dramatized the gravity of the situation causing them. These solemn, public actions are thus directed not only to the saints themselves but to society. Most events that led to coercion of saints were social disturbances—too many pilgrims to a remote monastery, disrespect of monastic rights by local landholders, abuse of a monastery's peasants. Relief could come only from social change. Thus the physical mistreatment, threatened or actual, of the most important person in the mediated relationship between the natural and supernatural worlds dramatized what had been done to this person and simultaneously helped polarize public opinion against the individual or group causing the disturbance. Humiliation almost invariably resulted in third-party arbitration to pressure the offending noble into agreement with the religious. The punishment of Saint-Calais succeeded in raising the consciousness of the monks to the plight of peasants on their distant property, and obviously, closing the church doors and suspending the cult of saints created disorder throughout the society that looked to that cult to secure divine favor and prosperity. Thus coercion of saints, like coercion of people, clarified the implicit assumptions of medieval society about the proper relationship between saints and men while it also served as a mechanism by which not only saints but sinners could be controlled.

This brief examination of the ways society viewed relationships between saints and men and their possible means of interaction must raise certain fundamental questions about the nature of medieval religion. Should coercion of men by saints and vice versa be seen as religion at all, or is it, rather, a form of magic that existed without serious opposition alongside genuinely religious aspects of Christianity through the twelfth century, was gradually condemned beginning in the thirteenth century, and then was slowly eliminated in the course of the later Middle Ages and Reformation? The exchange between the anthropologist Hildred Geertz and Keith Thomas, author of *Religion and the Decline of Magic*,[12] which appeared in the *Journal of Interdisciplinary History*, clarified the terms and boundaries of the debate on the nature of medieval Christianity.[13] As Thomas argued in his book and then pointed out again in his response to Geertz's critique of it, the various definitions of magic and religion with which historians, theologians, and until recently, anthropologists have attempted to assess systems and practices are themselves products of the early modern period. Reformers of the sixteenth century, trying to eliminate those remaining elements of medieval religion which they opposed, first formulated such distinctions as "religion is intercessionary, magic is coercive"[14] and *religion* is a term that covers the kinds of beliefs and practices that are comprehensive, organized, and concerned with providing general symbols of life, whereas *magic* is a label for those beliefs and practices that are specific, incoherent, and primarily oriented toward providing practical solutions to immediate problems but not referable to any coherent scheme of ideas.[15] Thus whatever the justification for using such labels, they are hopelessly culture bound and can be applied to other cultures and periods only with great risk to an integral understanding. Even Thomas's own chapter title, "The Magic of the Medieval Church,"[16] indicates how poorly such categories serve to illuminate the realities of the prereformation period. Certain essential characteristics of medieval religion—the sacraments, the cult practices associated with the saints—would be viewed by subsequent reformers as "magical" and, in their fragmented survivals in postreformation Europe, certainly did present a picture of incoherent, specific means of coercing supernatural powers to achieve particular ends.

Yet in the context of medieval society, these phenomena appear quite different. Punishing saints through their corporeal remains may be directed at particular ends, but it is an integral part of a broad,

12. Keith Thomas, *Religion and the Decline of Magic* (New York, 1971).
13. Hildred Geertz, "An Anthropology of Religion and Magic," *Journal of Interdisciplinary History* 6 (1975): 71–89, with a response by Keith Thomas, 91–109.
14. Ibid., 96.
15. Ibid., 72.
16. Thomas, 25–50.

cohesive view of the vertical and horizontal relationships in a society that includes both the living and the dead. The relationships of obligations and rights binding these groups, although not articulated and defined by law or creed, appear, nonetheless, to have been quite widely accepted, to judge by actions such as coercion and chastisement of men and saints. That these structures did not conform to postreformation and counterreformation views of Christianity is immaterial. Medieval religion was neither magic nor religion in the modern sense of these terms. More all-encompassing than modern, compartmentalized religion and less rationalized, codified, and articulated, medieval religion was an expression of a perception of the world, at times through joyous liturgical dance, at times through desperate physical abuse.

7 Living with Conflicts in Stateless France: A Typology of Conflict Management Mechanisms, 1050–1200

☯

Along with keeping the peace, administering justice has been a paramount function of government in the Western political tradition.[1] Public justice is a keystone of modern social and political order and for six centuries and more has been the goal, and often the mechanism for the creation, of the nation-state. Western societies, in contrast to others (today, most notably Japan, where contracts and conflicts, private and corporate, seldom require legal intervention),[2] have become accustomed to using more or less centralized, formal institu-

---

1. Preliminary versions of this chapter were presented at Loyola University of Chicago, the Western Society for French History, and the Ecole des Hautes Etudes en Sciences Sociales. I am grateful to Kermit Hall, Francis X. Hartigan, Barbara Rosenwein, Jean-Paul Poly, Stephen White, and Bertram Wyatt-Brown for their criticism and advice.
2. Martin Mayer, *The Lawyers* (New York, 1967); James Willard Hurst, *The Growth of American Law: The Lawmakers* (Boston, 1950). For a transnational examination of the literature on dispute settlement, see Mark Galanter, "Reading the Landscape of Disputes: What We Know and Don't Know (and Think We Know) about Our Allegedly Contentious and Litigious Society," *UCLA Law Review* 31 (1983): 4–71. Galanter points out (52) that much of the current attention to comparative litigation is based on false perceptions; e.g., note the following comparative statistics for judges, lawyers, and civil cases per million of population:

	Judges	Lawyers	Civil cases
France (1973)	84.0	206.7	30.67
Italy (1973)	100.8	792.6	9.66
U.S. (1980)	94.9	2348.7	44.00
Japan (1973)	22.7	91.2	11.68

On the interpretation of these statistics, which indicate that though Japan may have fewer professional judges and lawyers than Italy, its litigation rate is in fact higher, see Galanter, 57–61.

tions of justice to iron out the normal disputes and frictions of living in complex society. This is not of course to say that in contemporary French or American society conflicts and disputes normally lead to the courtroom; on the contrary, the vast majority are settled through informal or extralegal compromise.[3] But such private conclusions are encouraged by the general knowledge that public courts exist which, at considerable time and expense, will provide definitive judgments to which all parties will be required, or even forced if necessary, to adhere. Thus, whether the judicial system is actually engaged, or simply invoked, overtly or tacitly, courts capable of rendering relatively impartial, definitive decisions and of enforcing those decisions are an essential part of Western society.

It is not surprising, therefore, that medieval historians, reflecting on a time when such courts either were nonexistent or extended their jurisdiction only over unfree elements of society, should have been perplexed to apprehend no means of social control and conflict management. From a modern perspective, or even from that of the fourteenth century, such societies appeared anarchic. Legal and institutional historians in particular have found themselves on unfamiliar terrain and tended either to pass over the feudal period as a primitive state of organization, to dwell on private courts exercising jurisdiction over dependents, or to dismiss such actual means of conflict resolution as feuds as more evidence of "feudal anarchy."

The traditional view, held by legal historians such as Y. Bongert,[4] was that between the demise of the Carolingian comital court system in the tenth and eleventh centuries and the rise of royal and comital courts in the late twelfth, there existed no institutions by which the "feudal anarchy" of the period could be mitigated. Georges Duby's pioneering work on the judicial institutions of Burgundy, first published in 1946,[5] seemed if anything to reenforce this belief because, as

3. On the percentage of grievances that actually end up in court filings, see Richard E. Miller and Austin Sarat, "Grievances, Claims, and Disputes: Assessing the Adversary Culture," *Law and Society Review* 15 (1980–1981): 525–566. A study conducted in the United States (544) in 1980 indicated that for every 1,000 grievances (defined by the authors as the combination of an event and the willingness on the part of individuals to label that event as a grievance), only 50 actually resulted in court filings.

4. Y. Bongert, *Recherches sur les cours laïques du Xe au XIIe siècle* (Paris, 1944).

5. Georges Duby, "Recherches sur l'evolution des institutions judiciaires pendant le Xe et le XIe siècle dans le sud de la Bourgogne," *Le Moyen Age* 52 (1946): 149–195

he brilliantly demonstrated, the traditional forms of public judicial institutions, in particular the courts of the count and bishop, gradually evolved into voluntary tribunals of arbitration. By the end of the eleventh century, he concluded, "moral obligations and the persuasion of their peers were all that could impose a limit to their violence and greed."[6]

Yet while seeming to confirm the conclusion of generations of legal historians, Duby's examination subtly undermined it and pointed the way to a new understanding of the institutions and social control that replaced the old Carolingian legal structures in feudal Europe: true, one could not look to the courts of decentralized France for these mechanisms; rather, one had to examine the moral horizons and extralegal forms of social pressure. In other words, an understanding of the means by which conflict was handled in feudal France cannot be achieved through the methods of traditionally conceived institutional and legal history; it demands the methods of the social and cultural historian.[7]

Both American and European medievalists responded to Duby's challenge. The first to begin to give some shape to the social structures involved in these "moral obligations and persuasion of their peers" was Frederic Cheyette, who in a 1970 article examined the role of compromise settlements of disputes in the Midi, the proverbial *pays de droit écrit*.[8] He argued that before the middle of the thirteenth century, conflicts were seldom settled by authoritative courts in accordance with objective legal criteria. Rather they were worked out by arbiters, either formally chosen or simply friends and advisers, whose goal was not to judge according to a set of rules but to find a solution that would defuse a real or potentially explosive situation.

---

and 53 (1947): 15–38, reprinted in his *Hommes et structures du Moyen Age* (Paris, 1973), 7–46, and trans. as "The Evolution of Judicial Institutions: Burgundy in the Tenth and Eleventh Centuries," in Georges Duby, *The Chivalrous Society*, trans. Cynthia Postan (Berkeley, Calif., 1977), 15–58.

6. Duby, "Evolution of Judicial Institutions," 58.

7. The work of Frederic William Maitland had a similar effect on the study of the English Parliament. Although he denied "departing very far from the paths marked out," the actual effects of his analysis of the 1305 Memoranda de Parliament amounted to a revolution in the understanding of Parliament. See Edward Miller's introduction to E. B. Fryde and Edward Miller, eds., *Historical Studies of the English Parliament*, 1, *Origins to 1399* (Cambridge, 1970), ix.

8. Frederic Cheyette, "*Suum Cuique Tribuere*," *French Historical Studies* 6 (1970): 287–299.

Stephen White examined Cheyette's general thesis, namely, that in the West of France in the eleventh century, conflicts not settled by war were settled by compromises arranged through informal and voluntary use of arbiters. He concluded that "compromises were not reached, as judgments were, through the application of only a few rules deemed legally relevant to a dispute. Instead, they took account of conflicting obligations and of concerns about social ties as well as property rights . . . [and] served . . . to reconcile disputing parties and to create social ties of the sorts that collectively constituted the formal social structure of the communities in which disputes took place."[9] Stephen Weinberger then examined conflicts between clerics and laity in Provence and found that such conflicts, rather than being evidence of "feudal anarchy," reveal instead that the laity were attempting to defend hereditary rights against church claims based on legal titles.[10] The studies by Lester Little and others of rituals by which religious communities attempted to coerce opponents are also closely related;[11] for these rituals appeared most frequently in monastic liturgical books of the tenth through twelfth centuries, precisely the period when such justice was not available through human institutions. All these studies make it increasingly clear that feudal concept of conflict was extremely complex and more closely related to social and cultural structures than to legal tradition. Medieval society had numerous nonlegal means of dealing with conflict, and they appear to be evidence of anarchy only when observed from a particularly narrow and formalist legal historical perspective.

Much remains to be done before the nature of conflict in feudal France can be adequately understood. Many specific regions' judicial institutions are being examined, so that a chronology of the transformation of Carolingian judicial institutions should become possible.[12] More studies of these transformations along the model of Duby's Burgundian work and Henri Platelle's on Saint-Amand are yet

9. Stephen White, "*Pactum . . . Legem Vincit et Amor Judicium:* The Settlement of Disputes by Compromise in Eleventh-Century Western France, "*American Journal of Legal History* 22 (1978): 308.
10. Stephen Weinberger, "Les conflits entre clercs et laïcs dans la Provence du XIe siècle," *Annales du Midi* 92 (1980): 269–279.
11. Little, "Formules," 377–399, and "La morphologie des maledictions monastiques"; Platelle, "Crime et châtiment," 155–202; and see above, Chap. 5.
12. See the magisterial synthesis on the subject by Robert Fossier, *Enfance de l'Europe: Aspects économiques et sociaux* 1 (Paris, 1982), 394–401.

needed, as are more such examinations of the makeup and functioning of courts of arbitration as those of Cheyette, White, and Weinberger. Likewise essential is more research into the rituals by which conflicts were directed and transformed,[13] of the kind Little is doing on the liturgical clamor in France, Italy, and Spain.

In addition, we must also rethink the conceptual models within which we understand the place of conflict in feudal society. The traditional legal model of dispute settlement is, as is now clear, inadequate. Instead, medievalists must begin to look for different conceptual frameworks, and those most likely to be of use to us are found in the rich and often contradictory literature of legal anthropology.[14] Medieval historians are by no means the first scholars to encounter societies that deal with conflict and dispute without benefit of impersonal, centralized institutions of justice capable of rendering and enforcing definitive verdicts. Many such societies exist, and though medieval Europe was radically different from the worlds of, for example, the Barotse of Northern Zimbabue or the !Kung Bushmen of the Kalahari, the experience of anthropologists studying how these and other societies deal with social tensions can assist us in formulating categories with which to understand medieval Europe. Bearing all this in mind, let me, then, suggest a preliminary model for understanding medieval conflict.

13. One such ritual that has been the subject of considerable attention is the ordeal; see in particular Rebecca V. Colman, "Reason and Unreason in Early Medieval Law," *Journal of Interdisciplinary History* 4 (1974): 571–591; Peter Brown, "Society and the Supernatural: A Medieval Change," *Society and the Holy in Late Antiquity* (Berkeley, Calif. 1982), 302–332; Charles M. Radding, "Superstition to Science: Nature, Fortune, and the Passing of the Medieval Ordeal," *American Historical Review* 84 (1979): 945–969; and Paul R. Hyams, "Trial by Ordeal: The Key to Proof in Early Common Law," in *On the Trials and Customs of England: Essays in Honor of Samuel E. Thorne*, ed. Morris S. Arnold et al. (Chapel Hill, N.C., 1981), 90–126; and a critique of this literature by Robert Bartlett, *Trial by Fire and Water: The Medieval Judicial Ordeal* (Oxford, 1986).

14. English and American anthropologists have been particularly interested in the problem of conflict resolution in acephalous society, largely for the historical reasons, closely related to the English colonial experience, discussed by Simon Roberts in his excellent synthesis, *Order and Dispute: An Introduction to Legal Anthropology* (Harmondsworth, 1979), 11–13. Other fundamental studies of legal anthropology include Richard L. Abel, "A Comparative Theory of Dispute Institutions in Society," *Law and Society Review* 8 (1973): 217–347; the collection of essays edited by Laura Nader in *The Ethnography of Law, American Anthropologist*, supple. to 67 (1965); and Laura Nader and Harry F. Todd, eds., *The Disputing Process: Law in Ten Societies* (New York, 1978).

The Example of Chorges

A late eleventh-century dispute between the monks of Saint-Victor of Marseilles and a group of knights in the area of Chorges (in Haute-Alpes, near Embrun) has all the salient characteristics of medieval conflicts. The apparent issue was a quarrel over the possession of the *sponsalicium*, that is, the foundation endowment, of the priory of Chorges. The endowment had been donated to Saint-Victor in 1020. Prior William's determination to present his version of what transpired between the monks and the laymen resulted in the inclusion in the cartulary of Saint-Victor of a long (ten pages in the Guérard edition)[15] narrative of the conflict. In fact a sort of minichronicle, the text presents what may be perceived as a social drama within which certain fundamental issues of hierarchy, local community structure, and relationships were acted out.

This drama was performed against a background of a regional crisis of authority that began with the death in 1062 or 1063 of Count Joffred of Provence and became overt when his son, Bertrand, the last representative of the comital house, died in 1090 or 1094, precipitating a rivalry between the counts of Barcelona and Toulouse for control of the region.[16] To this political crisis was added the turbulence of the Gregorian reform in Provence, which was particularly hard fought and violent. The simoniac bishop Ribert of Gap had been deposed, probably by Pope Nicholas II, in spite of great opposition on the part of the local knights, which resulted in Pope Alexander II placing the diocese under interdict. The bishop's successor, a monk of the Trinité de Vendôme, Arnulf, so displeased the local knights that he was assassinated by one of them in 1074.[17] There resulted a vacuum of public authority and, in the words of a charter from Montmajour, "Because of this there was at that time no duke or marquis who could make right justice, but every lay order from the lowest to the highest daily practised its injustice."[18]

---

15. B. Guérard, ed., *Cartulaire de l'abbaye de Saint-Victor de Marseille* (hereafter cited as *CSV*) 1 (Paris, 1857), no. 1089, 555–564.
16. Jean-Pierre Poly, *La Provence et la société féodale, 879–1166: Contribution à l'étude des structures dites féodales dans le Midi* (Paris, 1976), 204–209, 318–359.
17. Ibid., 261–262.
18. Ibid., 208 n. 216: " . . . propter hanc causam quid tunc temporis non erat dux nec marchio qui rectam justiciam faceret, sed a minimo usque a maximum omnis laicalis ordo quotidianum iniustiam exercebat."

The text begins in medias res with the death of Poncius de Turre, one of the knights who had held the *sponsalicium* in spite of the monastery's protests. Poncius and his family and supporters had been excommunicated because of their refusal to return the property to the priory, so the monks and clergy were unwilling to give him a Christian burial.[19] To have him buried in consecrated ground, his kin agreed at a meeting presided over by "Count" Isoard of Gap to abandon all the property that could be demonstrated to have belonged to the original donation, provided that in return they could hold in fief certain *mansiones*, or farmsteads.[20] The following day the prior, who was asked to agree to this arrangement, demurred, saying that the final accord had to be given by Cardinal-archbishop Richard, who was abbot of Saint-Victor.

At a subsequent meeting presided over by Count Isoard, the knights and the monks representing the abbot approved an accord but left the problem of identifying the property unsolved. In particular, according to Prior William, the identification had been complicated by the fact that the manse of Benedet Pela had later been divided into two manses, those of Salamus and Ferreng. On the grounds that the charter of donation did not mention these two properties by their later designations, the knights insisted that they had never been part of the *sponsalicium*. This meeting ended inconclusively, with the count having succeeded only in convincing the parties to swear that they would abide by his future decision.[21]

The knights then went to their lord, Archbishop Lantelmus of Embrun, to inform him that the prior, by bringing the matter to the count, had acted against the archbishop's interests.[22] Lantelmus was furious and reprimanded William but went, nevertheless, to see the count and agreed to allow Isoard to arbitrate the issue. In the meantime, however, the knights and the monks, equally unhappy, began preparing to wage a private war.[23]

19. *CSV*, 555: "Monachi autem et sacerdotes noluerunt eum sepelire usquequo archiepiscopus venit."
20. Isoard de Mison was actually a viscount, originally an agent of the count subordinate to the bishop, who had profited from the situation to assume the comital title; see Poly, *La Provence*, 203.
21. *CSV*, 556–557.
22. *CSV*, 577: " . . . abierunt ad archiepiscopum et dixerunt quia monachi contra eum hoc fecerant."
23. *CSV*, 557: "Ipsi vero preparabant singulos homines ad prelium."

To prevent violence, the count and the archbishop convened the parties once more and began by inviting their advisers (termed "iudices") into the Church of Saint Christopher to ask how best to conclude the dispute. The advisers suggested that Peter Poncius should ask his mother about the extent of the *sponsalicium* and then that he should disclose it under oath. Prior William was then called into the church and offered this solution. He rejected it, insisting that if Peter would point out the entire property, he would accept it without an oath; for otherwise, the saints and the monks might lose simply through the ignorance of Peter. William was assured, however, that such would not be the case: if he could prove more property belonged to the endowment than Peter had shown, the monks could have it. William accepted these terms. Then Peter Poncius and his friend Peter de Rosset were called and informed of the agreement (*placitum*). They were compliant, and Peter Poncius gave a pledge (*fideiussor*) in the amount of one hundred solidi in the hands of the archbishop as guarantee that within four days he, Peter, would indicate the totality of the *sponsalicium* and swear his oath. On the appointed day, however, he indicated only that property which he had previously acknowledged and denied that certain properties including the manses of Salamus and Ferreng were included. He agreed to swear his oath to confirm this demonstration the next day, but on the morrow he was nowhere to be found in the entire village.[24]

The situation remained at this impasse until some time later, when Peter de Rosset wanted to arrange a double marriage uniting his family and that of the deceased John de Turre. He would marry John's widow, and his son, John's daughter. Peter de Rosset went to Prior William and asked him to intervene before John's lord, the count, and obtain permission. William was hesitant because John had been Poncius de Turre's brother and thus his widow was under excommunication for continuing to hold part of the *sponsalicium*. William feared that through Peter's marriage to a participant in the dispute, he would lose Peter's *amicicia* (friendship).[25] Peter promised that if William would assist him, he would make John's widow renounce the property before marrying her. William agreed and arranged the betrothals. When the knights and monks met to discuss

---

24. *CSV*, 558: "Et in mane [Willelmus prior] quesivit eum set non est inventus de toto die in illa villa."
25. *CSV*, 559: "Nolo hoc facere, quia vestram amiciciam timeo perdere."

this agreement at a placitum, however, the former insisted that the monks give them forty solidi in return for their *gripicionem* (quit-claim). The monks refused, and the groups parted *sine amore*. Not surprisingly, the monks refused to bless the marriages (hordinem facere, sicut mos est), and the knights went off with threats against the monks and celebrated the marriages without them.[26]

The knights soon found a way to revenge themselves. They attacked a priest of Saint-Victor who was passing through Rosset with wine for the priory, took his horse and mules, and confiscated the wine. When William went to demand them back, he was roundly cursed. He then appealed to the count for justice. Isoard called Peter de Rosset before him, had Peter give him gages, then ordered him to surrender the entire portion of the *sponsalicium* which, through the marriage, he held unjustly, to end his "*malefacta*," and to recompense the monks for the injuries done them. A few days later, Peter and his sons went before the archbishop and surrendered the property into his hands in the presence of the monks. In turn, the archbishop released Peter from excommunication.[27]

This conclusion lasted only as long as the count was in the area. As soon as he went on crusade in Spain, Peter de Rosset, his sons, and the sons of Poncius de Turre, seeing that the disputed property was without protection, again began to harass the monks.[28] Again the knights were excommunicated, but this only encouraged them to redouble their attacks. They pastured their animals on the sown fields, cut down trees on the property for firewood, appropriated offerings destined for the church, and even prevented the monks from bringing the last sacraments to the dying bailiff Martin, going so far as to throw the Eucharist and the cross out of the house when the monks arrived at the bedside.[29] When Martin died, the monks buried him, but from the money he had willed to the priory, Peter Poncius

26. Ibid.: "At illi cum ira et indignatione et minas recesserunt et fecerunt nupcias."
27. Ibid.: "Post paucos dies venit Petrus de Rosset et filii eius ante archiepiscopum . . . et in manu eius relinquerunt totum quod habebant de sponsalicio. . . . Et tunc solvit eos ab excommunicatione."
28. *CSV*, 560: "Viderunt . . . quod terra remanserat sine potestate. Oppres[s]erunt valde monachos Sancti Victoris et familia eorum."
29. Ibid.: "Ipsi [Petrus Poncius et Petrus de Rosset] insurgentes adversus eos [monachos] ejecerunt foras corpus et crucem Domini nostri Jesu Christi cum fustibus igneis, et sic per tribus vicibus hoc fecerunt." One might wonder if such a violent attack on the Eucharist and crucifix did not already suggest the presence of the heresy that would appear in the region a short time later.

and Peter de Rosset took ten solidi and gave them instead to another monastic community, Saint-Michel.

The monks appealed to the countess, who called the knights to appear before her. Only Peter de Rosset bothered to come, and then only to vilify William. Later, when their lord, Archbishop Lantelmus, visited Chorges, Peter de Rosset and Peter Poncius agreed to surrender the property they held from him in fief, as he commanded them[30] and they secured their promise with a warranty of two hundred solidi and two *fideiussores*. The archbishop ordered a bailiff (his?) named Peter to come before him in the church and, threatening him with excommunication, ordered him, by the fidelity that he owed,[31] to speak the truth. Peter was terrified but admitted that the manse of Benedet Pela belonged to the *sponsalicium*. On leaving the church, the archbishop then ordered Isoard, son of Poncius de Turre, and Girald, son of John de Turre, to relinquish the property of the Church of Saint Mary and the *sponsalicium* as Peter Poncius had done. This they did. They claimed, however, that the manse in dispute they held from the archbishop himself and that they would admit that it belonged to the *sponsalicium* not because they knew this to be true but simply in compliance with the will of their lord, the archbishop. Lantelmus urged them to acknowledge the property not simply because he desired it but because it was so, to which they replied that they did not *know* that it *had* belonged to the *sponsalicium*. Then the archbishop forced Bailiff Peter to repeat his sworn oath publicly. He did so but urged the archbishop to retain the knights as vassals nevertheless, a request likewise urged by the archbishop's advisers. The archbishop replied that he did not know how he could retain them if they did not know what property had made up the *sponsalicium*. At this point, the knights finally acknowledged the extent of the *sponsalicium* and begged to be retained.[32]

---

30. *CSV*, 561: "Petrus Poncius et Petrus de Rosset venerunt ante eum et promiserunt se de illo honore pro quo erant excomunicati ut facerent sicuti ipse [archiepiscopus] mandaret, et ut retinerent eos de hoc quod ei placeret." The knights clearly considered that the disputed property belonged to the archbishop.

31. Ibid.: "Constrinxit eum per excommunicationem, ex parte Dei et sanctę Marię et sancti Victoris, et per fidelitatem quam ei debebat." Bailiffs of the counts and of the bishops were a relatively recent innovation in the region. The "bail" they held was more precarious than a fief, and hence Peter is under great pressure to cooperate; see Poly, *La Provence,* 203.

32. *CSV*, 561–562.

After this formal recognition, the archbishop sought a compromise. He assembled the two parties and offered to retain the knights as vassals from the half of the *tasche* or share of the crop of Benedet Pela and from certain *manses*. The knights refused, claiming that they would rather conclude a settlement according to one of two conditions: either they would surrender one-half of the manse of Benedet Pela and would give the monks other property, the exact amount to be determined by their friends and those of the monks;[33] or they would be willing to hold the entire property in fief of the monks and to pay an annual census. These counteroffers displeased the archbishop, and the attempt to settle the affair ended with no change: the knights continued to hold the disputed property as before.

Prior William continued his campaign to have the archbishop and the count force a settlement and was able to bring the matter up once again when the count of Urgelle came to Chorges.[34] Once more the monks and knights appeared and repeated their claims and counterclaims. Much of the sparring this time involved finding reliable witnesses whose testimony would be acceptable to both parties. William suggested the sons of one Guina Tasta Ceias, but one of the knights, Bruno Stephanus, replied that they were too young to be suitable; William then offered the deathbed testimony of the father, but Bruno, perhaps with sarcasm, asserted that a dead man was too old to serve as a witness.[35] Finally the bailiff Peter was again selected. He repeated the oath he had sworn at the previous meeting, acknowledging that the disputed manses and several other properties had been part of the original *sponsalicium*, and all agreed to accept his testimony. The knights returned the property into the hands of the archbishop, and Count Isoard urged William to accept the knights as his vassals (thus returning the property to them in fief). William

---

33. *CSV*, 562: " . . . quantum amici nostri et sui laudaverint."

34. Count Ermengaud, who died ca. 1090; see Poly, *La Provence*, 272.

35. *CSV*, 262–263: "Willelmus dixit, 'Sunt quedam filii Guina Tasta Ceias quem ego credam, si per scramento constringeritis eos.' Bruno Stephanus dixit: 'Non sunt tested idonei, quia nimis sunt iuveni.' Respondit Willelmus: 'Et si isti iuventes sunt, pater illorum vetulus fuit, qui mihi ad obitum mortis suẹ testificavit.' Tunc Bruno Stephanus: 'Neque ille idoneus testis fuit, quia nimis erat vetulus.'" This deathbed confession made to the prior in the presence of his children would have been inadmissible in a court of Roman law because it was not firsthand. Even in such negotiations as these, one sees the memory of Roman law, which was once more beginning to make its way into daily life.

agreed in principle but insisted that such a decision could only be made by the absent abbot of Saint-Victor. He attempted to arrange a meeting between Peter de Rosset and Peter Poncius and the abbot, but the two knights refused to attend.[36]

Only when Abbot Richard came to Chorges itself did they meet with him.[37] This time, they were willing to admit that the manse of Benedet Pela and several other disputed properties had been part of the *sponsalicium*. William pressed them, however, to acknowledge not only the properties Bailiff Peter had specifically enumerated but also others that he had said had once belonged to the *sponsalicium* but did no more. This the knights refused to do without further sworn testimony from Bailiff Peter. Because Peter was not the abbot's vassal, however, the abbot could not force him to provide an oath. At this point, the abbot stated that he would therefore have to wait for Archbishop Lentelmus and Count Isoard to report what the bailiff had testified. Whether this ever took place is unknown, as the account ends at this point with the bitter comment, *"And thus it remained."*[38]

Analysis: Conflict as Structure

This greatly simplified account of the dispute at first seems to support the traditional image of conflict in eleventh-century society as something close to anarchy: the avaricious knights, the weakness of the count, the inadequacy of the various attempted settlements, all might imply a society without order or control. On closer examination of the background and various phases of the dispute, however, there emerges a carefully structured series of events that touches on the fundamental issues of status, power, and lordship in the region of Chorges during a period of rapid social and institutional change precipitated by the reform movement and the conflict over the disputed Provençal succession.

We must begin with the recognition that in eleventh-century

36. *CSV*, 562–563.
37. Although they did finally appear, they indicated their displeasure by making Cardinal Richard wait two days before they did so; *CSV*, 563–564.
38. *CSV*, 564: "Et ita remansit." I am grateful to Paul Hyams for assistance in making sense of this ambiguous text. The conflict, which would gradually be transformed in the twelfth century into a question of the competing jurisdictions of the count and the archbishop, would continue for well over a century; see Poly, *La Provence*, 203 and notes.

Chorges, as indeed in most societies including our own, strife played an integral, and on the whole constructive, role in daily life.[39] Strife was an organic part of the organizational structure of this society. The social units had different interests, the pursuit of which naturally led to disputes both with other similar groups (kindred vs. kindred, monastery vs. monastery, lord vs. lord) and between kinds of groups (lay vs. ecclesiastic, family vs. feudal following, regular clergy vs. secular clergy). The prior, the archbishop, and the knights were each involved in their own pursuits in harmony with their own values, some of which conflicted with those of others. The prior was concerned with the territorial integrity of his institution's property, a concern for which he would have to render an account to Saint Victor himself; the archbishop was likewise concerned with the temporalities of the diocese, as well as with his relationship as feudal lord with his vassals. The knights were eager to protect what had become hereditary family rights in their locality.

In addition, conflicts arose from the pursuit of interests by different orders or social levels (lord vs. peasant, town vs. countryside, bishop vs. lower clergy). Nor were the origins of conflict limited to tensions within the social fabric; for the very religious understanding of the relationship between the natural world and human actions prevalent in the culture also led inevitably to altercations. Because every aspect of the world was understood as having a direct meaning in human life, what we would today call "natural disasters" were then understood as endowed with meaning and demanding retribution, or at least some sort of human reaction directed at those judged culpable. Plagues, famines, floods, or crop failures thus meant that the Jews, witches, heretics, sinners, or kings perceived to have directly or indirectly caused them had to be destroyed, expelled, punished, or corrected, depending on the circumstances and how the community interpreted them.

In medieval society, daily or at least frequent contact with opponents was inescapable; thus conflict was a constant and ongoing part of life. Enemies frequently were forced to encounter one another, perhaps even to work together, and certainly to pray together, and

---

39. Roberts, 45–48. The positive nature of conflict was first explored by Georg Simmel in his *Soziologie: Untersuchungen über die Formen der Vergesellschaftung*, 5th ed. (Berlin, 1968).

this constantly reinforced atmosphere of hostility ultimately involved not only the opponents themselves and their immediate families but the entire community. Every conflict drew into it a wider society; as individuals and families were forced to take sides, to define their relationships to the principal participants. In the dispute at Chorges we see a conflict that involves not only the prior and the de Turre brothers but also their respective vassals, lords (the abbot and the archbishop respectively), and kin and, ultimately, the neighbors who are forced to testify for one side or the other. The circle of conflict becomes progressively wider.

The fatal magnetism that feuds exercised on society at large is perhaps best illustrated in contemporary literature. The essence of the tragedy in medieval epics and sagas is often exactly this: that a man, burdened by complex obligations to estranged parties, is ultimately and fatally drawn into their conflict. Neutrality is unthinkable. The most obvious example is the conflict between Roland and his father-in-law, Ganelon, which ultimately leads to the deaths not only of the two principals but also of the peers, numerous Frankish knights, and thirty of Ganelon's kinsmen (not to mention thousands of Saracens).[40] At Chorges, the prior tries to avoid having Peter de Rosset drawn into the web of conflict for fear of losing his friendship; the bailiff Peter attempts to avoid testifying because he knows that to do so will place in the conflict. Both efforts come to nought.

From this process of taking sides, of testing bonds, came not only social antagonism but cohesion as well. Dispute thus served to define the boundaries of social groups: kindreds, vassalic groups, patronage

---

40. The trial of Ganelon has long attracted the interest of legal historians; see, most importantly, R. M. Ruggieri, *Il processo di Gano nella Chanson de Roland* (Florence, 1936); J. Halverson, "Ganelon's Trial," *Speculum* 42 (1967): 661–669; R. Howard Bloch, *Medieval French Literature and Law* (Berkeley, Calif., 1977), 37–39; and Paul R. Hyams, "Henry II and Ganelon," *Syracuse Scholar* 4 (1983): 23–35. On conflicts in saga literature see Jesse L. Byock, *Feud in the Icelandic Saga* (Berkeley, Calif., 1982), but note the criticisms of Byock's approach made by William Ian Miller in his review, *Speculum* 59 (1984): 376–379. Miller's own work on dispute processing in Icelandic society is one of the most important examinations of conflict in medieval society; see in particular his "Choosing the Avenger: Some Aspects of the Bloodfeud in Medieval Iceland and England," *Law and History Review* 1 (1983): 151–204, "Justifying Skarphedinn: Of Pretext and Politics in the Icelandic Bloodfeud," *Scandinavian Studies* 55 (1983): 316–344, "Avoiding Legal Judgment: The Submission of Disputes to Arbitration in Medieval Iceland," *American Journal of Legal History* 28 (1984): 95–134, and *Bloodtaking and Peacemaking: Feud, Law, and Society in Saga Iceland* (Chicago, 1990).

connections, and the like. Moreover, conflicts created new groups as individuals or parties sought new alliances to assist them in pressing their claims. Finally, every conflict tested the implicit, preexisting social bonds and hierarchies, and every new outbreak caused existing ties to be either reaffirmed or denied. The Chorges dispute tests and reinforces the bonds uniting the de Turre and de Rosset groups, tests and strengthens the loyalty of their vassals and *amici,* and forces the entire local community to define itself in relationship to the two sides. By the end of the account (which is not the same as the end of the dispute), the knights have reason to doubt the strength of their bonds with their lord, the archbishop, and to take comfort in the loyalty of Bruno Stephanus and their other vassals who have proven their devotion. The archbishop and the monks, who had often faced each other as opponents, have drawn closer together in their mutual effort to end the conflict.

Like the dispute over the *sponsalicium* itself, the narrative of it does not begin at the "beginning" and carry through to the "end." This is typical of such records because these conflicts were such an essential part of the social fabric that one can hardly speak of them in this society as having a beginning, a middle, and an end. Conflicts were more *structures* than *events*—structures often enduring generations. The basis for social forms themselves was often a long-term, inherited conflict without which social groups would have lost their meaning and hence their cohesion. As historians, then, our interest must be less in how these long-standing antagonisms were resolved than in how they were handled. The *uses* of conflict are more significant than either the "causes" or the "resolutions" of discrete incidents, inasmuch as both the beginnings and the endings that appear in our sources are seldom really that. What they are is evidence of significant moments when deeper conflictual structures break into the open, are used for certain social purposes, and then seem to disappear, only to reemerge still later.[41]

These manifestations of conflict are not random; for they involve the issues particularly critical to that portion of society which we can

41. Legal anthropologists speak increasingly of "dispute processing" to describe the mechanisms with which conflicts are handled. As Richard Miller and Sarat point out (526), however, such an emphasis tends to obscure the social context of disputing. By speaking of disputes as dynamic structures, one emphasizes their integral role in society.

glimpse in our texts. These issues are land and its use, lordship, and honor, the latter being at once a concrete term encompassing the first two and a broader category of the public, ritual recognition of status and enjoyment achieved through the other two, its opposite being the *honte,* or disgrace, feared above all else in chivalric society. Likewise, the forms taken by dramatic outbreaks of conflict in this society are far from random. They often include the violent seizure of property, the killing or capturing of opponents, and the real or ritual exercise of power over persons or things in dispute. In the Chorges example, the apparent issue is land. To understand the background, however, we must return to the foundation of the priory and the original donation of its *sponsalicium* by Archbishop Rado of Embrun and Isoard de Mison in 1020.[42] The foundation gift included a manse identified by the name of the person who worked it, one Benedet Pela (Benedictus Peladus), and donated by Rado. Over the next fifty years, the family of the viscount of Embrun (to which Isoard de Mison probably belonged) made a series of donations to Saint-Victor, but relations between the local powers of Embrun and the great Marseillais monastery were not always calm: the archbishop was involved in a series of conflicts concerning rights over the priory's temporalities.[43] Likewise, the knights involved in the dispute were hardly less closely connected with the priory; their families had formed ties to it by exchanges and various relationships over generations. They were more old friends than enemies of the priory, although they were also vassals of the archbishop, who had apparently given them the disputed property in fief. Peter de Rosset in particular had made previous donations to Saint-Victor.[44] Having done much for the priory, these men now wanted a particular relationship with this institution which, in the sixty years since its foundation, had developed into an increasingly

42. Poly, *La Provence,* 84, n. 59, and "Lignées et domaines en Provence Xᵉ–XIᵉ siècles" (appendix to the unpublished version of Poly's thèse Droit, Université de Paris II, 1972, app. K); *CSV,* nos. 691 and 1057.

43. *CSV* no. 699 records an attempt to settle a dispute between Archbishop Lantelmus and the monks of Saint-Victor over several churches.

44. *CSV,* no. 691. In addition, Peter de Rosset, Peter Baill, and others involved in the conflict appear as signatories to two charters of donation to Saint-Victor by the viscount Isoard and Archbishop Guinamannus (the predecessor of Lantelmus); see *CSV,* nos. 692 and 698. On the complex and enduring relationships between monasteries and their "enemies," who are often also their friends and supporters, see Rosenwein, *To Be the Neighbor of Saint Peter,* esp. 49–77.

important landholder and power in Chorges. What they were seeking was not simply property but a clarification of the proper *structural relationships* among themselves, their lord archbishop Lantelmus, and the priory, which is clear from their repeated efforts to become vassals of the priory enfeoffed with all or part of the *sponsalicium*. The importance of such a positive bond of friendship is emphasized by the terminology: William fears to lose Peter de Rosset's *amicicia*;[45] after their quarrel the knights depart *sine amore*. This friendship must be created or restored in order to settle the issues at stake; without an explicit delineation of the relationships among the parties, no settlement of the property question can have any likelihood of success. Nor is there any possibility of a neutral relationship between the monks and the knights. Lacking a real settlement, the two groups will remain enemies, the one excommunicated, that is, under attack by the Church; the other harassed and bothered at every turn by the knights.

The problems underlying the conflict are thus deeply tied to the changing power structures of the region in which purely local groups—knights—are attempting to define their relationships with a great, geographically diversified, and powerful monastery. But when did the latent conflictual structure result in overt, explicit hostilities— that specific, charged episode one would traditionally term a *dispute?* It is impossible to know. The dispute was already underway at the document's beginning, continued after the document ended, and although "settled" several times, continued to erupt again and again.

These conflictual structures latent in the social fabric seem to have flared into overt conflict at specific, critical moments when social bonds (and hence the conflicts that helped to create and to sustain them) had to be reassessed and rearticulated. At Chorges, the moments of particular stress were instances of transition in the two communities: the death of John, the marriages of Peter de Rosset and his son. These were the points in the aristocratic life cycle when relationships had to be spelled out and property holdings had to be clarified. At least as significant in these circumstances was the fact that the sacramental offices of the Church were needed, giving the monks greater leverage than at other times. Like the conflict itself, which could smolder for years, a sentence of excommunication was not

45. *CSV* no. 559.

necessarily as difficult a burden to live with as the Church might have liked, but it was certainly a difficult burden to die with, and perhaps even more difficult to be buried with. Likewise, the delicate negotiations around the remarriage of a widowed heiress required the assistance of the prior, both to negotiate with the widow's lord and to bless the union.

Such conflictual structures are by no means unique to medieval Europe. What was unusual about "dispute processing" in the eleventh and twelfth centuries is that, in much of Western Europe, there existed no effective, centralized means of channeling or limiting outbreaks or of converting them into other forms of social action. In the course of the tenth and early eleventh centuries, public comital courts, which had functioned more or less well in the Carolingian period, had disappeared in large areas of Europe.[46] Those courts that did continue either already were, or rapidly became, private. Individual landowners or landholders (that is, the old aristocracy), the newly emerged free warrior society, and the ecclesiastical institutions all had their own courts, but these served only to provide justice to their unfree or semifree dependents. Here "justice" was severely dispensed, and real judgments were "recognized" through oaths, ordeals, or, in areas of Roman legal tradition, testimony. The jurisdiction of these courts did not, however, extend beyond the circle of a lord's dependents, and often he was unable even to require his own

46. On Carolingian courts see Robert-Henri Bautier, "L'exercise de la justice publique dans l'empire carolingien," *Positions des thèses, Ecole nationale des Chartes* (1943): 9–18; François Louis Ganshof, "Charlemagne et l'administration de la justice dans la monarchie franque," in *Karl der Große: Lebenswerk und Nachleben*, 1, *Personlichkeit und Geschichte*, ed. Helmut Beumann (Düsseldorf, 1965), 394–419, and trans. as "Charlemagne and the Administration of Justice," in François Louis Ganshof, *Frankish Institutions under Charlemagne*, trans. Bryce Lyon and Mary Lyon (New York, 1968), 71–97. The nature and degree of the transformation of the Carolingian system of justice varied widely across Europe. On the transformation of public justice in post-Carolingian Europe see—in addition to Duby, "Recherches," and Bongert for West Francia—Heinrich Mitteis, *Der Staat des hohen Mittelalters: Grundlinien einer vergleichenden Verfassungsgeschichte des Lehnzeitalters*, 8th ed. (Weimar, 1968), 161–168, and P. Dollinger, *L'evolution des classes rurales en Bavière depuis la fin de l'époque carolingienne jusqu'au milieu du XIIIe siècle* (Strasbourg, 1949), 47–77, for the relatively conservative empire; François Louis Ganshof, "Les transformations de l'organisation judiciaire dans le comté de Flandre jusqu'à l'avenement de la maison de Bourgogne," *Revue belge de philologie et d'histoire* 18 (1939): 43–61; Henri Platelle, *La justice seigneuriale de l'abbaye de Saint-Amand: Son organisation judiciaire, sa procédure et sa compétence du XIe au XVIe siècle* (Louvain, 1965); and in general, Fossier, 394–401, and the bibliography there cited.

vassals to resolve their disputes in his court. These private courts were thus less institutions of public order than important sources of revenue and social control.

It cannot be said that those powerful enough to escape such private jurisdictions that is, the *milites*, or knightly order, and the Church— were subject to no public system of law or justice; but the system that prevailed was immanent in the community and found expression in just such negotiations as those at Chorges rather than in a transcendant, central authority like a count. In fact, counts such as Isoard of Gap should be seen less as impotent public authorities than as individuals attempting to coerce or cajole their neighbors into submitting to their private justice. This does not mean that law and legal systems were unknown. On the contrary, one could almost speak of a superabundance of legal systems: the traditional Germanic laws as transmitted and emended by the Carolingians; Roman law still alive in many southern regions of Europe; a body of Church laws; and an emerging feudal law.[47] What was lacking was a mutually obligating sense of community with a jurisprudential system or other means by which individuals could be controlled and constrained. Where comital courts continued to meet, participation by the free population was largely voluntary, and decisions, often deceptively termed "judgments" (*iudicia*) in the documents that preserved the form but not the content of the Carolingian tradition, were not enforceable by the count or judge. Even when a particularly strong count was able to

47. As White and others point out, courts did continue to function in this period, but they were primarily intended for lower levels of society. Some disputes were dealt with by judges who rendered real decisions, finding for one side against the other. As in the case of Chorges, however, such decisions often were unenforceable, and disputants therefore sought a deeper resolution of the conflict through a mutually acceptable compromise. In addition to the literature cited in note 46 above, see A. C. F. Koch, "L'origine de la haute et de la moyenne justice dans l'ouest et le nord de la France," *Revue d'histoire du droit* 21 (1953): 420–458; and F. L. Lemarignier, "La dislocation du pagus et le problème des consuetudines, X^e–XIe siècles," in *Mélanges Louis Halphen*, ed. Charles-Edmond Perrin (Paris, 1951), 401–410. In the late eleventh century, Provence was already beginning to experience a renaissance of Roman law; see R. J. Aubenas, "Quelques réflections sur le problème de la pénétration du droit romain dans le midi de la France au Moyen Âge," *Annales du Midi* 76 (1964): 371–377; Marie-Louise Carlin, *La pénétration du droit romain dans les actes de la pratique provençal, XIe–XIIIe siècle* (Toulouse, 1967); and Jean-Pierre Poly, "Les maîtres de Saint-Ruf: Pratique et enseignement du droit dans la France méridionale au XIIe siècle," *Annales de la faculté de droit des sciences sociales et politiques et de la faculté des sciences économiques de l'université de Bordeaux* 1, no. 2 (1978): 183–203.

impose his justice on the free society of his region, this imposition was usually possible only through fear, and his disappearance, through death or absence, was sufficient grounds for his judgments to be ignored and violence to break out anew.[48] No community based on an abstract "rule of law" checked or controlled the eruption of violent conflict.[49]

The situation at Chorges was exactly as outlined above. In spite of the presence of the nominal lords of the region, the archbishop and the count—and in spite of the vocabulary of the text, which speaks of *iudices, placita, iusticiam facere, iusticiam dare, placitum facere,* and so forth—the sorts of proceedings can hardly be termed adjudications of the dispute. Rather than act as "judges," the archbishop, the count, and their advisers could do nothing more than suggest solutions or, at best, impose temporary resolutions that dissolved as soon as the count was out of the region. The moment Isoard left for Spain to fight the "barbarians," leaving the land *sine potestate,* the old conflict resumed.[50] Lacking such a community of mutually recognized authority and an internalized sense of the "rule of law," individuals and groups, for whom neutrality was impossible, related to each other as *amici*—that is, those who are bound by a *pax* or friendship—or as *inimici*—that is, those who face each other in a potential or actual state of war. Beginning in the tenth century, the Peace of God movement attempted to induce members of society to bind themselves together in a *pax* that would establish a common, positive relationship among neighbors and form the basis for community control. This attempt to substitute God's peace for that of the no-longer-effective king's peace met with opposition both from below, as free warriors considered it an

48. Another prime example of the precariousness of even those judicial systems that seemed well developed by the late eleventh century is Flanders, where the structures established by the counts rapidly disintegrated after the murder of Charles the Good; see James Bruce Ross's excellent introduction to his translation of Galbert of Bruges's account of the murder: Galbert of Bruges, *The Murder of Charles the Good Count of Flanders: A Contemporary Record of Revolutionary Change in Twelfth Century Flanders* (New York, 1967), 46–47. On the judicial institutions of the counts and the communes, see R. C. Van Caenegem, *Geschiedenis van het Strafrecht in Vlaanderen van de XIᵉ tot de XIVᵉ eeuw* (Brussels, 1954), and *Geschiedenis van het strafprocesrecht in Vlaanderen van de XIᵉ tot de XIVᵉ eeuw* (Brussels, 1956).

49. On the development of modern notions of rule of law, see the provocative synthesis by Harold J. Berman, *Law and Revolution: The Formation of the Western Legal Tradition* (Cambridge, Mass., 1983).

50. *CSV,* 559–560; Poly, *La Provence,* 266–267.

imposition on their freedom, and from above, as kings, emperors, and counts recognized it as a form of competition. Not surprisingly, except in those areas where magnates were able to co-opt the Peace of God and to use it to expand their territorial authority, it failed to produce lasting institutions of public justice or peace-keeping based on a spiritual consensus.[51]

Mechanisms for Conflict Management

To assert the absence of a public court system with recognized jurisdiction is not to say that society existed in a state of anarchy. Groups and individuals belonged to a society and a culture that were remarkably homogeneous, and within this homogeneous system, they dealt with their conflictual relationships according to a complex of shared values and implicit rules.

The primary model for dealing with others with whom one had a dispute was armed self-help, the feud.[52] This was the natural means

---

51. On the Peace of God in general, see Thomas Head and Richard Landes, eds., *The Peace of God;* Hartmut Hoffmann, *Gottesfriede und Treuga Dei*, Schriften der Monumenta Germaniae Historica 20 (Stuttgart, 1964); Georges Duby, "Les laïques et la paix de Dieu," in *Hommes et structures*, 227–240, trans. as "Laity and the Peace of God," in *Chivalrous Society*, 123–133; Duby, *Les trois ordres ou l'imaginaire du féodalisme* (Paris, 1978), esp. 35–61; and Jean-Pierre Poly and Eric Bournazel, *La mutation féodale X^e–XIIe siècles*, 2d. ed. (Paris, 1991), 222–274. On the appropriation of the Peace of God by the magnates, see Fossier, 317–318. An excellent example of the appropriation of peace movements to other ends is provided by Archbishop Guido of Vienne (1083–1119), who, during a long dispute with Bishop Hugo of Grenoble over the region of Salmorens, used a group of knights organized to preserve the Peace of God as a strike force to occupy the disputed territory; see Jules Marion, ed., *Cartulaires de l'élise cathédrale de Grenoble dits cartulaires de Saint-Hugues* (Paris, 1869), no. 23, 49: "Sed Viennensis archiepiscopus noluit audire juditium, quoniam eo tempore milites illius terrae ad pacem faciendam conjuratos in manum sua tenebat."

52. There is an enormous amount of literature on the feud in medieval Europe. On the feud as a fundamental structure, see Otto Brunner, *Land und Herrschaft: Grundfragen der territorialen Verfassungsgeschichte Österreichs im Mittelalter*, 5th ed. (Vienna, 1965), 1–110, trans. as *Land and Lordship: Structures of Governance in Medieval Austria*, trans. Howard Kaminsky and James Van Horn Melton (Philadelphia, 1992), 1–94. Although Brunner is treating a much later period, the political and social structures of late medieval Austria resemble those of France at an earlier period. On Brunner's concept of feud and its significance to his understanding of medieval power, see the introduction to Kaminsky and Melton, xiii–lxi, esp. xviii–xix. On the earlier period see Geoffrey G. Koziol, "Monks, Feuds, and the Making of Peace in Eleventh-Century Flanders," in Head and Landes, 239–

of righting wrongs in a social group that based its existence on, and
justified its social role in, warfare. The model of the feud was not
confined to the laity. The clergy, and especially the monastic communities that dominated the religious society of the period, shared the
ideal of their martial brothers and were ready to wage a spiritual war
and even a physical one against their enemies.[53] Such conflicts, often
termed *guerrae* in contemporary sources, were by no means, however,
conducted as unlimited wars aimed at extinguishing the family or
party in opposition. Usually such a *guerra* was intended to reestablish
a balance in real or imagined offenses (an eye for an eye) and thus to
restore an equilibrium of honor, or else it was waged to achieve
temporary advantage and force the enemy into negotiating the
deeper, underlying issues. These issues might be possession of property, the clarification of hierarchical relationships, or the recognition of traditional bonds and obligations. When, for example, Hugo
"Chiliarchus," frustrated in his attempts to win what he considered
proper treatment from his lord, William IX of Aquitaine, disavowed
his bonds of fealty and began a *guerra* against his lord, going as far as
seizing some of his castles, he had no intention of making the break
permanent. The "war" was but a limited, ritual attack designed to
indicate the seriousness of the situation and to win for him a stronger
bargaining position with his once and future lord.[54]

258; Stephen White, "Feuding and Peace-Making in the Touraine around the Year
1000," *Traditio* 42 (1986): 195–263; and William Miller, *Bloodtaking and Peacemak-
ing*. On feud and conflict in the Germanic world, see, in particular, Hanna Vollrath,
"Konfliktwahrnehmung und Konfliktdarstellung in erzahlenden Quellen des 11.
Jahrhunderts," in *Die Salier und das Reich*, 3, *Gesellschaftlicher und ideengeschichtlicher
Wandel im Reich der Salier*, ed. Stefan Weinfurter (Sigmaringen, 1991), 279–297;
Timothy Reuter, "Unruhestiftung, Fehde, Rebellion, Widerstand: Gewalt und
Frieden in der Politik der Salierzeit," in ibid., 297–325; and Gerd Althoff, *Ver-
wandte, Freunde und Getreue: Zum politischen Stellenwert der Gruppenbindungen im
früheren Mittelalter* (Darmstadt, 1990), and "Königsherrschaft und Konfliktbewäl-
tigung im 10. und 11. Jahrhundert," *Frühmittelalterliche Studien* 23 (1989): 265–
290. For analyses of feuding in cross-cultural perspective, see Jacob Black-
Michaud, *Cohesive Force: Feud in the Mediterranean and the Middle East* (New York,
1975); and Max Gluckman, "The Peace in the Feud," *Past and Present* 7 (1955): 1–
14.
53. On the militant ideology of monasticism see Barbara H. Rosenwein and Lester K.
Little, "Social Meaning in the Monastic and Mendicant Spiritualities," *Past and
Present* 63 (1974): 4–32.
54. Jane Martindale, "*Conventum inter Guillelmum Aquitanorum comes et Hugonem Chili-
archum*," *English Historical Review* 332 (1969): 528–548. See the analysis of this

Of course, a feud need not be carried on only by warfare: it could equally well be pursued through occasional harassment, interference with the daily activities of the enemy, or even verbal attacks in assemblies or law courts.[55] The knights and monks at Chorges had various means to press their ends, each particular to their social position. The knights sought to exercise lordship over the property in dispute, or at least to prevent the monks from doing so, by seizing the property, destroying crops, and in general disrupting the exploitation of the land. They also attempted to hamper the monks in the exercise of their religious activities, particularly when those activities, such as the administration of the last rites, would be likely to benefit the monks materially.

For their part, the monks sought to interrupt the continuity in the lay community through refusal to perform the sacraments and through excommunication (launched of course by the archbishop). Just as the *guerra* was a ritual war intended to exert pressure on the enemy, these liturgical measures could be brought to bear for the same effect.[56] The repertoire included rituals of excommunication,[57] liturgical cursing,[58] public shaming (see Chap. 5), and the like. These rituals served both to announce to society at large the wrong that had

---

document by George Beech, "A Feudal Document of Early Eleventh-Century Poitou," *Mélanges offerts à René Crozet* (Poitiers, 1966), 203–213. For very different interpretations of the *conventum*, see M. Garaud, "Une problème d'histoire: A propos d'une lettre du Fulbert de Chartres à Guillaume le Grand, comte de Poitou et duc d'Aquitaine," in *Etudes d'histoire du droit canonique dediés à Gabriel le Bras* 1 (Paris, 1965), 559 ff.; and Poly and Bournazel, 137–141 and 148–150.

55. As Laura Nader points out in "The Anthropological Study of Law," in *Ethnography of Law*, 18–19, litigation has many other functions than to maintain order, including not only settling conflicts but performing punitive functions, preventing or deterring breaches in law or custom, and maintaining order in politics and economics. Court proceedings are also used to ruin enemies, to defeat competitors, to harass the less-than-ideal citizen, to serve as a moral "turning point" just as the drama of the court provides a mechanism for socialization or enculturation, to test values other than legal ones, to achieve economic gain, and even to provide entertainment.

56. On the channeling of conflicts into ritual, see Roberts, 59–61.

57. On excommunication see Gabriel Le Bras, *Institutions ecclésiastiques de la Chrétienté médiévale*, Histoire de l'église depuis les origines jusqu'à nos jours 12 (Tournai, 1959), 226–230 and 246–248; Elisabeth Vodola, *Excommunication in the Middle Ages* (Berkeley, Calif., 1986); and Heinrich Fichtenau, *Living in the Tenth Century: Studies in Mentalities and Social Orders* (Chicago, 1991), 392–397.

58. Little, "Formules" and "La morphologie." On the close relationship between ritual cursing and excommunication, see the latter, 49–53.

been done and to reaffirm the proper structural relationship, which, according to the clerics, had been upset. They were also intended to force the wider society to take sides in the conflict and thus marshal community pressure for settlement or at least containment of their enemies. These rites should properly be seen not as rituals of conflict resolution but as means of *continuing* the conflict in such a way as to strengthen the relative position of the church in the conflictual structure of society.

All these rituals were public. Excommunications and ritual curses, for example, normally took place during the Sunday mass immediately after the reading of the gospel.[59] A ritual humiliation, in which the relics and other sacred objects of the church were placed on the floor and covered with thorns, took place after the consecration and before the kiss of peace. The meaning of the ritual was clearly and graphically explained to those present. In the case of excommunication, the bishop explained to the congregation just how the person to be excommunicated had offended God and, through his or her extravagant pride, had cut himself or herself off from the communion of the faithful.[60] The ritual cursing practised in monasteries, which did not have the episcopal power to excommunicate, likewise sought to make clear the offenses of the enemy and to claim, through impressive if fictional episcopal and papal confirmations, the right to curse opponents.[61] The ritual humiliation sought the same clarification by a physical inversion of the proper hierarchical status: the relics and sacred images of the church were placed on the floor and covered with thorns to show how, through their pride, the enemies had overturned the divine order. At Saint-Amand, after the crucifix had been placed on the floor of the church, a list of the offenses committed by the monastery's enemies was placed in the outstretched hand of the Christus so that he, and presumably everyone else, would know the exact cause of the humiliation.[62]

59. Excommunication: "Episcopus cum excommunicare vel anathematizare aliquem pro crucis et manifestis sceleribus dispositum habet, post lectionem Evangelii clerum et plebem ita debet alloqui" (*Ordo excommunicationis, PL* 138.1123). Curses: " . . . in die dominico et cotidianis diebus in dicto monasterio, finito evangelio a diacono, stans presbiter ante altare dicat" (Little, "Formules," 392–393).

60. *PL* 138.1123: "Sed ipse proh dolor! diabolo cor eius indurante, monita salutaria sprevit, et in incepta malicia perseverans, Ecclesiae Dei, quam laesit superbiae spiritus inflatus satisfacere dedignatur."

61. Little, "Formules," 381–382.

62. Platelle, *La justice seigneuriale*, 421–427.

Though a clamor, a ritual cry to God for help, formed the heart of these rituals, the religious did not stop at a divine appeal; for the liturgies were designed to enlist the public as well. The excommunicate became an exile in his own community.[63] Under pain of joining her or him in excommunication, no one was to give the culprit food or shelter, or even to converse with her or him unless it was with the purpose of bringing about repentance.[64] The terrible curses called down upon the heads of the monastery's enemies were likewise to visit anyone who aided them.[65] And after the ritual of humiliation, the closing of the church to the local laity deprived everyone in the area of divine access until the conflict was resolved.

In these rituals we can discern three goals: first, to isolate the enemy both from God and from man; second, to disrupt the normal social relations of the community—to bring usual daily intercourse to a halt; and third, to present an image of the proper hierarchical structure of the world as well as a graphic, ritual image of the unnatural inversion caused by the offender. By suggesting how the divine system had been threatened, the clergy could orient the understanding of every natural accident, injury, or reverse of fortune in the enemy camp as divine retribution falling on the evildoer and his allies.[66]

Just as at Chorges, such rituals were particularly effective at certain critical moments in life. In the hour of death, an excommunicate or long-time enemy of the local monastery might be led by fear of damnation to reach a settlement. Failing that, the Church had another powerful weapon: denial of Christian burial. It is not unusual to find accounts of agreements reached between heirs and monasteries while the body of the old opponent lay uninterred in their midst.[67]

63. On exile see Roberts, 65–67; on excommunication as exile see Le Bras, 226–227.
64. *PL* 138.1125: "... et qui ille (excommunicato) quisi christiano communicaverit, aut biberit, aut eum osculatus fuerit, vel cum eo colloquium familiare habuerit, nisi forte ad satisfactionem et paenitentiam eum provocare studierit, aut in domo sua receperit, aut simul cum eo oraverit, procul dubio similiter sit excommunicatus." Le Bras, 246 n. 12.
65. Little, "Formules," 10: "Maledicti sint uxores eorum et infantes eorum et omnes qui eis consentiunt."
66. Little, "Pride Goes before Avarice."
67. Another example of the pressure that could be exerted on an opponent's party at the moments of death and burial is that of Wichardus of Ruffey, preserved in a charter of Cluny in A. Bruel, ed., *Recueil des Chartes de l'abbaye de Cluny* 3 (Paris, 1876), no. 2009, 221–222: "Wichardus de Rufiaco, moriens, et nil loqui prevalens, deportatus apud Cluniacum, antequam sepeliretur, affuerunt eius propinqui et

Likewise at the time of a marriage, which in knightly society was an important alliance between kindreds as well as the crucial means of continuing the family, the laity were eager for a church blessing, which was highly desirable although not absolutely essential to ensure a fruitful and legitimate union.

These pressures, both on the individuals in conflict and on the wider community, were intended not to destroy the enemies of the Church but to bring about negotiations. Although texts written from the perspective of the clergy often read as though the results of their rites were the abject surrender of the evildoers, a closer examination usually suggests that, under the pressure of the wider public and the friends and the lord of the opponent, a negotiated compromise was reached.

The ultimate purpose of negotiation was to establish a *pax* or *amicitia* between the opposing parties, that is, to create a positive relationship to replace the state of war. At Chorges, both sides were quite willing, if other forms of direct action failed to restore *amicitia*, to resort to arms, and this threat of open warfare seems to have been a major cause of the wider community's attempts to arbitrate the dispute.[68] The negotiation might be carried on directly between the leaders of the opposing parties. Thus the abbot or prior of a monastery might meet face-to-face with a knight who disputed the monastery's claim to a piece of property.[69] More often, as at Chorges, negotiations were carried on by an arbiter agreeable to both parties.[70]

---

parentes, qui inter se colloquentes coeperunt iniquirere quid pro anime illius salute agere deberent. . . . Dederunt etiam franchisiam sitam in Rufiaco villa, quam ipse Wichardus quęrelabat servis Sancti Petri." The document and the conflict between the kindred of Wichardus and the monks of Cluny which it records is discussed by Georges Duby in his *La société au XIᵉ et XIIᵉ siècle dans la region mâconnaise*, 222.

68. The count and archbishop were particularly concerned "ut bellum non esset inter monachos et milites" (*CSV*, 557).

69. On private *convenientiae* in general see White, "*Pactum*," 292–307; and Fossier, 396. Fossier sees these negotiations as efforts to "courtcircuiter" established justice, whereas White argues, as I do, that these *convenientiae* may have been more effective at resolving basic, structural problems than mere judgments might have been. Penelope D. Johnson, *Prayer, Patronage, and Power: The Abbey of la Trinité, Vendôme, 1032–1187* (New York, 1981), 93, finds the percentage of settlements reached by negotiation during the period she has studied increasing from 57 percent to 86 percent. She points out, however, that just as we shall see below, these negotiated settlements were not necessarily any more successful in resolving disputes than were judicial proceedings.

70. Karl S. Bader, "Arbiter arbitrator seu amicabilis compositor," *Zeitschrift der Savigny-*

The position of arbiter was not institutionally designated. It was a job given to someone who by virtue of his social or charismatic position could exercise a certain moral force in the community and who had some sort of relationship with both parties.[71] A perfectly neutral arbiter probably could not have been found in such a society, but even if one could have been, it is likely that each side hoped that the ties binding the arbiter to their own party would prove strongest. Often the arbiter was a count, bishop, or abbot, but in any case he exercised his role only with the agreement of the parties. In our example, neither the archbishop nor the count was a disinterested observer. The archbishop in particular was the feudal lord of most of the knights involved in the dispute—indeed, they contended that *he* had given them the disputed property in fief. John de Turre had also been the vassal of the count, as it was from Isoard that Peter de Rosset had to obtain permission to marry John's widow. It was because of these personal ties, not because of their jurisdictions, that they were called upon to attempt the arbitration, as is clear from the archbishop's initial anger when he learned that the matter had been brought not to him but to the count, as well as from the count's apparent willingness to allow the archbishop to arbitrate the affair in his stead.

The count and the archbishop were assisted in their task by their advisers (*iudices, sapientes*), who participated in the interrogation of the parties, offered their *consilium*, and in general took an active part in the proceedings. These were the vassals of the count,[72] essential at every step of the deliberations because they represented the wider community. The arbiters were careful to make no suggestions without their advice.

The two groups of opponents were also present at the arbitration sessions, with their own supporters, their vassals and other *amici*, to

Stiftung, Kan. Abt. 47 (1960): 236–276. On the transformation of judges into arbiters, see Duby, "Recherches," esp. 11–13; Cheyette, 292–293; White, "*Pactum*," 294. See also T. Eckhoff, "The Mediator, the Judge, and the Administrator in Conflict-Resolution," *Acta Sociologica* 10 (1966): 148–172.

71. On the neutrality or involvement of arbiters in differently structured societies, see Roberts, 74, 120–122, 150–153. Roberts and other anthropologists distinguish among the mediator, who helps the disputants toward their own solution rather than imposing one on them; the arbitrator, who derives authority to decide the dispute from the invitation of the disputants themselves; and the adjudicator, who derives authority to impose a solution from some community office.

72. *CSV*, 555: "... coram domino Ysoardo comite et omnibus illis qui hic super nominati sunt."

give them advice and attempt to push the proceedings to a satisfactory conclusion. Attendance at these assemblies was largely voluntary. Although summoned, the knights did not always appear, and once present, they might leave if the proceedings seemed to go against them, as Peter Poncius left the village before having to swear an oath recognizing the *sponsalicium*. Often the arbitrator attempted to secure promises to abide by his decision through the giving of guarantors and by demanding oaths specifying a sum of money to be forfeited if the agreement was not accepted. These guarantors might be kinsmen or vassals of the interested parties and were in some cases to remain virtual hostages until an agreement was reached.[73] They also seem to have served to press their respective sides for a settlement, if for no other reason than to obtain their freedom. At the assemblies held before the count of Gap, the knights gave one of their vassals, Bruno Stephanus, "in manu [comitis]" as a *fideiussor*, and in turn the monks gave a *fideiussor* of their own.[74] This same Bruno Stephanus, along with Peter Cedal, was *fideiussor* at a later assembly before the archbishop.[75] These guarantors seem to have served not only to guarantee that their party would abide by the decision but also to have actively counseled them to reach an accord. At the initial proceedings, these *fideiussores* seem to have been the only guarantees provided by the parties. As the conflict escalated and the participants increasingly refused to accept the proposed compromises, subsequent assemblies began with the pledges of specified amounts of bond money. The initial oath pledging a bond, at first one hundred solidi, then two hundred, was sworn in the hands of the presiding archbishop or count.[76]

Just as oaths sworn at the outdoor, initial portions of the proceedings were necessary to begin the assemblies, oaths of witnesses were central to the deliberations that took place in the interior portions of the sessions. As central as they were, however, their effectiveness was limited both by the fact that the principals in the conflict could not be forced to accept the testimony offered under oath and by the fact that

---

73. On hostages in the process of settlement in Flanders, see Van Caenegem, *Geschiedenis van het Strafrecht*, 264–280.
74. *CSV*, 557.
75. *CSV*, 561.
76. *CSV*, 558: "Petrus Pontius dedit fideiussorem per centum solidos in manu archiepiscopi." *CSV*, 561: "Ita firmaverunt in manu archiepiscopi per ducentos solidos."

except under very specific circumstances people could not be forced to swear oaths. Thus Prior William could refuse to accept the oath sworn by Peter Poncius, not because he might be lying but simply because he might be ignorant of the truth.[77] Also, witnesses suggested by either party could be refused by the other for reasons we have seen such as age.

Since the arbiters were not acting in any official, public capacity, their ability to extract valid oaths from principals and witnesses was limited to whatever personal bonds they had with those they hoped to have swear. Thus the archbishop could force his bailiff Peter to swear, not because he was the judge of a public court but only because he was Peter's archbishop, who could excommunicate him. Possibly more to the point, Peter was his agent.[78] For the same reason, Richard, the cardinal-archbishop abbot of Saint-Victor, was unable to extract a valid oath from one William Peter, because the latter was apparently neither vassal nor agent of the archbishop.[79] Finally, even when a person seemed ready to swear, it was possible to avoid the oath by simply disappearing. When Peter Poncius failed to appear to swear the oath he had promised to swear, the monks apparently had no recourse, and the count and archbishop took no action against him. Again, the voluntary nature of the entire proceeding is striking.

Just as in the case of excommunications, ritual curses, humiliations, and the like, the time and place of negotiation sessions were important parts of the mise-en-scène. These sessions took place on public festival days, usually Sundays, or, in the case of one of the assemblies at Chorges, the Saturday before Palm Sunday. As the dates emphasized the public nature of the assemblies, so too did the settings. The Chorges assemblies normally took place at the church of Saint Christopher, both outside (apparently on the porch) and within. We detect a certain rhythm of motion from the exterior to the interior and back again. Opening and formal phases of the negotiations, such as initial complaints, oaths to accept the recommendations of the arbiters, and the giving of hostages and gages, took place in the more public exterior assembly. Count Isoard, in good Carolingian tradition, was

---

77. *CSV*, 558: "Et si Petrus Poncius totum sponsalicium non scit, . . . pro qua re vos dicitis hoc quod nos amplius scimus, propter suum sacramentum et proper suam insipienciam, sancti et nos perdamus?"

78. See above, note 31.

79. *CSV*, 564: "Nos non habemus potestate super eum ut per nos faciat sacramentum."

holding his assembly in open air when the knights, fearing that things were going against them, went to inform the archbishop that the prior was acting against his interests. Likewise, the initial complaints in the second assembly, held before the count and the archbishop, took place outside, before the "judges" entered the church to deliberate among themselves how best to terminate the quarrel.[80] After the knights had prevented the monks from administering the last rites to the dying bailiff Martin, the archbishop began outside the church, where he had Peter Poncius and Peter de Rosset swear to abide by his decision before actually beginning proceedings.[81]

The more private, detailed, and complex aspects of the proceedings took place inside. There the arbitrators and their advisers questioned, cajoled, and threatened the parties. It was within the church, for example, that the archbishop reprimanded Prior William for having taken the affair to the count rather than to him. Likewise, at the assembly held on the Saturday before Palm Sunday, the *judices* interviewed each of the parties privately in the church. There also Peter the Bailiff was interrogated and forced, by the fidelity he owed the archbishop, to identify the entire *sponsalicium* under oath.

The arbiter operated not according to any one of the competing and contradictory laws more or less recognized in the society but rather according to what might be termed a form of equity.[82] That is, he attempted to change the structural relationship between the parties, not simply to negotiate the apparent issue. Thus while the overt reason for a negotiated settlement might have been the seizure of a person or property under the authority of the opponent, the actual subject of arbitration might be older, deeper, and more complicated problems merely symptomized by the seizure.

On the overt issue the arbiter, advised in turn by the respected members of the community both lay and spiritual, usually suggested a compromise.[83] Seldom did anyone emerge a clear winner or loser in such proceedings. At Chorges, every attempted solution, except for the disastrous attempt by the count to force the return of the entire

80. *CSV*, 557.
81. *CSV*, 561.
82. White, "*Pactum*," 303–305.
83. The notion of a compromise as the key to settlements is the central point emphasized by Cheyette and White and distinguishes these settlements or attempted settlements from judgments.

sponsalicium after the attack on the priest transporting wine, included some form of division of the property in question. Frequently, when the dispute was between religious and secular opponents, the compromise was presented as an act of charity: property long in dispute might be awarded to the lay party, who then would donate it to the church for the spiritual benefit of the donor and his family.[84]

Ideally, too, the arbiter maneuvered the opponents into a new structural relationship, and one of mere neutrality was unlikely to prove sustainable. The parties' daily interaction really required that a positive relationship replace the negative one, if conflict was not again to disrupt society. Thus between lay groups, the end of the negotiation was often cemented by a firm pact of friendship that specified concrete forms of mutual assistance. In disputes between lay and ecclesiastical institutions, the ecclesiastical institution was often urged to return the property in dispute to the layman in fief.[85] Thus the layman would have the property he had claimed and would be united with the monastery or church through the bonds of fealty. At the first session of arbitration at Chorges, it was suggested that the knights retain certain properties, which they would hold in fief from Saint-Victor.[86] Some variation on this proposal was again suggested at each

84. It is impossible to know how many charters recording donations "pro animis" actually record *guerpitiones* or quitclaims of property in dispute, as they often take the form of a simple donation. An example of such a case from the Southeast is the *noticia guerpitionis* made in 1054 by one Ramundus Gaucellinus; his wife, Petrolina; and his brother Petrus Gaucelinus on behalf of the monastery of Psalmodi; see Nîmes, Arch. dép. du Gard, MS. H 160, fols. 199v–200r. On the importance placed on *guerpitiones* over adjudications, see White, *"Pactum,"* 302.

85. In Provence, all or part of the disputed property might be returned to the opponent as a lifetime benefice. Examples include a dispute between one Eldegarda *femina deo devota* and Archbishop Rostagnus of Arles in 925 (Cartulaire de Arles, no. 33, fol. 34v–35r) and a settlement between one Salvator and Saint-Andreas-lez-Avignon in 1006–1014 (Georges de Manteger, ed., *Les chartes du pays d'Avignon [439–1040]* [Macon, 1914] no. 109). Similar settlements might be concluded with peasants as well. Around 1012, Abbot Archinricus of Montmajour concluded an agreement with the inhabitants of the property of the priory at Correns by stipulating that the property could remain in the family only as long as it did not pass outside of the community. Such property could not be used as dowery, nor could it be sold or mortgaged to anyone outside the community; see Paris, BN MS lat. 31915, fols. 51r–51v.

86. *CSV,* 555: "Ysoardus iussit talem diffinitionem inter illos . . . et ipsi filii Poncii haberent illas mansiones quas monstraverant de sponsalitio, propter fidelitatem Sancti Victoris et monachorum." *CSV,* 562: "Nos [Petrus Poncius et Petrus de Roset] tale placitum fecerimus . . . habemus totas mansiones per fidelitatem il-

subsequent session. Even if no formal vassalic relationship was formed, the layman might well receive a "gift" from the monastery. Weinberger has considered that the likelihood of receiving a gift at the end of a dispute may have encouraged lay people to press the most absurd claims.[87] Although this possibility cannot be excluded, we should view the gift as a gain for both receiver and giver; for acceptance of a gift established a positive relationship between the two parties,[88] a relationship that, like those created by other ritual conclusions of hostilities, defined and established structural connections. In conflicts between lay groups, the "gift" might be a daughter to form a marriage alliance.[89]

If compromise was accepted by both sides, a ritual of reconciliation was performed. Just as the public had been involved in the original announcement of the rupture, so it was included in the reunification. In lay society this ritual often included a banquet.[90] An excommunicate was solemnly met by the bishop at the door of the church and ritually brought back into the community.[91] In a reconciliation subsequent to a ritual humiliation, the lay person paid humble respects to the saints and then the relics were joyfully returned to their places of honor (see Chap. 5). Even if the conflictual structures remained, these public rituals indicated that the parties had returned them to latency, and the life of the community could proceed.

---

lorum [monachorum] et mittant in illas censum quod eis solvamus per singulos annos." *CSV*, 563: "Tunc [Comes] Isoardus rogavit Willelmum ut eos retinerent de eo sibi placeret."

87. Weinberger, 273. It is of course also possible that some compromises were face-saving means of disguising the failure of the ecclesiastical institution to achieve its goals. That dynamic can be seen in English disputes; e.g., John Hudson, "Life-Grants of Land and the Development of Inheritance in Anglo-Norman England," *Anglo-Norman Studies* 12 (1989): 67–80.

88. White, "*Pactum*," 302–303. We must not conclude too hastily that such rituals of gift giving were unambiguous or intended merely to restore peace. Gifts could be meant to humiliate, and their meaning could subsequently be subject to conflicting interpretations and become grounds for resuming the conflict.

89. See Van Caenegem, *Geschiedenis van het Strafrecht*, 280–307, on rites of reconciliation in Flanders.

90. White, "*Pactum*," 297; Van Caenegem, *Geschiedenis van het Strafrecht*, 280–307.

91. *PL* 138.1125–1126: " . . . cum aliquis [excommunicatus] . . . poenitentia ductus veniam postulat . . . episcopus, qui eum excommunicavit, ante januas ecclesiae venire debet . . . circumstare . . . tunc episcopus apprenhensa manu eius dextera eum in ecclesiam introducat, et ei communionem et societatem christianum reddat."

Just as no beginning was entirely new in the history of social conflicts, many endings were not definitive. Ideally, the community had
been restructured through the process: the overt period of conflict
had served as a social drama during which the community had experienced a catharsis and emerged changed for the better. This is much to
ask of any social system, however, especially of one in which conflicts
were a positive force in defining social groups and structures. Thus,
in spite of the vows, the exchanges of hostages, and the like, it was not
unusual for one or the other party to refuse to accept the solution
offered by the arbiter or, more commonly, to avoid having to break an
oath, to quit the proceedings, as did Peter Poncius as soon as it
became clear that things were going against his interests. Moreover,
even after a compromise had been accepted, underlying social tensions and opposing interests, if they had not been entirely resolved
for all members of each opposing group, could reemerge in the next
generation, upon the death of the principal parties, or even if, after
accepting the compromise, one party experienced a loss of honor in
public opinion.[92] Hariulf, in his life of Bishop Arnulf of Soissons, for
example, tells of just such a situation: a knight of Aldenburg, William
the Long, had a son notorious for his criminal behavior. The son was
caught in the act of housebreaking and killed by the homeowner, one
Siger. In spite of the manifest guilt of the son, William normally
would have had to avenge his death, but Saint Arnulf arranged a
peace between William and Siger. Soon after, however, people began
to wonder why William had accepted the death of his son so lightly,

92. On conflicts as social dramas see Nader, "Anthropological Study of Law," 16–17.
On the necessity and difficulty of obtaining adequate participation in such proceedings, see Stephen White, *Custom, Kinship, and Gifts to Saints* (Chapel Hill, N.C.,
1988). White, in *"Pactum,"* 297–298, describes some of the rituals used at Marmoutier to obtain approval of family members, including in one case three infant
sons too young to talk or at least to swear an oath, who indicated their consent by
touching the charter recording the agreement and receiving from the abbot one
denarius. The dispute concerning the settlement achieved at the death of Wichardus of Ruffey (see above, note 67) was later called into question by his heirs, who
objected to the means by which their consent had been acquired, and Abbot Odilo
of Cluny had to renegotiate the issue, finally giving them 23 solidi to confirm the
original donation; see Bruel, nos. 2008 and 2009. Johnson, 94–97, also comments
on the longevity of conflicts and suggests that often the monastery finally won
simply because it was "a wealthy corporate community that could keep alive and
defend its claims beyond the temporal and financial limits possible for most families" (95).

and this talk, which caused William to lose face, induced him to break his peace and to attack his son's slayer.[93]

The conflict between the knights and prior of Chorges is no exception to this pattern. No conclusion to the conflict was ever reached, at least not in the extant documentation, and the reasons are much deeper than simply the perfidy of the knights or the stubborness of the prior. For one thing, the evidence on which to make a settlement was extremely difficult to control. In Provence, a region of strong Roman legal tradition, it is not surprising to see that written evidence was considered important. But the written material (in this case, the charter of donation) was inadequate because so little of the complex social and economic activity of the day was recorded. True, an authentic charter recorded the initial donation of the manse of Benedet Pela, but the subsequent divisions of the property were apparently made without written record. Because lack of written records was the rule rather than the exception, the value of the one document was accordingly decreased. The real basis for decision was, then, the memory of the community. Yet the community was made up of people intimately involved with the claimants; thus the testimony, laboriously extracted by oaths, proved as limited in value as the written evidence.

Perhaps even more fundamental to the problem was the fact that the real issue was not the possession of the manse but the relationships uniting lay and ecclesiastical groups in the region. The priory at Chorges was only one of many, many such holdings of Saint-Victor, and while an amicable solution to its problems with the knights of the area may have been very important to the prior, he lacked the authority to conclude negotiations on his own. The abbot, who possessed that authority, was part of a much wider and more complex world in which the dealings with these particular knights would have had a much different meaning and lower priority.

The knights, too, were limited in their options and confined by their own involvement in a wider and more complex system, that of the archbishop's vassalage. Throughout the proceedings, they claimed not that the disputed property belonged to them but that they had received it in fief from the archbishop. Thus in their opposi-

---

93. Hariulfo *Exvita Arnulfi episcopi Suessionensis* 2.16, *MGH SS* 15:888: "Postea Willel-
    mus a quibusdam malignis increpatus, cur filii mortem tam leviter indulsisset,
    coepit penitere de benefacto et iterum coepit captare locum, quo vindictam
    sumeret de Sigero."

tion to the prior they were defending their lord's interests (although of course because of the de facto inheritability of fiefs, they were also defending their own). Being the vassals of the archbishop, they no doubt expected his support in the proceedings, so his acceptance of the claims of Prior William must have seemed to them an attempt to abrogate his obligations to them. From their perspective, what had happened was that their lord had formed a new relationship with the monks which excluded them from their traditional rights as his vassals. Thus one understands their anger, resentment, and suspicion at every suggested compromise that would have left them not in possession of the property they had traditionally held and not bound to the acknowledged owner of the property—be he archbishop or abbot— by clear bonds of fealty. Little wonder, then, that as long as the archbishop and the abbot pursued their wider ends in the increasingly complex world of late eleventh-century Provence, the knights and the prior of Chorges found themselves with no way out of their conflict.

We can say, then, that in the society of the eleventh and twelfth centuries conflictual structures had such fundamental and enduring importance that attempts to resolve conflicts were less significant than attempts to use them. Conflicts might be acted out through ritualized but nonetheless deadly violence, or they might be pursued through the transformation of these rituals of violence into rituals less dangerous to the society at large. When efforts were made to end conflict, they seem to have been directed largely to the transformation of the social structures giving rise to the conflicts—hence the attempts in arbitration to establish positive bonds rather than simply to eliminate hostility. That these efforts were often ineffectual should be hardly surprising given the need of social groups to preserve the conflictual structures that gave them cohesion.

I have said nothing about the gradual transformation of these voluntary courts of arbitration into institutions of binding arbitration and, ultimately, adjudication. This is because such a development probably never took place. The ability to impose judgments on parties in a dispute implies a relationship neither possible nor even considered desirable by contemporaries. Such a court would necessarily exercise a coercive power to enforce a peace, even when the basis for conflict continued.

Such courts did continue to exist during this period with jurisdiction but only over those not fully "free." These courts had real judges who "recognized" the judgment of God brought against those under their jurisdiction and meted out definitive decisions and penalties. But these courts were designed less to settle disputes and build a better, conflict-free society than to improve income, control dependents through coercive judicial force, and thus demonstrate the power of lordship.[94] When, in the course of the thirteenth and fourteenth centuries, new court systems were established across Europe with a jurisdiction that included those who had previously been outside of any jurisdiction, they developed not from an increasing acceptance of arbiters or some sort of social contract increasingly binding free men, or from the joyful acceptance of a better quality of justice. It appears rather that these courts were imposed from above as counts, kings, bishops, and popes managed to expand their coercive judicial authority from their serfs and slaves to the free warriors, nobles, and clerics of Europe.

94. See Van Caenegem, *Geschiedenis van het Strafrecht,* on the difference between what he calls "evolved penal law" and "law of reconciliation."

Reproducing

༄༅

8   The Saint and the Shrine:
The Pilgrim's Goal in the Middle Ages

⨳

"What did you go out into the wildnerness to see? A reed shaken by
the wind? What then did you go out to see? A man clothed in soft
raiment? Behold, those who are gorgeously appareled and live in
luxury are in kings' courts. What did you go out to see? A prophet?
Yes, I tell you, and more than a prophet."[1] The answer to Christ's
rhetorical question has varied across the centuries. Christians have
gone "out into the wilderness," that is, they have left their familiar
locales, their normal social positions, and their accustomed activities
in favor of the ambiguous, ill-defined "liminality" of the pilgrim to
pursue myriad quests.[2] For some, the life of the pilgrim itself was the
goal: as the Christian is a stranger and wanderer in this world until he
reaches the heavenly kingdom of the next, so were some pilgrims, like
the early Celtic missionaries to the Continent, lifelong wanderers
whose only goal was to extend their liminality until the end of their
journey on earth.[3]

For most other Christian pilgrims, pilgrimage was a temporary
hiatus in their normal lives. They abandoned their traditional milieus

---

1. Luke 7:24–26.
2. On the "liminality" of the pilgrim see in particular the work of Victor Turner,
   "Pilgrimages as Social Processes," in his *Dramas, Fields and Metaphors: Symbolic
   Action in Human Society* (Ithaca, N.Y., 1974), 166–230, and "Liminality and Com-
   munitas," in *Ritual Process: Structure and Anti-Structure* (Chicago, 1969), 94–130,
   and with Edith Turner, *Image and Pilgrimage in Christian Culture* (Oxford, 1978).
3. On the Irish pilgrims on the Continent, see Heinz Löwe, ed., *Die Iren und Europa im
   früheren Mittelalter* (Stuttgart, 1982); still important are Louis Gougaud, *Christianity
   in Celtic Lands* (1932; Dublin, 1992); and Wilhelm Levison, "Die Iren und die
   fränkische Kirche," *Aus rheinischer und fränkischer Frühzeit*, 247–263.

for a time in order to travel to a place where the power of God broke into mundane existence, and then they returned to their former lives. The grand, perhaps archetypal goals of such pilgrims have been the ancient "high holy places" of the Christian world located at the extremities of European experience. Through the centuries, Christians wealthy enough to undertake an expedition of several years' duration have traveled to the great pilgrimage sites of Christendom, to Rome and, above all, to Palestine, where they could visit places sanctified by the drama of sacred history enacted in them: Bethlehem, Jerusalem, and the empty tomb that marks the place of salvation. There was a noteworthy difference between pilgrims to the great sites and those going to local sites: apparently the former were not usually seeking miracles.[4]

The vast majority of Christians, for whom the costs and dangers of a distant pilgrimage were too much, sought instead to escape the structures of their normal existence by finding a place of local liminality—a place not so removed physically from their familiar surroundings and yet sharing with the great pilgrimage sites of Palestine a direct connection with divine power. These places have been regional or local cult sites, some of recent origin, others much more ancient than Christianity. This chapter is about these local pilgrimage sites and the role of their cult objects.[5] Such sights were not sanctified by the footsteps of Christ or the events of his passion. Their sanctity did not come from where or what they were. It came from what was to be found there—what physical link with the divine sphere remained incarnate in the material world. What then did these pilgrims go out into the desert to see?

Ad Sanctos

In late antiquity one often went out into the desert to see a holy man—one of the "friends of God" who, like John the Baptist himself, demonstrated his special relationship with God through his radical rejection of the normal social roles and aspirations, his extreme asceticism, the unusual and often violent forms of self-discipline he prac-

---

4. See Benedicta Ward, *Miracles and the Medieval Mind*, 119–120.
5. On other types of pilgrimages see the essays in *Wallfahrt kennt keine Grenzen*, ed. Lenz Kriss-Rettenbeck and Gerda Mohler (Munich, 1984), and especially the very valuable bibliography on pilgrimage compiled by Edith Chorherr, 543–568.

ticed, and the miraculous cures and exorcisms he performed.[6] Even after his physical death, the power of the holy man remained in the places where he had lived and died. Mere physical death did not end his importance, and his tomb continued to attract Christians seeking his help.[7]

These living links with divine power were not the only objects of the pilgrim's journey nor, after the sixth century, the most common. In the eastern Mediterranean, the object was often a sacred image, an icon.[8] These pictures were far more than simple artistic representations painted by human artists and intended to inspire the faithful or to educate the illiterate. Like the holy men, they enjoyed a special relationship with the divine power. Often they were supposed not to have been painted by human hands but to have fallen from the heavens. They participated directly in the existence and the being of the person they represented, so that the image brought the pilgrim into direct visual (that is to say, in the traditional understanding of optics, tactile) contact with the person represented. To be in their presence was to look through a window into the other world and, correspondingly, to be seen by the person in the other world.[9]

In the West, this profound sense of the participation of images in the person depicted was largely lacking, and here the attention of the faithful turned instead to the corporeal remains of holy men. The *Libri Carolini*, the polemical treatise composed as the official answer of the Franks to the "heresy of the Greeks," makes clear the Frankish preference for relics, rather than images, as the proper focus of saints' cults. Images might be more or less faithful representations and more

6. On holy men in late antiquity see the classic study by Peter Brown, "The Rise and Function of the Holy Man in Late Antiquity," in his *Society and the Holy in Late Antiquity* (Berkeley, Calif., 1982), 103–152, as well as Brown, *The Cult of the Saints.*
7. Brown reminds us that "the hillsides on which the stylites perched their columns would be ominously ringed by brand new, empty *martyria*, waiting to receive their guaranteed holy occupants," in "Eastern and Western Christendom in Late Antiquity: A Parting of the Ways," in *Society*, 185.
8. On icons see in general Jaroslav Pelikan, *The Christian Tradition: A History of the Development of Christian Doctrine*, 2, *The Spirit of Eastern Christendom, 600–1700* (Chicago, 1974), chap. 3, "Images of the Invisible"; Ernst Kitzinger, "The Cult of Images in the Age before Iconoclasm," *Dumbarton Oaks Papers* 8 (1954): 83–150; and Peter Brown, "A Dark Age Crisis: Aspects of the Iconoclastic Controversy," in *Society*, 251–301.
9. On the "face-to-face" encounter possible through the icon, see Brown, "Dark Age Crisis," 272.

or less beautiful, but they could have only a didactic function. Any greater honor or veneration was to be reserved for relics alone:[10] "They [the Greeks] place almost all the hope of their credulity in images, but it remains firm that we venerate the saints in their bodies or better in their relics, or even in their clothing, in the ancient tradition of the Fathers."[11] Thus did the eighth-century author of the *Libri Carolini* explain the difference between the veneration of saints' remains in the West and that of icons in the East.

These bodies of saints and their relics, that is, either actual portions of their bodies or objects that had been in close contact with them (*brandia*), became, in the West, the central focus of religious devotion.[12] Well into the eighth century, these objects were firmly fixed in the sacred geography of Latin Christendom: the holy men of Europe were venerated after their deaths where they had lived and died.[13] Originally, the objects of veneration had been the early Christian martyrs. Roman law had always mandated burials outside the city walls, so the suburban tombs of the martyrs became the sites of annual ritual commemoration of the martyrs' passions. The faithful, led by the clergy of the city, would go out into the "wilderness" to celebrate the memory of the martyrs.[14] From the fourth century, increasingly elaborate basilicas were erected over these tombs, and these martyria became the object of pilgrimages. The significance of this transformation of the sacred geography should not be underestimated. Roman tradition marked the sacred confines of the city, the center for worship and ritual, in contrast to the "unclean" suburban cemeteries ringing the ancient city. The new Christian geography placed the centers of sanctity outside the city, a reversal of values consistent with the revolution in cultural values that accompanied not

10. *Libri Carolini, MGH Concilia* 2, suppl., 3.24:153–154 and 3.16:137–138.
11. Ibid., 3.16:138.
12. The bibliography on relics and relic cults has grown enormously. In general, see Martin Heinzelmann, *Translationsberichte;* Heinrich Fichtenau, "Zum Reliquienwesen,"; Peter Brown, "Relics and Social Status in the Age of Gregory of Tours," in *Society,* 222–250; and the annotated bibliography on saints' cults by Stephen Wilson in his *Saints and Their Cults,* 309–417.
13. On the traditional reluctance of Western churchmen to divide the remains of saints, see J. M. McCulloh, "The Cult of Relics in the Letters and 'Dialogues' of Pope Gregory the Great: A Lexicographical Study," *Traditio* 32 (1976): 145–184.
14. In general, see B. Kötting, *Der frühchristliche Reliquienkult und die Bestattung im Kirchengebäude* (Cologne, 1965); and B. de Gaiffier, "Réflexions sur les origines du culte des martyrs," *La maison-Dieu* 52 (1947): 19–43.

simply the Christianization but also the ruralization of Western Europe.[15]

The Christianization of northern Europe and the Franks' growing political domination of the West brought about a transformation in the distribution of these sacred sites. The old Roman towns of Gaul, Spain, and Italy had their Roman cemeteries and their martyrs and holy men; the more recently converted areas of the North were lacking such places. Sacred sites existed, but they were sacred only in pagan tradition. The spread of Christianity had been accomplished with relatively little shedding of Christian blood—with the exception of Boniface and his followers, the martyrs had been on the other side. Beginning in the middle of the eighth century, the ancient Western tradition that the remains of martyrs were not to be moved about or divided came to an end as Roman martyrs' remains, with or without the consent of the pope, began to find their way north.[16] The significance of this distribution would have major implications for the future of Western Christianity. Sacred places could now be created by the transfer of holy men of the past to new sites with which they had never before been associated, in life or in death. The "wilderness" in which Christians could seek "a prophet . . . and more than a prophet" could now be everywhere. As the *Glossa ordinaria* suggests, "the world is compared to a desert."[17]

This initial redistribution of saints' relics in northern and eastern Europe was far from random. It was part of a careful program of Carolingian ecclesiastical policy carried out by the leading bishops and abbots of the Frankish church.[18] Indeed, the control over the

15. Heinzelmann, 26–27; A. Grabar, *Martyrium: Recherches sur le culte des reliques et l'art chrétien antique*, 2 vols. (Paris, 1946); Jean-Charles Picard, "Espace urbain et sépultures épiscopales à Auxerre," *Revue d'histoire de l'église de France* 62 (1976): 205–222.

16. On translations into northern Europe in the Early Middle Ages, see K. Honselmann, "Reliquientranslationen nach Sachsen," in *Das Erste Jahrtausend* 1 (Düsseldorf, 1962), 159–193; W. Hotzelt, "Translationen von Märtyrerreliquien aus Rom nach Bayern im 8. Jahrhundert," *Studien und Mitteilungen zur Geschichte des Benediktiner-Ordens und seiner Zweige* 53 (1935): 286–343; H. L. Mikoletzky, "Sinn und Art der Heiligung im frühen Mittelalter," *Mitteilungen des Instituts für österreichische Geschichtsforschung* 57 (1949): 83–122; K. Hauck, "Die fränkisch-deutsche Monarchie und der Weserraum," in *Kunst und Kultur im Weserraum, 800–1600* (Corvey, 1966), 97–121.

17. *PL* 114.270: " . . . deserto mundus comparatur."

18. See Nicole Herrmann-Mascard, *Les reliques des saints*, 49–70, 84–86; Geary, *Furta Sacra*, 15–27.

distribution of relics was one of the keys to ecclesiastical control over the sacred. Unlike the living holy men of the Near East or the occasional Celtic pilgrim or local wonder-worker such as the Aldebert who ran afoul of Boniface in the mid-eighth century (see Chap. 9), dead saints could be controlled by the episcopacy. Since at least the time of Gregory of Tours, the Frankish episcopate had managed the memoria of the saints so as to present to the laity its chosen image of sanctity and its ideal of the relationship between the sacred and the profane.[19] The cults established after the massive translations in the later eighth and ninth centuries continued this tradition. Carolingian synods sought to limit the proliferation of shrines containing sacred relics and not directly under the supervision of approved clergy; the proliferation of new, unauthorized cults; and the authorization by secular and episcopal authorities of transferral of saints' remains to new locations, as we see in Chapter 9.

Patrons and Protectors

The successful implementation of this program of Christianizing European geography required more than the passive acquiescence of the pope or even the active involvement of Frankish bishops. It was not sufficient that sacred space could be moved about; it was also necessary that the faithful accept the particular form in which it was being presented—the relics of the saints—and the possibility of the mobility of sanctity along with the mobility relics.

The acceptance of relics presented few problems. The cult of relics was widely accepted across Europe and became, in post-Carolingian Europe, the primary means of human contact with the divine. Perhaps a major reason for this acceptance was that saints, either indigenous or brought into a locality, could become involved in the same sorts of face-to-face, personal relationships that characterized feudal society.[20] People's understanding of the relationship between the human and divine spheres often tends to mirror relationships in the human sphere, and in a society that experienced radical decentraliza-

19. Brown, "Relics and Social Status," 245–249.
20. On the role of relics in personal interactions, see R. Michalowski, "Le don d'amitié dans la société carolingienne et les 'Translationes sanctorum,'" in *Hagiographie cultures et sociétés IVᵉ–XIIᵉ siècles: Actes du colloque organisé à Nanterre et à Paris 2–5 mai 1979* (Paris, 1981), 399–416.

tion and erosion of public authority, this very process took place. Thus, outside of court circles, the cult of Christ underwent a relative eclipse. Just as the influence of official public authorities connecting local communities to central institutions was weakened where ever it did not positively cease to exist, so too did the role of Christ as the primary mediator cede to local personalities, his saints.[21] Perhaps great men or educated clerics could deal directly with Christ just as they might, under other circumstances, deal with counts or kings whose influence was immeasurably distant from the reach of ordinary people. The saint was physically present in his tomb, where he could be approached, implored, cajoled, even under certain circumstances threatened (Chap. 6), to provide for the needs of the local community.

These needs were great and various. Essential to all forms of assistance was the miracle-working power of the saint. The possibility of miracles, which was a strong aspect of classical religion, had long held a major place in the development of Christianity.[22] Indeed one could point to the miracles of the New Testament as evidence that the power to heal and to cast out demons was at least as important as predication in Christ's ministry. The variety of miracles, performed by Christ through his saints prior to the thirteenth century, varied but little and tended to fill the needs of a rural population with only the most rudimentary alternatives for health care and public assistance: cures, particularly of various sorts of paralysis and blindness, predominated.[23] In the traditional, Augustinian understanding of the relationship between God and creation which dominated medieval religious thought, all nature was at least potentially miraculous, and God's involvement in creation was such that the explanation of events as miraculous often ranked as the preferred one rather than as an outside possibility only to be considered after all others had been excluded.[24]

21. On the cult of Christ in the Carolingian period and its relationship with the cult of the emperor, see C. Heitz, *Recherches sur les rapports entre architecture et liturgie à l'époque carolingienne* (Paris, 1963).

22. On the theory of miracles in antiquity and the Middle Ages, see Ward, 1–19.

23. Numerous scholars have attempted to examine the physiological aspects of disease through collections of miracle stories; see in particular Finucane, *Miracles and Pilgrims;* and Rouche, "Miracles, maladies et psychologie de la foi à l'époque carolingienne en Francie."

24. Ward, 32.

Though miracles could take place anywhere and any time, they tended to be performed in physical proximity to the touchstones of divine power that were the saints' remains.[25] The means by which the faithful approached the saints' relics was essentially the same by which their polytheistic ancestors had approached sites of healing: after preparation by prayer, fasting, and the essential pilgrimage from the normal world to that of the sacred, the pilgrim would attempt to touch the tomb or at least to come as close to the saint's remains as possible. Often he or she would pass the night near the tomb, the traditional incubational rite of the Asclepius cult.[26] A graphic illustration of this tradition is the windows of Trinity Chapel, Canterbury cathedral, completed around 1220, which picture miracles performed by Thomas Becket.[27] The recipient of the miracle is often depicted asleep near the saint's shrine, and in one scene, the saint himself is shown emerging in the night from the end of the shrine to appear in a vision to a monk.[28] As in the ancient healing cult, the cure would often be effected by the saint, who would appear to the pilgrim in a vision, taking the form of the iconographic representation of the saint presented in a reliquary. Thus, for example, Saint Foy (Fides) of Conques often appears in the form depicted in her reliquary, the *Majesty of Saint Foy,* one of the masterpieces of medieval metalwork.[29]

As important as these cures were, however, they are only one aspect of the significance of the saints in society. Saints also performed miracles to assist and to protect their devotees. They found lost objects and strayed livestock, helped their "friends" in times of financial need, and protected them from enemies. To this latter end, saints performed various "negative" miracles, chastising and occasionally even killing those who had mistreated them or their supporters.[30]

---

25. On the rhythm of miracles in a specific region, see Pierre-André Sigal, "Maladie, pèlerinage et guérison au XIIe siècle: Les miracles de saint Gibrien à Reims," *Annales: ESC* 24 (1969): 1522–1539. For other analyses of the process of cures, see Ward's examinations of eleventh- and twelfth-century miracle collections, 33–109.
26. On the traditional cults of antiquity see Lionel Rothkrug, "The Cult of Relics in Antiquity," in *World Spirituality: An Encyclopedic History of the Religious Quest,* 1, *European Archaic Spirituality,* ed. Charles Long (New York, in press).
27. Ward, 89–109.
28. Ibid., 90–92.
29. On Saint Foy see Geary, *Furta Sacra,* 58–63 and 138–141; Ward, 36–42.
30. Pierre-André Sigal, "Un aspect du culte des saints: Le châtiment divin."

But miracles were only the most public part of the saints' role in medieval society. They advertised the virtues and importance of the saints and thus increased the number of pilgrims to their shrines. More important, saints by their physical presence were a primary means of social integration, identity, protection, and economic support for the communities in which they were found. The religious communities living around the tomb of a saint were identified and united primarily by their attachment to the saint himself. They, along with the peasants working the church lands, made up the "family" of the saint, a wide and often powerful group. As in a lay or episcopal family, the head was expected to provide protection and assistance to the members. Protection was both of the supernatural variety (imminent justice visited upon enemies of the community) and of a more subtle, practical variety as an important focus of public opinion that could be brought to bear on opponents.[31] The saint assured the prosperity of the family both by guaranteeing the fruitfulness of the land (which received his or her benediction during periodic processions that brought the saint's remains to the fields) and by attracting pilgrims, an important source of income.[32]

Mobility of the Saints

For all of these needs, an active cult of the saint was essential, the physical presence of the saint was the basis of an active cult. To develop a cult, then, normally required, sooner or later, the establishment of the saint's remains at the cult site. One can detect, as it were, a tendency to concretize the cult of a saint in his or her physical remains: whether or not the saint's relics had been at the place of origin

---

31. Geary, *Furta Sacra;* and see above, Chap. 5.
32. An example of the financial importance attached to relics appears in the protracted dispute between the monastery of Saint Eloi of Noyon and the cathedral of that city over which institution possessed the remains of the saint. In the thirteenth century the bishop had excommunicated anyone who made a pilgrimage to the monastery or made offerings there to Saint Eloi. The monks had claimed 3,000 marks in damages for their loss of revenues. See Paris, BN MS lat. 13777, fol. 7v; also Erica J. Laquer, "Ritual, Literacy and Documentary Evidence: Archbishop Eudes Rigaud and the Relics of St. Eloi," *Francia* 13 (1986): 625–637; and Olivier Guyotjeannin, "Les reliques de Saint Eloi à Loyon: Procès et enquêtes du milieu du XIIIe siècle," *Revue Mabillon,* new ser. 1, no. 62 (1990): 57–110.

of the cult, the veneration of the saint would ultimately, over time, produce the firm belief that the saint was physically present in the monastery or church.

A prime example of this tendency is the evolution of the cult of Mary Magdalene at Vézelay in Burgundy. The Mary Magdalene venerated in the West was a composite saint who was at once the penitent sinner who anointed Christ's feet (Luke 8:36–50) and Mary, the sister of Martha (Luke 10:38–42) and of Lazarus (John 11:1–45). The origins of her cult in the West are obscure, although as early as 1022, Bishop Erminfroi of Verdun had dedicated a church to her. Within a few years, the *Gesta episcoporum Cameracensium* recorded that a monk had brought the remains of the Magdalene to the West from Jerusalem,[33] and by 1050 a papal bull acknowledged that the body of Mary Magdalene was to be found in Vézelay.

Explaining exactly how the saint might have come to be in the particular location could be a problem inasmuch as saints were notorious for their unwillingness to have their remains transferred from their place of burial to new shrines: the hagiography of the early Middle Ages is filled with stories of relics that miraculously became so heavy when attempts were made to transport them that they were ultimately left in place.[34] Attempts to move saints about also met with very human obstacles: the local community that had looked to the saint buried in its midst was naturally unwilling to see her or him taken away. Moreover, in an age in which spurious relics circulated widely, communities were naturally suspicious of relics acquired from elsewhere: After all, if the community in which the saint had been found was so willing to give him or her up, could the saint really be a powerful protector? If a saint allowed herself or himself to be taken from another community, what sort of protector could that saint be?

The meditation on the benefits derived by a particular region from the presence of a particular protector, animated both by the firm conviction of the saint's physical and spiritual presence and by an awareness of competing claims on the remains of important saints, led to the elaboration of various explanations of how saints who had lived and died in distant areas had come to rest in local churches. For some saints, such as Saint James or Santiago de Compostella, the

33. Geary, *Furta Sacra*, 74–78.
34. On *translationes* see Heinzelmann, 46–77.

presence of the body was explained by a miraculous event: after death the saint had been carried by supernatural power to his or her new resting place. Of others, it was explained that the saint had miraculously made manifest her or his intention of being transferred to a new location, often because of insufficient veneration in the place of original interment. In this case, the saint was said to have been translated, with or without the consent of the proper ecclesiastical and civil authorities, at the saint's own express desire.[35] In all the accounts of these translations, the tension between the two communities and the hesitations about the propriety of moving the saint at all, are made clear in the difficulties encountered in the transfer and in the elaborate justifications with which the perpetrators explained by what right they could presume to move the saint's remains.

In the most extreme of these accounts, the transfer was often presented as a theft, or more aptly as a kidnapping, which, like the contemporary practice of bride stealing, was carried out with the active assistance of the "victim."[36] This was the case of Mary Magdalene, Saint Fides of Conques, Saint Benedict at Fleury, and many others, famous and obscure, across Europe.[37] In the versions of the translation narrative written within or for the institution claiming to possess the saint's remains, one usually hears that the saint had appeared to a holy member of the community, complained that he or she was not presently receiving adequate veneration, and asked to be transferred to a new and proper community. After this vision was made known to the community, two or more members were sent on the mission of obtaining the saint's body, a task usually accomplished in spite of the resistance of the saint's rejected community, jealous of its honored patron and eager to prevent the theft. The saint's mirac-

35. Translations were formal procedures in which remains of saints were officially recognized and transported from one place to another. Geary, *Furta Sacra*, 108–128; Heinzelmann, 33–42.

36. Geary, *Furta Sacra*, 125–126. Bride stealing, one of the oldest forms of Germanic marriage, was still common in the ninth and tenth centuries. As in traditional European societies today, this form of ritual kidnapping could function in a variety of ways: it could make possible a marriage opposed by the family of the wife (for after the fact, the woman's virtue was lost and her chances of another marriage were nil), but it could also be a way for families to avoid the scandal of a voluntary marriage considered too far below the woman's status. This latter aspect might be the most appropriate point of comparison with the theft of saints. See Heinrich Brunner, *Deutsche Rechtsgeschichte* 1, 3d ed. (Berlin, 1906), 94–96.

37. Geary, *Furta Sacra*, 125–126.

ulous intervention generally was instrumental in effecting the transfer. As the thieves and their new saint approached their community,
they were met by their superior and the community and accompanied
into the monastery in a joyful procession reminiscent of the imperial
adventus of late antiquity.[38]

Although these theft accounts record an extreme form of relic
acquisition, they nevertheless indicate the importance of these relics
to the religious communities of Western Europe. Their presence was
essential to the prosperity of the monasteries and churches that
looked to them for identity and protection, just as they were essential
to the pilgrims who sought from the saints the help that they could
obtain nowhere else.[39] In the course of the later eleventh and twelfth
centuries, however, the close relationship between the physical proximity of saints and the strength of their cults began to wane, and this
change was to have profound effects on the spiritual geography of
Western Europe.

Transformation of the Pilgrim's Goal

One can detect three transformations in the nature of local pilgrimage sites. The first was caused by the enormous increase in the
number and diffusion of corporeal relics of biblical and patristic
saints' remains as a result of the increased pilgrimage and crusade
traffic to Palestine.[40] In particular, after the aberrant Fourth Crusade
captured and sacked Constantinople in 1215, a vast flood of Byzantine relics spilled into the West, making available to churches across
Europe relics of the early martyrs and saints of the Old and New
Testaments.[41] To cite but one example, pilgrims no longer needed to
travel to Compostella to find Saint James; he was also physically

38. Heinzelmann, 66–77; Brown, *Cult of the Saints*, 99–100, and "Relics and Social
    Status," in *Society*, 247–249; Sabine MacCormack, *Art and Ceremony in Late Antiquity*
    (Berkeley, Calif., 1981).
39. On the relationship between patrons living and dead and their communities, see,
    in particular, Otto Gerhard Oexle, "Die Gegenwart der Toten," and above, Chap.
    4.
40. See, in general, Jonathan Sumption, *Pilgrimage: An Image of Mediaeval Religion*
    (London, 1975), 114–145.
41. See the mass of data on the relics and sacred images acquired by the West as a result
    of the crusade, collected in the nineteenth century by Edouard Riant, *Exuviae
    Sacrae Constantinopolitanae*, 3 vols. (Geneva, 1877–1898).

present in Namur, Paris, and Troyes (see Chap. 11), to name but a few
of his communities. As a result, the distinction between local and
international prilgrimages lessened, only to be lessened still further
by the increasing practice of indulgences, particularly the granting of
indulgences traditionally reserved for the great pilgrimages for participation in local ones.[42]

Second, whereas in the tenth and eleventh centuries the veneration
of the faithful was directed primarily to local protectors, either associated with the region in life or installed there in death, by the twelfth
and thirteenth centuries the cults of universal saints were making
serious inroads into local veneration. This is not to say that the third
transformation was from a physical to an immaterial focus; the actual
process was a transformation *of* the physical. Across southern Europe
the cult of the Virgin began to compete seriously with the cults of local
thaumaturges.[43] Often, as in the south of France, these "new" cults
were focused on an image, usually a statue. The romanesque virgins
of Targasonne and Angoustrine, to mention but two, closely resemble
the majesty of Saint Fides.[44] All are seated female figures, but the
former differ from the latter in that they hold the Christ Child and
contain no relics. The cult of the Eucharist, greatly strengthened after
Lateran IV, likewise focused on a different form of physical object,
the consecrated host that had been affirmed in the ninth and again in
the eleventh centuries as the "body of Christ, not only in figure but in
truth."[45] The development of the cult of Mary and that of Christ in
the Eucharist made the first serious inroads into the tradition of the
quasi-necessity of corporeal remains as cult centers.[46]

---

42. See, e.g., Chap. 11, on indulgences granted for pilgrimages to the relics of Saint
Helen of Athrya.
43. On images of the Virgin see Ilene H. Forsyth, *Throne of Wisdom: Wood Sculptures of
the Madonna in Romanesque France* (Princeton, N.J., 1972); on the cults of the Virgin
see Ward, 132–165.
44. On these two statues, both stolen in November 1975, see *La religion populaire en
Languedoc*, 446.
45. See Pelikan, *Christian Tradition*, 3, *The Growth of Medieval Theology, 600–1300* (Chicago, 1978), 184–204; Richard W. Southern, "Lanfranc of Bec and Berengar of
Tours," in *Studies in Medieval History Presented to Frederick Maurice Powicke*, ed. R. W.
Hunt et al. (Oxford, 1948), 27–48; and Brian Stock, *The Implications of Literacy:
Written Language and Models of Interpretation in the Eleventh and Twelfth Centuries*
(Princeton, N.J., 1983), 241–325.
46. On the Eucharist see Gary Macy, *The Theologies of the Eucharist*. On the growth of
Marian devotion see Richard W. Southern, *Medieval Humanism* (New York, 1970),
173–174.

Whether as cause or effect of these transformations in the availability and nature of cult objects, historians have detected from the late eleventh century a shift in popular piety away from strictly local protectors, thaumaturges, and patrons and toward a wider and more individualistic form of veneration.[47] The wider choices as well as the wider horizons of Europe's population made the selection of patron increasingly a question of individual choice. The local pilgrimages, the search for that sacred wilderness in which the Christian could come into contact with the divine presence, did not decrease in importance, but once again, the answer to the question "What did you go out into the wilderness to see?" was open.

47. G. Zimmermann, "Patrozinienwahl und Frömmigkeitswandel im Mittelalter, dargestellt an Beispielen aus dem alten Bistum Würzburg," *Würzburger Diözesan-Geschichtsblätter* 20, no. 21 (1958–1959): 24–126.

9   The Ninth-Century Relic Trade—A
Response to Popular Piety?

ᗢ

If by "popular piety" is meant a uniquely lay religious tradition separate from that of the clergy, then the obstacles to understanding the
popular dimensions of religion in the Carolingian period are such
that one must approach the subject with extreme care and leave it,
when all that can be said has been, with equally extreme frustration.
The first obstacle is the scarcity of useful documentation. All the
sources are Latin texts written by clerics or members of the high
aristocracy—direct evidence from the "people" is entirely lacking.
When the witnesses speak of the devotions and practices of the laity,
they do so either to present what they wish to find in the laity or to
condemn practices, popular in origin, which had developed outside
the framework of the official church. In both cases the accounts are
usually too polemical to provide accurate information on these phenomena, and, without independent evidence, interpreting them is
extremely difficult.

The second problem is the deep gulf between the culture of those
literate writers and that of the mass of Europeans. What scattered
references to "popular" practices do exist indicate that in the eighth
and ninth centuries an enormous gap separated the masses from the
tiny elite participating in the so-called Carolingian renaissance. Educated monks and bishops, many of them foreigners from England,
Ireland, Italy, or Spain, lived in a world apart from that of most of
Europe's population and pursued religious and cultural interests that
often were quite alien to those of the people, whom many churchmen
understood but little. The one group of foreigners who provide
interesting if biased insights into popular customs are the Septima-

nian Goths such as Agobard of Lyons, Claudius of Turin, and Theodulf of Orléans. These men, whose Spanish cultural horizons were
much different from those of the Franks and Latins with whom they
found refuge, opposed various customs in the North and felt com-
pelled to attack them. Thus their writings on popular beliefs, on
images and relics, and on assorted other topics are significant evidence of Carolingian society and culture as seen by outsiders. If
official Christianity was ever a "hothouse" phenomenon, this was the
age.

The last obstacle is the nature of early medieval religion itself.
Across Europe, even in the former Roman areas of the Carolingian
empire, Christianity was qualitatively different from the "popular
Christianity" of postreformation Europe and indeed even from that
of the later Middle Ages. Action was more important than belief, cult
and liturgy far more important than confession. In brief, religion
both for lay masses and the vast majority of clerics was physical, not
intellectual—danced, not believed.

For all these reasons, exclusively lay religious practice (if there
be such a thing) of the Carolingian period must remain extremely
obscure. If by popular piety we can mean, however, those aspects of
this danced religion—such as the cult of saints' relics—which were
shared by laity and clerics of all social and cultural strata, then a great
deal more can be said. Through writings of the clerical elite and
through their efforts to control and direct mass practices, we can
at least examine commonalities and differences within this popular
piety. Although not entirely satisfactory, such an effort is valuable and
indeed necessary if we are to understand the roots of later medieval
popular movements.

The first documented mass participation of Europeans in religious
programs took place in the tenth and eleventh centuries, when the
laity, noble and peasant, became involved in monastic reform and the
Peace of God.[1] Scholars such as Bernard Töpfer and Harmut Hoffmann have recognized the central role of devotion to saints' relics in
changing these movements from merely another series of ecclesiastical reforms into genuinely popular mobilizations.[2] Töpfer in particu-

1. See the introduction to Thomas Head and Richard Landes, eds., *The Peace of God*
1–20.
2. Bernard Töpfer, "Reliquienkult und Pilgerbewegung zur Zeit der Klosterreform
im Burgundisch-Aquitanischen Gebiet," in *Vom Mittelalter zur Neuzeit: Zum 65.
Geburstag von Heinrich Sprömberg*, ed. Hellmut Kretzschmar (Berlin, 1956), 420–

lar, in a brilliant Marxist analysis of the relationship between reform and saints' cults, suggests that the monastic exploitation of popular devotion to relics was the specific means by which clerical elites influenced and mobilized mass support. But such mobilization presupposes popular devotion to saints and their relics. Thus we must ask when Europeans developed this great devotion to saints which could be tapped in the tenth century. Although saints' cults grew slowly from the beginning of Christianity in Gaul and Germany, a crucial period was the century from 740 to 840, the reigns of the early Carolingians. This chapter first outlines the process by which Carolingian prelates and kings of that century attempted to control, direct, and encourage the preexisting popular demand for holy men, and then it assesses the relationship between these elite efforts and popular religion.

Examinations of the cult of relics and the establishment of patrocination in this period, particularly the work of Friedrich Prinz and Leo Mikoletzky, have established the broad outlines of elite interest in Roman saints.[3] Although transalpine Christians had been interested in the cult of Roman martyrs since at least 397, when Victor of Rouen brought relics of twenty-three martyrs home to that city from Rome,[4] it was the alliance between Pepin the Brief and Pope Stephen II; sealed by Pepin's adoption of Saint Petronilla (held to have been the daughter of Saint Peter) as *auxiliatrix* or helper, which gave the cult of Roman martyrs its major impetus in the North.[5] The second great period of interest in Roman saints was during the reign of Louis the Pious, when numerous Roman saints were translated from Rome.[6] Both Prinz and Mikoletzky acknowledge a relationship between these elite interests in saints and some sort of widespread piety, but both are

---

439, trans. as "The Cult of Relics and Pilgrimage in Burgundy and Aquitaine at the Time of the Monastic Reform," in Head and Landes, 41–57, and also in German a more developed form in his *Volk und Kirche zur Zeit der beginnenden Gottesfriedensbewegung in Frankreich* (Berlin, 1957); Harmut Hoffmann, *Gottesfriede und Treuga Dei.*

3. Friedrich Prinz, "Stadtrömisch-Italische Märtyrerreliquien und Fränkischer Reichsadel im Mass-Moselraum," *Historisches Jahrbuch* 87 (1967): 1–25; Leo Mikoletzky, "Sinn und Art der Heiligung."

4. Wilhelm Hotzelt, "Translationen von Martyrerreliquien aus Rom."

5. Prinz, 10.

6. Mikoletzky has explained this furious activity as a reaction against the rationalist tendencies of the Carolingian renaissance and the state-dominated church of Charles the Great. In fact, these translations are part of a continuing tradition of interest and support for the cult of saints, of which Charles was a supporter.

concerned with elite participation in relic cults, Prinz from a political perspective, Mikoletzky from a cultural one. Their work might support the argument that the fascination with Roman saints was the result of the interests of a tiny minority of lay and clerical members of the aristocracy and was entirely divorced from the religion of the people. I argue instead that the cult of Roman saints was introduced and encouraged in an effort to supplant the cult of other persons across the Frankish empire. The policies of Pepin, Charles, Louis, and their ecclesiastics were a consistent attempt to control and co-opt this sort of popular devotion and to use it to their advantage.

As Heinrich Fichtenau has pointed out, Europeans in the eighth and ninth centuries were inclined to see human beings, rather than impersonal forces, behind those events they could not understand.[7] He cites, for example, the writings of Agobard of Lyons: "In these parts [the Lyonnais]," Agobard complains, "almost everyone, nobles and commoners, city dwellers and rustics, the aged and youth, think that hail and thunder can be caused by human volition."[8] Agobard likewise ridicules the widely held belief that a plague among livestock in the region had been caused by agents of Duke Grimald of Benevento.[9] Just as people were seen as the causes of disasters, so, too, were they the objects of religious devotion. Hence European religious activity focused on saints, but the "holy men" who were the objects of popular devotion were not always the ones chosen by Frankish elites.

The most famous example of a popular holy man in the eighth century is the Gaul Aldebert, whom Boniface persuaded Pope Zacharias to condemn at the Roman synod of 745.[10] Though Boniface was seldom objective in his accusations against those who opposed his pro-Carolingian political-religious expansionism, Adebert's enemies did present him as a self-appointed demagogue. They alleged that he claimed to have received a special letter from God as well as miraculous relics by which he could obtain whatever he wished; he could forgive sins without the need of confession; he opposed pilgrimages to the tombs of the apostles and martyrs and refused to dedicate

---

7. Heinrich Fichtenau, *Das karolinische Imperium*, 178–179.
8. *PL* 104.147. On Agobard's investigations into popular beliefs see Henri Platelle, "Agobard, évêque de Lyon (†840), les soucoupes volantes, les convulsionnaires," in *Problèmes d'histoire des religions*, 2, *Apparitions et miracles*, ed. Alan Bierkens (Brussels, 1991), 85–93.
9. *PL*, 104.158.
10. *MGH Concilia* 2:39–43.

churches in their honor; he founded oratories and set crosses where
he pleased and dedicated oratories to himself. Boniface even accuses
him of distributing bits of his own hair and nail parings as relics.
Aldebert can perhaps be seen more accurately as one of the numerous wandering bishops who opposed the strongly pro-Roman
ecclesiastical structure espoused by Boniface and perhaps also opposed the private penitential-confessional system then being introduced on the Continent by Anglo-Saxon and Irish missionaries. He
does seem to have developed a wide following, and one can easily
believe that his disciples saved bits of his hair and fingernails as
relics.[11] It was precisely to oppose such outlaw holy men that Boniface
and Pepin encouraged the cult of Roman saints, who, by their origin,
were intimately involved in the Roman-Frankish alliance.

Even when the saints honored were the "right sort" in the eyes of
the Carolingians, the forms of devotion shown them were often considered objectionable. In Germania Prima, Boniface discovered that
the "people of God" were actively pursuing pre-Christian cult practices transferred to Christian saints. A council held under his direction in 742 decreed that "in accordance with the canons each bishop
should take care . . . that the people of God should not do pagan
things but should abandon and repudiate all the filthy practices of the
gentiles, be it sacrifices to the dead or divination or immolation of
sacrificial animals, things which ignorant people do in the pagan way
next to churches in the name of the holy martyrs or confessors."[12]
Clearly, in this most recently converted area of Europe, conversion
had meant simply the substitution of saints for gods.

These substitutions were not peculiar to the fringes of Christianity.
In the same year that his council condemned the pagan practices
observed in Germania, Boniface wrote Pope Zacharias to complain of
pagan festivals such as the winter solstice and January first still being
celebrated in Rome. His complaints led to the condemnation of such
practices the following year,[13] although half a century later, pagan
celebrations were still being held in Rome on saints' days.[14] References to the adaptation of pagan practices to Christian saints' cults

11. On the complex role of hair as sacred object, see E. R. Leach, "Magical Hair,"
    Journal of the Royal Anthropological Institute 88, pt. 2 (1958): 147–164. On holy men
    see the work of Peter Brown, especially "The Rise and Function of the Holy Man."
12. *Karlmanni principis capitulare*, c. 5, *MGH Capit.* 1:25.
13. *Concilium Romanum a. 743*, c. 8, *MGH Concilia* 2:15–16.
14. Ibid., 581–582.

suggest that although popular devotion to saints was strong, it was not particularly Christian.

Even when the practices of devotion to recognized saints conformed to "official" standards, Carolingian churchmen found much that was objectionable in them. Charles the Great (or his ecclesiastical advisers) at the Council of Châlon-sur-Saône in 813 expressed grave concern about the motivations of those from all levels of society who were flocking to such pilgrimage sites as Rome and Saint-Martin of Tours. Priests and other clerics leading immoral and negligent lives thought that simply by making pilgrimages to such places they would discharge their obligations. Many lay people thought that as long as they frequented these holy places they could continue to sin with impunity. Magnates used the excuse of raising sufficient funds to travel to Rome or Tours as an opportunity to oppress the poor. Charles suggested that even paupers traveled to Tours and Rome for no more lofty reason than that they might have better luck begging in such places.[15]

If pilgrims were acting out of base motives, clerics promoting pilgrimages were often seen as no better. In a capitulary of 811, Charles asked his bishops and abbots what was to be done about those "who, as though acting out of love of God and of his saints and martyrs and confessors, transfer bones and relics of saints' bodies from place to place and construct new basilicas and strongly urge whomever they can that they give their belongings to it."[16] Later in the century, Bishop Agobard of Lyons expressed similar concern about the motivations of those promoting the cult of Saint Fermin, an early bishop of Uzès. Around 829 a severe infection of unknown origin, symptomized by seizures similar to those of epilepsy and sores like sulphur

---

15. *Concilium Cabillonense a. 813*, c. 45, *MGH Concilia* 2:282–283. Charles encouraged pilgrimages, provided they were accepted by the parish priest as a form of penitence. The capitularies of Pepin and Charles provided for the care and supervision of pilgrims to Rome and elsewhere. See, for example, under Pepin, *Concilium Vernense*, c. 22, MGH *Capit.* 1:37; Charles on sheltering and caring for pilgrims, *Admonitio generalis* of 789, c. 75, ibid., 60; protection from harm, *Capitulare missorum generale* of 802, cc. 5 and 14, ibid., 93–94; and on supervision of pilgrims, *Capitulare missorum* of 803, c. 6, ibid., 115. I am grateful to Ludwig Schmugge for pointing out to me that the terms *peregrinus* and *peregrinatio* did not necessarily mean pilgrim or pilgrimage in the ninth century. Hence one must avoid attributing all Carolingian discussion of *peregrini* to religious pilgrims. The terms still could be applied to any foreigner or voyager.

16. *Capitula de causis cum episcopis et abbatibus tractandis*, c.7, *MGH Capit.* 1:163.

burns, spread throughout the countryside around Uzès. In terror, people flocked to the shrine of Fermin, bringing offerings in return for hoped-for cures. No cures were effected, and Agobard was particularly critical of the willingness of the clergy who accepted these offerings to keep them to their profit. He suggested that plagues visited on men by God required not simply payment but repentance and that offerings made under such circumstances should be distributed to the poor.[17]

In dealing with these problems of misdirected cults, improper cult practices, and exploitation of popular piety, the early Carolingians proceeded as in their other reform efforts: from Pepin through Louis they sought not to abolish saints' cults but rather to standardize them, regulate them, and then promote them to their own advantage. If Pepin was not to allow the cults of Aldebert and his kind, the obvious objects on which to refocus devotion would be those saints most closely tied to his political-religious program, the Roman martyrs. Thus, as Friedrich Prinz and, earlier, Wilhelm Hotzelt have pointed out, this period marked the beginning of the great influx of Roman martyrs' relics into the North. By providing specifically Roman focuses of religious devotion, Pepin was reinforcing, at a truly popular level, the substitution by which he had replaced the old dynasty: that of papal charisma for the sacred Merovingian blood. Just as Pepin had needed papal approval for his usurpation, he needed it for his appropriation of Roman relics, and it is certain that, as John McCulloh has noted, the new policy of Paul I (757–767) of distributing corporeal relics of roman martyrs was essential to this first phase of the promotion of Roman saints.[18]

The next phase of what might be termed a Carolingian policy toward the cult of relics occurred under Charles the Great. Relatively few translations took place during his reign, but he supported the cult of Roman saints directly and indirectly even while attempting to bring it under ecclesiastical control. As we saw in the previous chapter, the cult of relics received official support in the 790s in connection

17. *MGH Ep.* 5:206.
18. I am greatly in debt to McCulloh for allowing me to read his unpublished paper on the papal role in the Carolingian cult of Roman relics, which he delivered at the 1975 annual meeting of the American Historical Association. This chapter has greatly benefited from his observations on the relationship between the rhythm of translations from Rome and papal policy on translations.

with the Franks' reply to Second Council of Nicaea's treatment of images.[19] The author of the *Libri Carolini*, Theodulf of Orléans, one of the Goths described above, insists further that there could be no equality between relics and images, because relics alone would share in the resurrection at the end of the world.

At the same time that the Frankish church was reaffirming the importance of relics, it was seeking to control the proliferation of the cults attached to them. Two canons of the Council of Frankfurt in 794 dealt specifically with saints' cults. Canon 15 called for the establishment of oratories within the cloister of monasteries containing saints' bodies, where the monks could pray their office without being disturbed by pilgrims visiting the shrine.[20] The council urged a means by which both pilgrims and monks might carry out their respective religious practices without disturbing each other, but it also directed, in Canon 42, "that no new saints be honored or invoked nor memorials to them be erected along roadways, but only those who have been chosen by the authority of their passions or the merit of their lives are to be venerated in the church."[21] This final measure might be seen as the "closing of the frontier" on new saints, whether chosen by the spontaneous attraction exercised by such men as Aldebert or by clerics eager to attract generous pilgrims to a new wonder-worker. And this measure came at a time when the demand for acceptable relics was at its height.

The popular desire for contact with holy men had been reinforced by the gradual introduction of the Roman liturgy in the empire and in particular by the increasing practice of including relics of saints in altar stones when dedicating churches.[22] By the end of the ninth century it was assumed that all churches contained or should contain relics. Thus the capitulary of Aix (801–803) mentioned among the aspects of parish life that bishops were to investigate "churches where are found relics."[23] Similarly, a capitulary of circa 802 ordered that

19. See above, Chap. 8, at notes 10 and 11.
20. *Concilium Francofurtense a. 794*, c. 15, *MGH Concilia* 2:168. See Töpfer, "Reliquienkult," 422. This canon is a reiteration of a capitulary of 789, *Duplex legationis edictum*, c. 7, *MGH Capit.* 1:63: "That where bodies of saints repose there should be another oratory where brothers might pray in private," and of chap. 52 of the *Regula Sancti Benedicti*, which prescribes an oratory for private prayer.
21. *Concilium Francofurtense a. 794*, c. 42, *MGH Concilia* 2:170.
22. On this complicated subject see Nicole Herrmann-Mascard, *Les reliques des saints*, 150–163.
23. *Capitulare Aquisgranense*, c. 1, *MGH Capit.* 1:170.

"each priest should build his church with great diligence, and should look after the relics of the saints with the greatest diligence in night vigils and the divine office."[24] By 813 it was apparently assumed that all parish churches had relics, inasmuch as the Council of Mainz, listing the feasts to be observed throughout the empire, concluded with the "feasts of the martyrs or confessors whose holy bodies rest in each parish."[25] Whether or not we can assume a direct reenactment of the canon of the Council of Carthage, understood as ordering that all altars contain relics,[26] it is apparent that the fathers at Mainz supposed that each parish church had relics.

If every parish church was to have relics, if saints' relics were to be made the officially supported objects of popular veneration, if monasteries were to contain bodies of saints, where were these relics to come from? Obviously, the finite supply of acceptable relics had to be redistributed, and at times the demand for relics must have outstripped the supply. The most striking evidence for a shortage by the end of the reign of Charles comes from England, but it probably indicates conditions on the Continent. In 816 bishops at the Council of Chelsea felt called upon to provide for the possibility that no saints' relics might be available for the consecration of a church: "When a church is built, let it be consecrated by the bishop of its diocese . . . let the Eucharist which is consecrated by the bishop be placed by him along with other relics in a reliquary and let it be deposited in that same church. And if he is unable to find any other relics, nonetheless this alone is surely sufficient because it is the body and blood of our Lord Jesus Christ."[27] The practice of including a bit of the consecrated bread in the altar had been part of the Roman ritual of dedication for some time.[28] Apparently, in the early ninth century, the Eucharist, considered a relic of Christ, was substituted for other relics when none of the latter could be found.[29] This shortage resulted in a rash of unscrupulous and unauthorized translations of relics, as Charles's above-mentioned capitulary of 811 suggests. By 813 the situation had become so acute that it was necessary at the Council of

24. *Capitula a sacerdotibus proposita*, c. 3, ibid., 106.
25. *Concilium Moguntinense a. 813*, c. 36, *MGH Concilia* 2:269–270.
26. *Concilia Africae a. 345–a. 525, Corpus Christianorum: Series Latina* 149:204–205.
27. Arthur West Haddan and William Stubbs, *Councils and Ecclesiastical Documents relating to Great Britain and Ireland*, 3 vols. (Oxford, 1869–1878), 2:580.
28. Herrmann-Mascard, 160.
29. Geary, *Furta Sacra*, 39–40.

Mainz to <u>forbid unauthorized translations:</u> "Let no one presume to transfer bodies of saints from place to place without the counsel of the prince and or [vel] of the bishops and the holy synod."[30]

<u>By the end of Charles's reign, then, saints' relics were</u> vital in the <u>religious life of the empire,</u> not just in the <u>great pilgrimage centers</u> but in the <u>most humble parish church.</u> <u>But these</u> relics had to be of officially recognized saints whose written lives and passions assured their orthodoxy. For long-Christianized areas of the empire, like Aquitane and Italy, such saints could be found among the early martyrs, hermits, and bishops of the region, such as Fermin at Uzès. As Chapter 8 explained, in the <u>more recently Christianized areas, saints had to</u> be brought in, and the most obvious source was Rome. In 780, however, <u>Pope Hadrian I discontinued the policy of his predecessors, declining to release relics of Roman martyrs to the North and basing</u> his decision on a mysterious "revelation of terror."[31] Nicole Herrmann-Mascard argues that shifts in papal policy may have been in part owing to the Roman populace's disapproval of such donations.[32] McCulloh has seen this change as evidence of the <u>cooling relations</u> between the pope and Charles, who, by 780, had left unkept many of <u>his promises to the pope made</u> in the 770s. <u>In any case, few</u> translations were authorized <u>from Rome over the next forty years.</u>

The 820s, however, saw a significant change in papal-imperial relations. After the executions of the papal notary Theodore and the nomenclator Leo in 823, the Franks seized the opportunity to intervene in papal affairs as never before. Lothair, coemperor since 817, was able to obtain oaths from Eugenius II that effectively placed the papacy under the tutelage of the emperor.[33] <u>Soon after, Frankish churchmen began to extract from the pope some of Rome's most valuable assets—the remains of its martyrs.</u>

The first such translation was that of Saint Sebastian, effected to Saint-Médard of Soissons by Abbot Hilduin of Saint-Denis, Louis the Pious's chancellor, in 826.[34] This translation, accomplished only with grudging approval from the Roman clergy, resulted in great popu-

---

30. *Concilium Moguntinense,* c. 51, *MGH Concilia* 2:272.
31. *MGH Ep.* 3:593.
32. Herrmann-Mascard, 59.
33. Louis Halphen, *Charlemagne et l'empire carolingien* (1947; reprint, Paris, 1968), 221–225.
34. *Ex translatione S. Sebastiani auctore Odilone, MGH SS* 15:377–391.

larity for Soissons, which soon became an important pilgrimage site. The success sparked envy among Hilduin's fellow churchmen as they watched the crowds of pilgrims leaving their dioceses to visit Soissons. They were no doubt concerned with their own loss of prestige and, perhaps, revenue. When Odiol of Saint-Médard wrote a highly fictitious account of this translation a century later, he placed a sermon in the mouth of Ostroldus, the contemporary bishop of Laon. Although a literary set speech, it probably reflects accurately the feelings of many ecclesiastics in Ostroldus's position. Addressing his congregation, Odilo has Ostroldus say: "What do you seek in journeying to Soissons, as though you would find the martyr Sebastian? You know that after his martyrdom he was buried in Rome and there he lies, moved by no one. You have here the church of the venerable Mother of God; frequent it, in it swear your vows and make your contributions. You should not wander to other places to seek external help. All that you ask faithfully through her will be given by the Lord."[35]

Such exhortations fell on deaf ears. The Roman martyrs became immensely popular, attracting crowds of pilgrims wherever they arrived and thus enhancing the prestige of the churches to which they were brought or which received fragments of their bodies. At Saint-Benignus of Dijon, for example, the presence of alleged Roman relics was sufficient to cause a mass hysterical reaction among women from throughout the diocese of Langres, even though the relics were clearly bogus.[36] At Fleury-sur-Loire, when Hilduin presented Abbot Boso with some of the relics of Sebastian, popular enthusiasm was so great that a special wooden structure had to be built outside the cloister so that the relics could be visited by the crowds of lay men and women who came to venerate them.[37] Thus bishops and abbots were drawn into intense competition to acquire famous relics from Rome, and over the next decades at least thirty such translations were recorded.

Most of the *translationes* written to describe these acquisitions are so greatly influenced by hagiographic topoi that it is very difficult if not impossible to ascertain the actual means by which the acquisitions

35. Ibid., 386.
36. Amulo episcopus Lugdunensis "Epistola ad Theoboldum episcopum Lingonensem," *MGH Ep.* 5:363–368.
37. Adrevaldus *Miracula Sancti Benedicti,* ed. Eugène de Certain (Paris, 1858), 65.

took place. It is clear, however, that many ecclesiastics bypassed official channels—which were still often blocked or at least slowed by
papal and Roman opposition—and made use of professional relic
merchants, who operated what Jean Guiraud has accurately described as a "commerce in contraband."[38]

One of the first and surely the most famous of these merchants was
the Roman deacon Deusdona, who contracted with Einhard to steal
the relics of saints Peter and Marcellinus in 827.[39] Deusdona was an
expert at his trade, and the picture of his organization and operation
is fascinating. He is described as a deacon of the Roman church living
near the basilica of Saint Peter in Chains. While it is not probable that
he was charged with the ecclesiastical jurisdiction of the third cemetery area of Rome, as has been suggested,[40] he was certainly well
acquainted with catacombs. He evidently had free access to them, no
doubt because they had been in ruins for centuries and were for the
most part deserted, and he was able to use this familiarity to his profit.
He was aided by his two brothers, Lunisus, a dealer in southern Italy
at whose house relics were secured after being removed from the
catacombs, and Theodorus, who traveled with Deusdona to Germany
on a second expedition in 830.

The business of supplying relics to the Franks was apparently
lucrative. Einhard does not say how much he actually paid for his
relics, but the gift of a mule he mentions in his account is clearly only a
small part of the price. When another customer entered into a contract with Deusdona in 830, he promised that "he would be well paid
for it by him."[41] The outfitting of a caravan to cross the Alps with
wares was no small enterprise, and the particulars of Deusdona's
operation were similar to those of later medieval merchant ventures.
During the winter months, he and his associates systematically collected relics from one or another of the Roman cemeteries. Apparently they concentrated on a different area of the city each year. Thus
in 826 they provided relics primarily from the via Labicana. In 835,

38. Jean Guiraud, "Le culte des reliques au IXe siècle," in *Questions d'histoire et d'arch-
    éologie chrétienne* (Paris, 1906), 235–257. See also H. Silvestre, "Commerce et vol de
    reliques au Moyen Age," *Revue belge de philologie et d'histoire* 30 (1952): 721–739;
    Heinrich Fichtenau, "Zum Reliquienwesen"; and Geary, *Furta Sacra.*
39. Einhard *Translatio SS. Marcellini et Petri, MGH SS* 15:238–264.
40. Ibid., 238–264.
41. Rudolphus *Miracula sanctorum in Fuldenses ecclesias translatorum, MGH SS* 15:332.

nine of the thirteen relics came from the area of the via Pinciana-Salaria. The following year the associates concentrated on the via Appia, as they did again two years later, when ten of the fourteen relics brought north came from that area.[42] In spring the merchants timed their visits to various monasteries to correspond with the important feast days of their customers. On June 2, 835, the feast of saints Marcellinus and Peter, Deusdona appeared at Mühlheim with his wares. Two days later he arrived at Fulda, on the eve of the feast of Saint Boniface.[43] Just as merchants were to find in the later Middle Ages, the pilgrims to these celebrations made ideal customers. Seeing the glory that the bodies of Marcellinus and Peter had brought to Mühlheim, for example, customers would be eager to acquire relics that would bring fame to their own institutions.

Deusdona operated on a large scale with a considerable organization. Others engaged in smaller but similar operations. Among these was a certain Felix, who dealt in all sorts of relics from various places of origin rather than specializing in Roman ones. For example, he sold Archbishop Otgar of Mainz the body of Saint Severus stolen from Ravenna,[44] and the monastery of Fulda, a large collection of relics from Rome.[45] He also visited Freising, where he sold the body of Saint Bartholomew to Bishop Erchambert.[46]

This commerce, which was the source of many relics that appeared in the North during the ninth century, was beneficial to all concerned. For the merchant, relics were an excellent article of trade. They were small and easily transported; even entire bodies of saints centuries old were nothing more than dust and a few bones that could be placed in a small cloth bag. As highly desirable luxury items, they brought an excellent price for very little capital investment. The risks were immaterial except for the wrath of a local populace at having their patron stolen (if one bothered to steal genuine relics) and the danger of

42. The traditional locations of the tombs of the martyrs sold by Deusdona can be determined from Usuardus's martyrology edited by Jacques Dubois, *Le martyrologe d'Usuard: Texte et commentaire*, Subsidia hagiographica 40 (Brussels, 1965), and from the early itineraries of pilgrims to Rome in *Itineraria et alia geographica* 1 and 2, *Corpus Christianorum: Series Latina* 175 and 176. See Geary, *Furta Sacra*, 56–57, nn. 18–20.
43. Rudolphus, 332.
44. *Liutolfi vita et translatio S. Severi, MGH SS* 15:292.
45. Rudolphus, 337.
46. Erchambertus episcopus Frisingensis "Epistola ad suos," *PL* 116.31–34.

losing the relics to another thief. Perhaps best of all, owing both to lack of communication and the peculiar nature of the items traded, the fact that the body of a popular saint had already been sold did not prevent one from selling it again to another customer at some future time.[47]

There was considerable political advantage for the pope in allowing the commerce to flourish. It was certainly in his best interest to keep the Frankish ecclesiastics well disposed toward him by not interfering in the relic trade, if indeed he could have done anything to stop it. Furthermore, the popularity of Roman relics in the North could only enhance the prestige of the Roman pontiff. Every martyr's remains that found their way into a Frankish church served to impress upon the Franks the dignity and importance of Rome as a center of Christianity. Moreover, owing again to the peculiar nature of relics, Rome and its pope lost very little in allowing some to be removed or even in giving them away. The fact that Eugenius II had given the body of Saint Sebastian to Hilduin in 826 did not prevent Gregory IV from solemnly translating the body of this same martyr from the catacomb in which it lay to an altar in the chapel of Gregory the Great in Saint Peter's.[48] Finally, the pope himself may have approved Deusdona's smuggling. The *Vita Hludowici imperatoris* by the so-called Astronomer suggests that the pope approved Einhard's acquisition of Peter and Marcellinus.[49]

The connections among popular piety, Carolingian politics, and ecclesiastical rivalry in the cult of Roman relics are intimate and complex. From Boniface's mission and indeed long before, relics had been recognized as a wedge with which to separate the masses from paganism and magic. Although specific abuses in the cult had been condemned, the power of relics had been experienced and recognized as something quite different from that of magic. The difference lies in the identification of the relics with the saint whose body they are. Unlike magical charms, relics identified with particular saints

47. Double sales could be accomplished in one of two ways: either parts of a body could be sold, as was the body of Alexandrus, which Deusdona divided and sold both in Switzerland and in Fulda (Rudolfus, 332), or the merchant could simply appear with another relic from a saint whose remains had already been sold in toto to another party, as the tooth of Sebastian was sold in 835 in spite of the earlier translation of the entire body to Saint-Médard ten years earlier.
48. Louis Duchesne, ed., *Liber Pontificalis* 2 (Paris, 1892), 74.
49. *MGH SS* 2:631.

were extremely personal and even capricious sources of power effective only for those they chose to aid. Moreover, this choice could change, and the saint could elect to favor different people or communities with his or her power.

This power was of two kinds. The most obvious was, of course, the ability to perform miracles, and this was the power sought by the thousands of pilgrims who flocked to the tombs of saints. The desire for cures fit well into traditional Christian attitudes toward penance and the increasingly important role of penitential pilgrimages. Had not Christ himself said, "Which is easier to say, thy sins are forgiven thee, or arise and walk?" But this thaumaturgic power was only the top of their enormous potential. Much more important to the communities that possessed relics was their ability to provide the continual action of divine Providence. Relics brought the special protection of the saint to the community, shielding it from enemies both spiritual and temporal and assuring its prosperity. The presence of an important saint in a monastery or cathedral inspired the laity both rich and poor to give alms. The miracles performed to heal the sick reminded the unscrupulous that this same power could be used against those seeking to harm a saint's chosen church.

This more general protection and favor could extend beyond the confines of the particular community in which dwelled the saint's body and benefit the larger community of the Frankish kingdom. Thus as the ninth century progressed, many saw the veneration of relics as the best hope for deliverance from the troubles that engulfed the later years of Louis's reign. Paschasius Radbertus, abbot of the Picard monastery of Corbie, suggests: "Nor would I say that it is without reason that miracles of saints long asleep in Christ have recently begun to flash forth. Never before have so many and so great things been done at one time by the relics of saints since the beginning of the world; for everywhere saints in this kingdom and those brought here excite each other to song even as cocks at sunrise."[50]

Finally, the relics of these sacred persons not only brought hope of cures to the poor and of stability to the great, but because they had a historical past, they could bring political and cultural focus to Carolingian policy. Relics belonged, in the words of Richard Southern, not only to "this transitory world [and] eternity" but also to an un-

---

50. *Vita Walae, PL* 120.1608.

changing, historical past that could be co-opted, integrated into the
present, and used to direct men's loyalties to Rome, and thus to
Rome's anointed defender.[51] It is no coincidence that the old practice
of using relics as oath objects was given particular support by Charles
and that the standard form of Frankish oath from the early ninth
century on was "May God and the saints whose relics these are judge
me that I speak the truth."[52] By incorporating these physical, tangible
links with Rome, the Carolingians sought to solidify at the popular
level, the new spiritual foundations of their empire.

In many essential aspects, the Carolingian effort to give a specifically Roman focus to the cult of holy men in the empire was a failure.
European peasant culture demonstrated a remarkable ability to adapt
elements of this form of elite religion without sacrificing what would
continue to be, in many ways, a separate culture. So-called pagan or
rustic forms of individual and group devotion to saints continued
throughout the Middle Ages and beyond.[53] The miraculous rather
than the penitential aspects of devotion to relics seem to have formed
for centuries the basis for popular devotion to local and regional
pilgrimage sites. And in spite of the extreme efforts of Carolingians to
procure Roman relics and establish them as cult centers, the great
majority of popular saints in the late Middle Ages would be either
local saints or saints in some way associated with local traditions:
Sebastian never replaced Medardus as the most popular saint in
Soissons, and Mary Magdalene (who by the eleventh century was said
to have ended her life in Provence) replaced the Roman martyrs
whose relics had been brought to Vézelay in the ninth century.

Nevertheless, the confluence of popular devotion, official Christianity, and Roman-Frankish politics did result in the consolidation of
the cult of relics in European religion in a more general way. Just as in

51. Richard W. Southern, *Western Society and the Church in the Middle Ages* (Harmondsworth, 1970), 31.
52. Charles prescribed that "all oaths be made in church or on relics, and what is to be
sworn in church . . . is 'May God and the saints of whom these relics are just him
that he says the truth'" (*Capitulare legi Ribuariae additum*, c. 11, *MGH Capit.* 1:118).
This formula appeared in the oath required by Charles the Bald in 853 (*Capitulare
missorum Silvacense*, c. 13, ibid., 2:274), and was employed by Louis the German in
860 (*Hludowici, Karoli et Hlotharii II conventus apud confluentes*, ibid., 155).
53. Keith Thomas, *Religion and the Decline of Magic*, chap. 2, "The Magic of the
Medieval Church."

other areas of Carolingian culture, little new was added to the cult of saints in the eighth and ninth centuries, but the emphasis on corporeal remains, the augmentation of the supply north of the Alps, and the encouragement of devotion to them laid the foundation for their great role in the mass movements of later medieval piety.

10   Sacred Commodities:
The Circulation of Medieval Relics

ぬひ

Any consideration of sacred relics as commodities in the Middle Ages may seem to be pushing to the extreme the definition of commodities as "goods destined for circulation and exhange."[1] Can we reasonably describe a human body or portions thereof as *destined* for circulation? Can we really compare the production and circulation of saints' remains to that of gold in prehistoric Europe, cloth in prerevolutionary France, or qat in northeastern Africa? The differences are of course great. Nevertheless, although relics were almost universally understood to be important sources of personal supernatural power and formed the primary focus of religious devotion throughout Europe from the eighth through the twelfth centuries, they *were* bought and sold, stolen or divided, much like any other commodity. The world of relics may thus prove an ideal if somewhat unusual microcosm in which to examine the creation, evaluation, and circulation of commodities in traditional Europe. Like slaves, relics belong to that category, unusual in Western society, of objects that are both persons and things.[2] Reflecting on their production, exchange, sale, and even theft can help us understand the cultural boundaries of commodity flow in medieval civilization. An analysis of relics as commodities

1. This chapter has benefited from the advice and criticisms of participants in the University of Pennsylvania Ethnohistory Seminar. I particularly thank James Amelang, Arjun Appadurai, and Bertram Wyatt-Brown.
2. Igor Kopytoff, "The Cultural Biography of Things: Commoditization as Process," in *The Social Life of Things: Commodities in Cultural Perspective*, ed. Arjun Appadurai (Cambridge, 1986), 64–91. On the process by which bodies or portions of bodies might be prepared for this transformed role, see the examples of Saint Helen and the alleged remains of the Magi in Chaps. 11 and 12 below.

requires the investigation of two complexes of cultural activity: the production and circulation of commodities in general, particularly the relative significance and values assigned to the modes of transfer (sale, exchange, gift, and theft) and the place of relics within this transactional culture, that is, the cultural context within which they moved.

Commodities in Medieval Society

A century ago medievalists looked upon the emerging society of feudal Europe as one based on a "natural economy," in which barter and payments in kind were the normal means of exchange. According to this view, Western Europe gradually began to develop a money economy only with the growth of towns, increasing long-distance communication, and the development of first Italian and later northern European trade, phenomena largely credited to the crusades, which began in 1095. This concept of medieval commerce owed more to the ideologies of nineteenth-century colonialism than to the evidence of medieval economy and trade in the West, and by the end of the last century economic historians were emphasizing the very real evidence that pointed to the important roles of money, coinage, and commerce in the eighth through eleventh centuries.

At no time in the Middle Ages was the European economy strictly speaking a "natural economy," in which barter and self-sufficiency characterized the production, exchange, and consumption of commodities.[3] Nor was it a "peasant economy" in the classical sense of the term. Peasants presumably use not capital but cash; profit and the accumulation of capital on an ever-increasing scale are not supposed to be a part of peasant strategies. In the West, even by the ninth century this image can be applied only with some difficulty. Since about 1960, scholars have been investigating the role of great monastic estates in the complex economy of Carolingian Europe. J.-P. Deveroy has examined the intricate network by which food surpluses

---

3. On commerce in the early Middle Ages, see Dietrich Claude, "Aspekte des Binnenhandels im Merowingerreich auf Grund der Schriftquellen," in *Untersuchungen zu Handel und Verkehr der vor- und frühgeschichtlichen Zeit in Mittel- und Nordeuropa*, 3, *Der Handel des frühen Mittelalters* (Göttingen, 1985), 9–99. See Peter Spufford, *Money and Its Use in Medieval Europe* (Cambridge, 1988), esp. 7–105, on coinage in northern Europe before the so-called commercial revolution of the twelfth century.

(principally grain and wine) from these estates were circulated in a flourishing local and regional trade.[4] Although Deveroy does not directly address the question of how much of this distribution was effected by barter as opposed to sale, the sources he examines clearly indicate the importance of both regional and international markets.[5]

Nor did the transformation of the Carolingian empire in the tenth century result in the creation or return of a "classic" peasant economy. Pierre Bonnassie has presented one example of the complexity of medieval peasant society from Catalonia, a region particularly rich in documentation on peasant families.[6] He describes the family of one Llorenç (died before 987) and his sons and grandsons. Llorenç was quite well off: he owned several houses, a freeholding, livestock, military equipment, and a reserve of grain and wine produced from his fields. Bonnassie describes him as typical of a peasant elite that was "enterprising, free, and capable of self-defense when necessary."[7] Within twenty-five years, the more enterprising of Llorenç's sons, Vivas, entered into forty-five land transactions, up to six a year. Land was no sooner bought than it was resold. Other types of property, too, were constantly sold: crops, horses, mules, armor. Vivas and his descendants improved their position in society considerably by the first half of the eleventh century. Their world included a fairly lively market and abundant specie as means of payment. These peasants were clearly moving up socially and economically, and they were using commodities produced from their increasingly specialized agricultural operations as the capital base of their move. Bonnassie considers this family "neither very typical nor very exceptional" and attributes its rise to the breakdown, already in the tenth century, of early medieval social relations, which he characterizes as "on the whole kindly, relatively undifferentiated as to status, still patriarchal in type."[8] To be sure, Barcelona is a unique place, but then so is every location. The forces at work in this region, which also appear in

---

4. J.-P. Deveroy, "Un monastère dans l'économie d'échanges: Les services de transport à l'abbaye Saint-Germain-des-Prés au IXe siècle," *Annales: ESC* 39 (1984): 570–589.
5. Ibid., 581–584.
6. Pierre Bonnassie, "A Family of the Barcelona Countryside and Its Economic Activities around the Year 1000," *Early Medieval Society,* ed. Sylvia L. Thrupp (New York, 1967), 103–123.
7. Ibid., 104.
8. Ibid., 116.

France and Germany in the twelfth century, may differ not so much in their nature as in their frequency, and these Catalan peasants may differ from those elsewhere in their success in achieving their goals more than in the goals themselves. The evidence of sale of land in Anglo Saxon England, on the other hand, suggests that land and land rights across England circulated through sale and purchase in the seventh through tenth centuries.[9]

The evidence of peasant involvement in markets and what might anachronistically be described as capitalist strategies seems to be paralleled by the evidence of long-distance commerce. Not only do mentions of cash sums to be imposed as fines or forfeits abound in charters and laws, but archaeologists have discovered coin hoards spread across Europe that contain moneys minted at places thousands of kilometers distant. Moreover, isolated but tantalizing references to merchants, to trading expeditions, to "eunuch factories," and the like seem to suggest that even during the darkest of the dark ages, commerce continued to play an important role, at both the local and the international levels. A generation of historians thus began to revise the image of the commercial world of the early Middle Ages and to present a picture of a rudimentary but nonetheless important commercial structure tying together the lands between the Mediterranean and the North Sea, a structure that differed from that of later medieval trade more in organization than in volume or nature.[10]

Yet even in the midst of this enthusiasm for commercial history, England's leading medieval numismatist, Philip Grierson, sounded an important warning.[11] He argued that the view of a largely monetized commercial economy was incorrect and had resulted from a failure to distinguish between three sorts of evidence: evidence of persons making their living by commerce; evidence of the sale of specialized or surplus goods directly by producer to consumer; and evidence of the distribution of luxury goods and money by unspecified means.[12] Too often, he warned, historians suppose that the

9. James Campbell, "The Sale of Land and the Economics of Power in Early England: Problems and Possibilities," *Hasking Society Journal* 1 (1989): 23–37, esp. 26–29.
10. Especially Alfons Dopsch, *Naturalwirtschaft und Geldwirtschaft in der Weltgeschichte* (Vienna, 1930); Henri Pirenne, *Mahomet et Charlemagne* (Paris, 1937); and Robert Latouche, *Les origines de l'économie occidentale*, IVᵉ–XIᵉ siècle (Paris, 1956).
11. Philip Grierson, "Commerce in the Dark Ages: A Critique of the Evidence," *Transactions of the Royal Historical Society*, ser. 5, 9 (1959): 123–140.
12. Ibid., 124.

existence of trade means the existence of traders, whereas most buying and selling of agricultural products seems to have taken place without middlemen. Likewise, historians tend to suppose that luxury goods were normally distributed by commerce and that specie was primarily a tool of commerce and its discovery prima facie evidence of commercial exchange. Grierson suggests, by contrast, that trade is by no means the only or even the usual means by which commodities change hands. Much of the exchange network connecting the monasteries of the ninth century probably operated by barter rather than sale (a view with which Deveroy would no doubt agree). The Catalan example of Llorenç, Grierson probably would argue, might represent 'the future, but it would remain a marked exception in Western Europe well into the twelfth century. In the early Middle Ages, Grierson argued, gift and theft were more important than trade in distributing commodities. Under gifts, he included all transfers that take place with the consent of the donor not for material and tangible profit but for social prestige. Under theft he included "all unilateral transfers of property which take place involuntarily," including simple larceny but, more important, plundering in warfare.[13] Of course, he pointed out, payments and exchanges such as ransoms and compensations might fall between the two.

Grierson strongly suggested, and Georges Duby later affirmed,[14] that gift giving and theft were probably the most important means of property transfers among the elite. Plunder, extortions from neighboring peoples or kingdoms, and ransoms demanded for the return of enemies taken in war formed the major means by which both luxury goods and money circulated in the medieval world. Certainly the circulation of gold seems less connected with commerce than with the payment of tribute, and gold acquired through such payments was often put into circulation again when the recipients were conquered by their neighbors.

Property exchanged through mutual consent was often less the material of trade than of gift and countergift.[15] Ritual exchanges of goods and services formed the normal means of distributing wealth acquired either through plunder or from agriculture. The dynamics of gift giving were quite different from those of commerce, even

13. Ibid., 131.
14. Georges Duby, *The Early Growth*, 48–72.
15. Marcel Mauss, *The Gift*.

though both involved exchanges of material goods. The goal of gift giving was not the acquisition of commodities but the establishment of bonds between giver and receiver, bonds that had to be reaffirmed at some point by a countergift. As Grierson puts it, "The 'profit' consists in placing other people morally in one's debt."[16]

Not only were theft and gift more basic forms of property circulation than trade in the early Middle Ages, but they enjoyed higher prestige. Between equals or near-equals, cordial relationships were created and affirmed by the exchange of gifts. Between individuals or groups of differing status, the disparity of the exchanges both articulated and defined the direction and degree of subordination. Similarly, hostile relationships were characterized by violent seizures of property or persons under the control of an enemy. In both situations, the relationship of relative honor and status was at stake, and the property that changed hands functioned symbolically to affirm or deny that relationship. Commerce suggests neutrality, a relationship that, though not unknown, was the weakest of the three alternatives; between the status of *amicus* (friend) and that of *inimicus* (literally, nonfriend, enemy), there was little middle ground. A stranger, someone not tied to the local community by a bond both formed and manifested in gift exchange, was dangerous and suspect. And conversely, he was himself in danger; for unless he could form such a bond with one of the powerful figures in the community, there was no one to guarantee his safety. From this perspective, it is little wonder that purchase was suspect: if one's goal was the realization of a profit, then such a transaction, if carried on with one's friends, was base, and if with one's enemies, cowardly. In fact, trade and piracy were often closely associated. Vikings, and no doubt others, engaged in both on the same expeditions as the opportunities presented themselves and social and cultural bonds dictated.[17] Only in the late twelfth century did the cultural perceptions of Europeans change sufficiently to allow for the possibility of a just price and the morality of mercantile activity.[18]

---

16. Grierson, 137.
17. See William Ian Miller, "Gift, Sale, Payment, Raid: Case Studies in the Negotiation and Classification of Exchange in Medieval Iceland," *Speculum* 61 (1986): 18–50.
18. John W. Baldwin, *The Medieval Theories of the Just Price* (Philadelphia, 1959); Lester K. Little, *Religious Poverty and the Profit Economy in Medieval Europe* (Ithaca, N.Y., 1978).

Even as we acknowledge the validity of this image of exchange in medieval society in general, however, we must also consider the exceptions. One can easily take the notion of gift exchange too far, assuming that it was the exclusive or normal means by which property circulated. Although early medieval Europe was a traditional society, it was by no means either simple or homogeneous. Goods exchanged may have served to create bonds between giver and recipient, but they were also desired for themselves. They could be, and at times were, converted into cash or even capital, so that both a system of objectified, alienable commodity exchanges and a system of subjective, inalienable gift exchanges coexisted. Rather than positing a developmental model of transition from a gift-based economy to a commodity-based economy, we should examine the specific social and political circumstances that might favor circulation of goods by the one or the other means.

This general examination of the nature of early medieval commerce is necessary for understanding the specific structure within which we find the production, sale, exchange, gift, and theft of sacred relics. The circulation of high-prestige articles in general, of which relics were but one sort (others were luxury imported cloth and illuminated manuscripts), did not occur primarily within a commercial structure. Moreover, even when a purchase lay at the heart of such exchanges, contemporaries were likely to look askance at such transactions or to understand them in the context of one or another of the two more significant forms of circulation of goods, theft and gift. Nevertheless, such purchases did take place, and at times a real production and marketing system did exist for the creation and distribution of prestigious commodities.

The Social Construction of Relics' Value

Relics of saints, whether particles of clothing or objects associated with them during their lives, particles of dust or vials of oil collected at the site of their tombs, or actual portions of their bodies, had no obvious value apart from a very specific set of shared beliefs. Such relics were of no practical use. Once removed from their elaborate reliquaries or containers, they were not even decorative. The most eagerly sought after relics of the medieval period—bodies or portions of bodies—were superficially similar to thousands of other corpses and skeletons universally available. Not only were they omnipresent and without intrinsic economic value, they were normally undesirable: an ordinary body was a source of contamination, and opening graves or handling remains of the dead was considered abhorrent. This was true even though the cult of the saints and the Christian belief in the resurrection of the dead had, by the eighth century, altered in some essentials the strict taboo of Roman society, which considered the dead a source of pollution and forbade burial within the confines of the city. Nor had the late medieval preoccupation with death and decay yet produced the image of the macabre that, in the fifteenth century, would permeate artistic and literary reflections on death. Nevertheless, remains of the ordinary dead were normally disposed of quickly and definitively through burial.[19]

The value attached to the special corpses that would be venerated as relics required the communal acceptance of three interrelated beliefs: first, that a person had been, during life and—more important—after death, a special friend of God, that is, a saint; second, that the remains of such a saint were to be prized and treated in a special way; and third, and for our purposes more important, that the particular corpse or portion thereof was indeed the remains of that particular saint.

The first aspect, that is, the belief that a person enjoyed special favor with God, was based on a received tradition of Christian veneration that originated in the Judaic cult of martyrs in the Maccabean period.[20] In Christian antiquity, martyrs, through their passion and death, were seen to have a special relationship with Christ, and the celebration of their *memoria* came to involve not simply a remembrance of the dead, but the petitioning of these special dead to continue to intercede before God for their friends in this world.

With the toleration and support of Christianity in the Roman Empire beginning in the early fourth century, the production of martyrs ended; henceforth, with rare exceptions, only opponents of Christianity died for their faith. Almost all the holy persons of the following centuries were those who lived heroic lives as friends of God rather than those who died heroic deaths. These confessors became the objects of the devotions previously reserved for martyrs, and both

19. Philippe Ariès, *The Hour of Our Death* (New York, 1981), 110–139.
20. Lionel Rothkrug, "The Cult of Relics in Antiquity."

during their lives and after their deaths, Christians came to them for
assistance of all sorts: cures, protection from oppression, finding lost
objects, settling disputes, and the like. In return for this assistance,
the faithful offered them veneration in the form of pilgrimages, vigils, prayers, and offerings—either symbolic (candles or votive offerings of wax or wood, for example) or material (property or money).

The determination of just who these friends of God were remained
well into the twelfth century a largely spontaneous and pragmatic
evaluation, based on the efficacy of a holy person's miracles and the
strength of his or her cult. Although it was the responsibility of local
bishops and increasingly, from the twelfth century on, of the pope to
recognize the feast of a holy person and include it among the official
feasts of the Church, the ecclesiastical official was recognizing an
already established cult, not creating it. Thus canonization did not
determine sainthood. If a dead person worked miracles that attracted
an enthusiastic following, then that person was a saint with or without
formal recognition. Conversely, without a cult, without a following, a
person, regardless of the holiness of his or her life, would not be
considered one of those special companions of God through whom
he chose to act in the world.

In the West, the preferred medium through which God used his
saints was their bodies. Their corpses were seen as the *pignora*, literally, the security deposits left by the saints upon their deaths as
guarantees of their continuing interest in the earthly community. At
the end of the world, the saint's body would rise and be glorified; in
the meantime, the saint continued to live in and to work through it.
This of course was the learned theory of educated churchmen. The
perception of the operation of relics on the part of most people, lay
and clerical, seems to have been much more immediate: relics *were*
the saints continuing to live among men. They were available sources
of supernatural power for good or ill, and close contact with them or
possession of them was a means of participating in that power. To the
community fortunate enough to have a saint's remains in its church,
the benefits in revenue and status were enormous, and competition to
acquire relics and to promote the local saint's virtues over those of
neighboring communities was keen.

Relics, then, were highly desirable—even essential, given that
every church altar was supposed to contain the remains of a saint. We
cannot quantify the demand for relics, but we can identify two par-

ticularly critical periods of demand. The first was roughly from 750 to 850. It resulted both from an aggressive Carolingian expansion in northern and eastern Europe—an expansion in which conversion to Romano-Frankish Christianity and specifically the cult of Roman saints was an essential feature—and from the development everywhere of rural parishes with their churches. The second period of high demand occurred in the eleventh century. It resulted in part from the growth of population across Western Europe with its concomitant need for new churches, in part from the competition between cult centers for the enormously increasing pilgrimage traffic.

The cultural assumptions about relics, their value and utility, were broadly shared. The few dissenters and critics such as Claudius of Turin in the ninth century and Guibert of Nogent in the twelfth (see Chap. 9), were the rare exceptions. From the twelfth century on, some heterodox groups denied the efficacy of relics, but often even these groups had their own versions of saints and even of relics. What was frequently at issue, however, was the identification of a corpse or grave with a saint: how could one be certain that a bone was not simply that of an ordinary sinner? Even those who had no doubts about the efficacy and value of relics could entertain great doubt as to the identity of any particular bones.

For remains to be valuable, they had to undergo a social and cultural transition from ordinary human remains to venerated remains of a saint—thus the aptness of Igor Kopytoff's suggestion that we examine the career or biography of objects as they pass from ordinary remains to treasured relics, and then perhaps back again.[21] With few exceptions, the career of relics was not one of unbroken veneration from the time of the saint's death through the Middle Ages. Some recently dead saints achieved such status. Indeed the remains of Simeon Stylites and Francis of Assisi were eagerly sought after even before they were dead—the danger of someone murdering an aging holy man to acquire his relics, or at least stealing his remains as soon as he was dead, was ever present. Much more common, whether for saints long dead (if indeed they had ever lived), or for more recently living persons, was the necessity of identifying a particular set of remains with a particular saint, using either extrinsic or intrinsic criteria. To the former category belong the tomb or reli-

21. Kopytoff, 64–91.

quary, documents called *authenticae* found either in the tomb or reliquary itself, and descriptions of the burial of saints in hagiographic texts. Formal examinations were usually carried out by the local bishop in public, solemn sessions attended by lay and clerical magnates. After the positive recognition of the relics' authenticity came a public ritual known as the "elevation," in which the relics were formally offered to the public for veneration.

These examinations of external evidence, although quite common, did not constitute the only, or indeed the most important, aspect of the recognition of relics in many cases. The most telling evidence usually came from the supernatural intervention of the saint, who indicated where his or her remains were to be found. Then, during the process of determining the relics' authenticity, the saint often showed by miraculous intervention that the relics were indeed genuine. Thus the initial impetus for the consideration of a possible relic often came in the form of a vision in which the saint appeared to a holy person and revealed where her or his remains were to be found. Often this person was a revered member of the local religious community, one who commanded respect and authority, by virtue of office or saintliness. When the vision came to a person of more humble status, its interpretation was often the responsibility of someone of superior status.[22] The vision led to a search by the community at large—often an entire monastery or village—for the relics, which, when found, exhibited their authenticity by working wonders. This need for relics to prove themselves efficacious was reinforced by the custom, in existence by the ninth century, of submitting relics to an ordeal by fire to determine if they were genuine.

These processes were essential to the creation of relics' value. The public, ritual discovery or invention (*inventio*) and examination of the relics publicized their existence and created or strengthened their cult. So important were these ceremonies that relics long recognized and venerated were periodically "lost" and "rediscovered." An excellent example is that of the remains of Saint Mark, who had been a major patron of Venice since the ninth century. His remains were rediscovered in the eleventh century in the course of restoration of

22. Klaus Schreiner, "'Discrimen veri ac falsi' Ansätze und Formen der Kritik in der Heiligen-und Reliquienverehrung des Mittelalters," *Archiv für Kulturgeschichte* 48 (1966): 1–53.

the basilica of Saint Mark—an orchestrated revitalization ritual that enhanced the value and importance of the saint in the community.

Thus corpses passed from the status of mere human remains to that of sacred relics through a public ritual emphasizing both the identity of the remains with those of a saint and the actual miraculous power exercised by that saint through those particular remains. This actual power was most important because communities often disagreed, even violently, over which one possessed the genuine relics of a particular saint. The identification of false relics and the determination of genuine claims ultimately rested on very pragmatic, functional evidence: if the relics worked—that is, if they were channels for supernatural intervention—then they were genuine. If they did not, they were not authentic, regardless of the strength of external evidence. Once relics had achieved recognition—had come to be perceived as genuine and efficacious—their continuing significance and value depended on their continued performance of miracles and on their relative value compared with other relics and other sources of power. Studies of relics' value indicate considerable fluctuations in both the short and the long term.

The long-term, Europe-wide fluctuation is most obvious and easily documented. Even though in antiquity, martyrs' remains were those most eagerly sought after, in time, the remains of hermits and bishops came to offer these earlier saints considerable competition. In the eighth and ninth centuries, Roman saints were the most eagerly sought after, to the relative detriment of local ones (see Chap. 9). In the eleventh century, apostolic saints such as James, Mary Magdalene, Dionysius, Lazarus, and Marcial, who were reputed to have had direct connections with the West during their lifetimes, became more popular, eclipsing Roman saints who had lived and died in Italy. During the crusades, biblical and Eastern relics became much sought after as booty carried back from Palestine and Constantinople.

Not only did the taste in specific relics change appreciably over the centuries, but relics' relative importance measured against that of other sorts of human and supernatural powers likewise changed. During periods of relatively weak central government, for example, in the later sixth and again in the eleventh centuries, relics were prized not simply for their thaumaturgic power but also for their ability to substitute for public authority, protect and secure the community, determine the relative status of individuals and churches, and

provide for the community's economic prosperity. When new political, social, religious, and economic systems began to develop in the
twelfth century, the relative significance of relics in providing these
services lessened: churches attacked by local laymen could appeal to
the king rather than to their saint for protection; a monastery able to
rationalize its budget and exploit its agricultural holdings was less
dependent on the income brought in by pilgrims.[23] Thus, although
saints' relics continued to be valued as sources of supernatural power,
particularly by pilgrims seeking miraculous cures, in other areas of
life they were effectively supplanted by new and more effective forms
of power and authority.

   Even at the local, individual level, the saints' relative value underwent considerable change. The fluctuation seems directly related,
first, to the impetus of the clerics responsible for promoting the cult—
their efforts at elevations or translations, the erection of new shrines,
the celebration of feasts, and the like—and, second, to a rhythm of
popular enthusiasm in which miracles seem to have led to more
miracles, only to die out again in the course of the year. New efforts
on the part of the clergy, or the celebration of the next feast, could
begin them anew.

   One of the most telling and detailed accounts of this process is the
study by Pierre-André Sigal of the cult of Saint Gibrian at Reims in
the twelfth century.[24] Gibrian was an obscure Irish hermit, long recognized but hardly venerated at Reims, until Abbot Odo of Saint-
Remi in Reims decided to develop the cult, to the profit of the newly
established monastery of Chartreux in Champagne. In 1145 the abbot commissioned a new reliquary shrine for the saint, and on April
16 the saint was solemnly translated into the new shrine in the presence of the archbishop of Reims. A careful record of miracles was
kept between that date and August 24 of the same year. Of a total of
102 miracles, only 20 occurred in isolation. Generally they occurred
in groups of at least four on the same day: 39 took place on Sundays
and feast days, for example, 24 on Monday, but only 1 on Tuesday.
Moreover, the miracles, which began with one on April 6, gradually
increased in frequency as the renown of the saint spread, until they
reached a peak of 10 on May 13, thereafter gradually receding across

23. Geary, *Furta Sacra.*
24. Pierre-André Sigal, "Maladie, pèlerinage et guérison au XIIᵉ siècle."

the months of June, July, and August. Unfortunately the record breaks off in August, possibly because the miracles had by then become so infrequent. One hears little of Gibrian for almost two centuries, until 1325, when again his relics were placed in a more worthy and impressive reliquary, and once more his cult began to attract pilgrims.[25]

The career of Gibrian's relics is similar to that of many more famous saints' relics. Thomas Becket, for example, began to attract miracles at the time of his martyrdom, but these soon fell off; they started up again years later, after the erection of a new and impressive shrine.[26] The career of a relic seems usually to begin with its elevation and continue with its exposure in a worthy and impressive shrine and with encouragement of the laity by the responsible clerics to make pilgrimages and seek cures (see Chap. 11). When cures ensue, they develop their own momentum, only to die out gradually until the cult receives another impetus.

These fluctuations were also influenced by competition between cult centers for the devotion of the faithful. It was not sufficient that a relic be merely efficacious—it had to be more attractive than other relics to which people might turn for assistance. A graphic example of the dilemma posed by competing shrines was that occasioned by pilgrimages to the body of Saint Sebastian, brought from Rome to Soissons in the ninth century, and Bishop Ostroldus of Laon's distressed plea to his congregation to patronize the cathedral rather than distant shrines (see Chap. 9). Competition between saints is seen most clearly in the devotional and propaganda literature produced at shrines, in particular the books of miracles such as that of Saint Gibrian, in many of which one reads that a cure took place only after the petitioner had tried and failed to find help from a long list of other saints. Sometimes these ineffectual saints themselves instructed the pilgrim to go to the saint who finally effected the cure.

This description of the process by which relics' values were constructed may seem to imply a certain cynicism on the part of the clerics responsible. Such was hardly the case. Clerics were among the most fervent pilgrims and often the recipients of miracles themselves; their desire to promote their cult over those of competing neighbor-

25. *AASS*, May 7, 651.
26. Benedicta Ward, *Miracles and the Medieval Mind*. Ward does not note the pattern.

ing shrines in no way indicates cynicism toward the cult of saints in general. Categories such as "popular" and "elite" have little meaning in terms of relic cults. Moreover, the existence of purely popular cults, such as the cult of the dog venerated in southeastern France from the twelfth through the nineteenth centuries as Saint Guinefort in the face of clerical and official condemnation, indicates the value laity attached to saints.[27] In promoting particular saints, the clergy were only attempting to win for their own patron a significant market share.

Circulation Mechanisms

We have seen the social and cultural structures within which some privileged remains of the dead acquired value. Given this value and the need to have such objects in every church across Europe, some sort of circulation mechanisms were necessary to supply churches far from the "production centers" (Rome, the Near East, the areas of Gaul and Spain that had formed part of the Roman Empire in late antiquity), and these mechanisms for the circulation of relics shared characteristics with those for the circulation of other valued commodities in the Latin West. But unlike the transfer of other valued goods, the transfer of relics necessarily breached the cultural context that created value. When a relic moved from one community to another, whether by gift, purchase, or theft, it was impossible simultaneously or reliably to transfer the function or meaning it had enjoyed in its old location. The relic had to undergo a cultural transformation to acquire status and meaning in its new context. Mere circulation was not enough; a newly acquired relic had to prove itself. Its authenticity, which the very fact that it had been transferred cast into doubt, had to be demonstrated, and in ways consistent with "authenticity"'s greater dependence on efficacy than on identification with a particular saint's body.

Gift. The normal means of acquiring relics was to receive them as gifts.[28] As Grierson points out, this is exactly how members of the elite went about acquiring other valuable objects in the early Middle Ages.

27. Jean-Claude Schmitt, *The Holy Greyhound.*
28. Roman Michalowski, "Le don d'amitié."

He mentions, among others, the example of Servatus Lupus, who wrote to King Aethelwulf of Wessex and to his agent to ask for lead for the roof of his church, promising prayers in return. The transaction would be accomplished entirely without recourse to merchants, as the lead would be collected at the mouth of the Canche by serfs of Servatus Lupus.[29]

Exactly the same sort of request lay behind the acquisition of many relics. Alcuin of York (ca. 730–804), the head of Charlemagne's palace school and abbot of several important monasteries, was particularly eager to obtain relics, as his correspondence indicates. He requested gifts of relics from such persons as Paulinus, the patriarch of Aquileia; Angilbertus, chancellor of King Pepin of Italy; Bishop Agino of Konstanz; and Abbot Angilbertus of Centula.[30] Such requests differ not at all from requests for other precious objects and can occur in the same breath as a request for gifts of other "objects of ecclesiastical beauty."[31] As in the case of Lupus, such transactions would normally take place without the assistance of merchants. The journey of Alcuin's messenger Angilbertus was the occasion for a request that Bishop Agino send Alcuin relics.[32] The trip of Angilbertus to Rome gave Alcuin the opportunity to ask him to acquire saintly relics there.[33] Again, as in the case of Lupus's request for roofing lead, the promising countergift was the daily prayers to be offered for the donor.[34]

The most important donor of relics was, of course, the pope, who had at his disposal the vast treasury of the Roman catacombs, containing the remains of the early Roman martyrs. Before the mid-eighth century, popes steadfastly refused to distribute these relics, preferring instead to distribute secondary relics, or *brandia*, objects that had come into contact with the martyrs' tombs.[35] As we saw in the previous chapter, from the mid-eighth century on, however, the Roman pon-

29. Grierson, 129.
30. To Angilbertus, no. 11, *MGH Ep.* 4:37; to Paulinus, no. 28, ibid., 70; to Agino, no. 75, ibid., 117–118; to Abbot Angilbertus, no. 97, ibid., 141–142; to Volucrus and Vera, nobles of Aquileia, no. 146, ibid., 235–236.
31. E.g., no. 97, ibid., 141.
32. No. 75, ibid., 117–118.
33. No. 97, ibid., 141–142.
34. No. 75, ibid., 118: "Et ubicumque sanctorum patrocinia preferuntur, ibi cotidie orationes pro vobis aguntur."
35. Michael J. McCulloh, "The Cult of Relics."

tiffs began to exploit their inexhaustible supply of relics in order to build closer relationships with the increasingly powerful Frankish church to the north.[36] The distribution of relics placed tangible evidence of papal importance in every region that received these gifts, either directly or through subsequent redivision of the relics. Moreover, as gifts, the relics were not alienated as they would have been had they been sold or traded. They thus remained the pope's, and their recipients remained subordinate to the pope by the ties created in the distribution.

Others who possessed illustrious relics could use them to develop similar patronage networks. Thus, for example, bishops distributed portions of important saints to the churches in their dioceses and even beyond. Rather than diffusing the importance of the central sanctuary, these gits increased both its prestige, as the central location of a now-more-widely-known cult, and the prestige of the ecclesiastic who had exercised the patronage. A prime example is the case of the relics of Saint Vanne, distributed throughout the diocese of Verdun in the eleventh century.[37] Such parceling of remains could only enhance their value because that value lay not in the bones themselves, as alienable objects, but in the relationships they could create as subjects.

An obvious and extremely significant aspect of the exchange of relics by means of gift was the establishment of personal bonds between giver and receiver, the creation of "fraternal love" between the two *amici*, as Roman Michalowski has emphasized.[38] Where such a bond did not exist, the parties were not *amici* but *inimici*, and for a transferral to take place, either such a bond had to be formed or, when one party, particularly the subordinate, would not establish a relationship of dependency, the transferral mechanism had to be purchase or theft.

Theft. Relic thefts covered the same broad spectrum of coerced transferrals as did other forms of theft discussed by Grierson:[39] In the ninth through eleventh centuries, the most frequent forms were isolated thefts of individual relics or the theft of the relics from an

36. Heinrich Fichtenau, "Zum Reliquienwesen im früheren Mittelalter," and in general see above, Chap. 9.
37. Geary, *Furta Sacra*, 65–74.
38. Michalowski, 404.
39. Grierson, 131.

enemy's church during a raid.[40] But theft could also take the form of the systematic extortion of Italian churches under the Ottonians,[41] or that of the ultimate theft, the pillage of Constantinople's relics after the sack of that city by the wayward Fourth Crusade in 1204.[42]

The usual target of the isolated theft was a distant monastery or church visited by a cleric who, judging that the saints whose relics were there were not receiving proper veneration, entered the church at night, broke open the shrine, and fled with the remains. One example will suffice. In 1058 a monk of the monastery of Bergues-Saint-Winnoc in Flanders was traveling to England in the company of merchants when the ship was blown off course and landed on the Sussex coast. The monk, Balgerus, explored the neighborhood and came upon a monastery in which were venerated the remains of Saint Lewinna. Impressed by the account of her life and miracles, which he heard from the local monks, he decided to steal the relics. He entered the church at night and attempted to take the relics but was thwarted by the miraculous resistance of the saint. Finally, after much prayer and effort, the saint agreed to accompany him, and he stole off to the ship with his prize.[43]

When, in the course of raids on neighboring nobles, an enemy's property was pillaged, relics were normally included in the spoils. Thus, for example, when Count Odo of Champagne in 1033 sacked and burned Commercy, amid the booty was the arm of Saint Pantalon.[44] Likewise, Count Arlulf the Old of Flanders (919–964) took the relics of saints Valerius and Richerius when he sacked the towns of Saint-Valery and Saint-Riquier.[45] Such appropriations of an enemy's sacred protectors to the benefit of the victor's community belong to an ancient tradition that could no doubt be traced to antiquity and the tradition of appropriating of the city gods of enemies. This sacred

40. Geary, *Furta Sacra*, 69.
41. E. Dupré-Theseider, "La 'granda rapina dei corpi santi' dall'Italia al tempo di Ottone," *Festschrift Percy Ernst Schramm* 1 (Weisbaden, 1964), 420–432.
42. Paul Edouard Didier, comte de Riant, "Dépouilles religieuses à Constantinople au XIIIᵉ siècle," *Mémoires de la Société nationale des antiquaires de France*, 4th ser., 6 (1875): 1–241; Giles Constable, "Troyes, Constantinople, and the Relics of Saint Helen in the Thirteenth Century," in *Mélanges offerts à René Crozet* 2, ed. Pierre Gallais and Yves-Jean Rion (Poitiers, 1966), 1035–1042; and below, Chap. 11.
43. Geary, *Furta Sacra*, 63–65.
44. Ibid., 69.
45. Nicole Herrmann-Mascard, *Les reliques des saints*, 380.

booty could, however, be treated exactly like other spoils: the arm of
Pantalon, for example, was subsequently sold to Abbot Richard of
Saint-Vanne in Verdun for one silver mark.

The greatest theft of relics in the Middle Ages was the sack of
Constantinople. Here the appropriation of saints was systematic and
thorough, lasting several months. All relics were placed in the hands
of Garnier de Traînel, bishop of Troyes, who saw to their distribution:
three-eighths each for the Venetians and the new Byzantine emperor,
the former count Baldwin of Flanders, and two-eighths for the West-
erners. The bishop and then, after his death, Nivelon de Cherizy saw
to the distribution of relics that eventually found their way into
churches across France and what is now Belgium.[46]

Commerce. The third means by which relics circulated was by sale.
Commerce in saints' remains took place not only simultaneously with
the more regular systems of gift and theft but even between the same
groups. Here one finds professional merchants, price negotiation,
efforts at quality control, and established patterns of transportation
and marketing existing side by side with the other, presumably more
archaic, systems of gift, countergift, and theft.

The best documented regular trade in relics was that between
Frankish churchmen and Italian merchants in the ninth century. The
most famous merchant was Deusdona, the Roman deacon we met in
the previous chapter, who negotiated to provide some of Alcuin's
associates, among them Einhard and Abbot Hilduin of Soissons, with
the remains of Roman martyrs in the 820s and 830s. Deusdona
represents the most highly organized and independent sort of relic
merchant. Others might be itinerant peddlers who traveled about
obtaining relics at random as the opportunity presented itself and
then hawking them in other dioceses. Still others, such as the English-
man Electus who operated along the Norman coast, sought primarily
relics to sell to a particular patron, in his case King Athelstan.[47]

The official and quasi-official involvement of central authorities,
ecclesiastical and royal, in the circulation of relics was part of a careful
program of centralized control over the sacred, as explained in Chapter 9. Carolingian control over the distribution of relics was in particular a means of orchestrating access to the sacred. Unlike living holy

46. Ibid., 370.
47. Ibid., 49, 115.

men in the Near East or the occasional Celtic pilgrim or local wonder-worker who appeared on the Continent, dead saints could be controlled by the episcopal hierarchy. The churches in which they were to be found were supposed to have regular clergy attached to them; the decision to move them about was reserved to the local count and bishop; and Carolingian synods sought to limit the proliferation of shrines containing relics of saints not recognized by the Church.

Similarly, one can see the frequently tolerated or even (as in the case of Athelstan) encouraged tradition of thefts as a deliberate attempt to acquire these important prestige objects in a way that would destroy the inalienable relationship between gift and gift giver that characterized the regular distribution of relics by popes and prelates. Carolingians needed important Roman relics for the control of their populations, but the price for relics acquired by gift was subordination to the pope. The theft or purchase of relics objectified these sacred objects; turned them, at least temporarily, into commodities; and allowed the new owner to escape being placed in the debt of the Roman church. The same process might be seen in the means by which the Anglo-Saxon Athelstan sought relics from the Continent.

Reconstruction of value. However it happened, the very act of transferral removed the relic, as I have said, from the cultural structure in which it had originally acquired value. It thus arrived in the new community as an unproven object, the target of considerable skepticism. Was the object really an efficacious relic? If it had been acquired by gift, why would the donor have parted with it if it were really worth having? If acquired by purchase, how could one trust a merchant not to be a fraud selling the "pigges bones" of Chaucer's Pardoner? Just like the oriental carpets entering the West, discussed by Brian Spooner, newly acquired relics had to undergo a process of social negotiation within the new community.[48] To allay suspicions, relics thus had once more to be subjected to the process of authentication described above. They had to be tested, and tested in such a way that the test itself would add to their fame. Thus transferrals of relics, referred to as "translations," were concluded with exactly the same rituals as "inventions."

Moreover, the account of the relics' translation had itself to become

48. Brian Spooner, "Weavers and Dealers: The Authenticity of an Oriental Carpet," in Appadurai, 195–235.

part of the myth of production: the story of how they had come to their new community was part of the explanation of who they were and what their power was. In this context, accounts of thefts, as opposed to gifts or purchases, were particularly appropriate and satisfactory. Between the eighth and twelfth centuries a traditional literary subgenre of hagiography developed in which translations were presented as thefts. The saints were clearly too precious to their communities to be parted with willingly. Thus they had to be stolen, or rather kidnapped. Moreover, the saints were too powerful to allow themselves to be taken unwillingly. A saint unable to prevent the sacking of his or her community or his or her own removal would hardly have been a desirable acquisition. Thus the thief had to have succeeded only by convincing the saint that he or she would receive more satisfactory veneration in the new location—a promise the flattered local community would have to keep.

A significant number of translations thus presented involve saints previously unknown. Whether this reflects missing documentation or saints who did not exist before someone took anonymous remains from a deserted churchyard is impossible to say. In either case, from the perspective of the community in which the remains came to be venerated, the construction of value and the mode of circulation reflected the same assumptions as the production context: acquiring the relic gave it value because it was worth acquiring, and this acquisition (often in the face of grave natural and supernatural dangers) was itself evidence that the relics were genuine. Circulation thus created the commodity being circulated, although to survive as a commodity it had to continue to meet the high expectations raised by the mode of its creation.

Value: Reflections and Questions

We have seen the creation and circulation of a particular type of sacred prestige commodity, saints' relics, within a complex traditional society. Although the existence and efficacy of such person-objects as relics were almost universally accepted, every individual case posed the problem of skepticism both because of the ubiquity of similar objects devoid of value (normal mortal remains), the recognition of widespread fraud, and the intense competition of different religious centers, each eager to discredit the main attractions of their neighbors. In addition we have seen that these commodities circulated in the broader context of an exchange system involving a variety of mechanisms, none of which were the exclusive domain of any social, economic, or educational group.

Human remains could go through a life cycle closely related to the wider production-circulation context: A human bone, given by the pope as a sacred relic, thereby became a sacred relic if the receiver were also willing to consider it as such. Likewise, a corpse once stolen (or said to have been stolen) was valuable because it had been worth stealing. Solemn recognition, by means of ritual authentication normally involving the miraculous intervention of the saint, provided assurance that the value assigned by the transfer was genuine. This value endured so long as the community responded by recognizing miraculous cures and wonders and ascribing them to the intervention of the saint. Enthusiasm tended to wane over time, and the value of the relic had to be renewed periodically through a repetition of transferral or discovery, which would then begin the cycle anew. So long as the relic continued to perform as a miracle worker, it maintained its value as a potential commodity and could be used to acquire status, force acknowledgment of dependency, and secure wealth through its whole or partial distribution.

These specific conclusions concerning relics as commodities suggest more general reflections on the theoretical problems of value and commodity exchange in medieval society. First, when discussing demand formed by need, taste, and fashion, the life history of relics suggests that we must be very careful to distinguish between demand in traditional societies and demand in industrialized (or industrializing) societies. Although the traffic in relics, like that of such commodities as textiles, pottery, and religious icons, was deeply affected by cultural values and collectively shared tastes,[49] the needs generated by the political economy of the Carolingian empire (and, at a later date, the Venetian empire) are no less relevant.

Second, the transformations of relics from persons to commodities and in some cases back to persons through a process of social and cultural transition suggests that we should examine the biographies of other sorts of objects that may have been both persons and com-

---

49. Jane Schneider, "Peacocks and Penguins: The Political Economy of European Cloth and Colors," *American Ethnologist* 5 (1966): 413–447.

modities. Along with slaves and relics, these might include sacred images, which in Byzantium and from the fourteenth century on in the West began to compete successfully with relics as sources of personal religious power, and other extremely important prestige objects such as royal and imperial regalia, art, and entailed estates. Under certain circumstances, all these might be the objects of commerce, but under other circumstances they more closely resemble persons. The boundaries between object and subject are culturally induced and semipermeable.

Third, as vital as cultural boundaries are for the social construction of value, the problem of the authenticity of relics indicates that there need not be consensus within a society on the value, equivalence, or even identity of specific commodities. On the contrary, high-prestige objects such as relics can play an important role in deeply divided communities. Disagreements and conflicts within society may be expressed and even conducted through disputes over the identity and value of such objects.[50]

If the foregoing examination of these "personal commodities" has elucidated something of the complex values of medieval society, we are still left with intriguing and ultimately perhaps unanswerable questions, which, for want of sources, I have been unable to address here. First, we must wonder whether it is possible to speak of value equivalences of relics and other commodities, or whether we ought to talk of rank. Much theoretical literature would suggest that a conversion between relics and, say, livestock ought to be impossible to establish—that in gift exchange, the emphasis is on quality, subjects, and superiority, rather than on the quantity, objects, and equivalence emphasized in commodity exchange.[51] And yet we know that relics were in fact dealt with both as gifts and as commodities, even though a price list could never be established. During the periods of their careers when relics were objectified, how was value equivalency determined? Did it cease to have any meaning once a relic had again become subjectified in a new social context?

Related to this first question is the second, that of the relative value of different relics: why was one relic more prized than another? In some instances—a local saint or a famous apostle—the answer is ob-

50. Peter Brown, "Relics and Social Status."
51. Chris A. Gregory, *Gifts and Commodities* (London, 1982).

vious. Usually, however, it is impossible to determine why, for example, Saints Peter and Marcellinus would be sought by the Franks, or why one would steal the remains of Saint Maianus or Saint Fides rather than those of some other saint. Were these merely targets of opportunity, or was there a process of comparison and selection?

Third, one would like to be able to establish the relative importance of gift exchange as opposed to the theft or sale of relics. Here again we have no idea. In the cases discussed of Carolingian ecclesiastics who were active in stealing relics as well as in purchasing them and receiving others from the pope, we see all three mechanisms. I have suggested above that the mechanism selected depended on the type of relationship the recipient desired to establish with the previous owner. Perhaps here the concept of kin distance (in the sense of artificial kin groups within the Christian community) might be helpful in determining the boundaries within which gift, sale, and theft were acceptable.

Fourth, one would like to know more about the acceptance of these objects as valuable within the broader, lay society of the regions into which they were introduced. We have seen that in the eighth and ninth centuries, much of the flow of relics was into the recently Christianized areas of northern Germany. Here they became the objects of officially sanctioned cults. In a controversial but fascinating study of pilgrimage sites in Germany in the later Middle Ages, Lionel Rothkrug has argued, however, that pilgrimages to saints' shrines are almost totally nonexistent in such areas as Saxony, which had been the major focus of these translations.[52] Could it be that despite the official propaganda attesting to the popularity of these relics, the native populations were never really drawn into the system of values within which they had meaning? Since Rothkrug shows, on both micro and macro levels, a startling coincidence between areas lacking pilgrimages and areas where the Reformation succeeded, it is tempting to argue that these regions never accepted the hagiocentric religion that was medieval Catholicism.

52. Lionel Rothkrug, "Popular Religion and Holy Shrines: Their Influence on the Origins of the German Reformation and Their Role in German Cultural Development," in *Religion and the People*, ed. J. Obelkevich (Chapel Hill, N.C., 1979), 20–86; "Religious Practices and Collective Perceptions: Hidden Homologies in the Renaissance and Reformation," special issue, *Historical Reflections/Réflexions historiques* 7 (1980).

Finally, we need more comparative studies and theoretical models of commodities that might elucidate some of the processes I have discussed. Most anthropologists tend to look either at industrialized societies in which the production and distribution of commodities operate in a very different context, or at traditional societies undergoing rapid transformation owing to colonization or at least increasing participation in alien markets and production systems. Neither model is appropriate for medieval Europe. Change was disjointed and internally generated and was not directed toward a colonial, capitalist, or industrialized economy imposed from without. It is within this very different economy that sacred relics as commodities must be understood.

Living

&

11 Saint Helen of Athyra
and the Cathedral of Troyes
in the Thirteenth Century

☙☙

The important role played by the saints in financing the construction of medieval churches is well known, thanks in large part to Pierre Heliot and Marie-Laure Chastang's researches on the tours of relics to raise funds for construction.[1] Monasteries and cathedral chapters, faced with the tremendous expenses of reconstruction and renovation, began around 1050 to send the remains of their important patrons on fund-raising tours of wide dimensions to reach those of the faithful unable to travel to the home of the saint or uninterested in doing so. It was indeed an unfortunate cathedral that did not have a saint in residence who could serve as a magnet for pious pilgrims and their offerings and travel as a fund-raiser as well. Such service was hardly either cynical or purely mercenary; nothing could have been more natural in the medieval church than that churches' patrons should come to the aid of their communities in times of financial need. The construction projects were worthy causes, and the clerical or lay preachers who traveled about in the company of these saints, offering indulgences and asking for contributions, were a necessity.

The only serious problem with this method of fund raising was that some churches lacked the remains of a popular saint. The obvious solution for such a church was to acquire a saint and create a cult in his or her honor. This feat was easier said than done, however, as it entailed, in effect, researching or even creating a market for the cult,

---

1. Pierre Heliot and Marie-Laure Chastang, "Quêtes et voyages de reliques au profit des églises françaises du Moyen Age," *Revue d'histoire ecclésiastique* 59 (1964): 789–822, and 60 (1965): 5–32.

publicizing it, promoting it, and selling it to the public, all while in fierce competition with other better known or better loved saints. Because such an advertising campaign requires the promoters to be particularly well attuned to the religious sentiment of the community they are attempting to reach, an examination of such a campaign can be highly informative, not only about the methods of fund raising in the Middle Ages but also about the religious sentiment of a medieval community. An excellent example is the progressive creation and elaboration of the cult of Saint Helen of Athyra to help finance the reconstruction of the cathedral of Troyes. In examining this process, we must keep in mind three interrelated aspects of the history of Troyes in the thirteenth century: the peculiar ecclesiastical and political organization of the town; the problematic genesis of the *Vita beatae Helenae;* and the halting efforts of the chapter to complete renovations in spite of a deteriorating economic situation.

Relics and the Fourth Crusade

The rape of Constantinople perpetrated by the participants in the Fourth Crusade resulted in a flood of sacred relics deluging Western Christendom in a volume never before or since equaled. Among the hundreds of relics and sacred objects sent to the West in the following decade, one of the most obscure was the body of Saint Helen of Athyra, reputed to have been the daughter of a fourth-century king of Corinth, Agiel, and his queen, Gratulia, which reached Troyes sometime before 1215.[2] The cathedral of Troyes received this and other relics through the efforts of its bishop, Garnier de Traînel, who had been appointed "procurator sanctorum reliquarum" by the Latin conquerors.[3] Although Garnier died in 1205 and was succeeded in office by Nevelon de Cherisy,[4] the relics he had set aside for his church were faithfully sent back to Troyes, probably through the agency of his chaplain. The collection, though small, was indeed impressive: in

---

2. Giles Constable, "Troyes, Constantinople, and the Relics of St Helen," 1038. Constable bases this *terminus ante quem* on the introductory letter discussed below, which states that in this year, John of Troyes arrived in Constantinople to learn something about the life of Saint Helen (1041).

3. Ricardus de Gerboredo *Adventus faciei S. Johannis Bapt., AASS,* June 5, 640; Edouard Riant, "Dépouilles religieuses à Constantinople," 32.

4. Riant, "Dépouilles religieuses à Constantinople," 32.

addition to the body of Saint Helen, Troyes received relics of the true cross, a cup purported to be the Holy Grail, the head of Saint Philip, and an arm of Saint James the Greater.[5] Although each of these relics was more important and better known than the body of Helen, in time she surpassed them all in popularity, becoming one of the principal saints of the diocese of Troyes, the object of a cult that seemed to far exceed any reason for such devotion.[6]

In trying to explain the great popularity of this Helen of Troyes, scholars have tended to disregard as a fabrication the *Vita beatae Helenae,* which purports to be an account of her life written by John Chrysostom, and to identify her either with the hermit Helynus, whose cult was already known in Troyes, or with the empress Helen, mother of Constantine.[7] The research of Edouard Riant in the nineteenth century and, more recently, of Giles Constable has, however, established beyond serious doubt that she should be identified with the Saint Helen honored in Athyra, a town near Constantinople, immediately before the Fourth Crusade.[8] But if the physical remains of Helen were transported to Troyes, it is not at all evident that anything of her actual life and virtues were recognized or appreciated in Champagne. Once in the West, Helen had to acquire a new identity

---

5. Edouard Riant, *Exuviae Sacrae* 2:178.

6. Her feats on May 4 ranked in Troyes with such feasts as the Assumption of the Virgin and All Saints; Constable, 1035.

7. The Bollandist Godfroid Henskens believed that Helynus and Helen, mother of Constantine, were confused in the minds of the inhabitants of Troyes because of the similarity of their names; *AASS,* May 1, 531. Although P. J. Grosley attempted to make the relics at Troyes actually be those of the mother of Constantine, this identification was never made in the Middle Ages; see P. J. Grosley, *Mémoires sur les Troyens célèbres* 1 (Paris, 1812), 436–441. The text on which some have tried to base this identification, the *Chronicon* of Alberic of Trois-Fontaines (*MGH SS* 23:685), clearly refers to the presence at Troyes of the body of Hilda, a servant of Helen, not of Helen herself: "Anno 332. Obiit sancta Helena mater Constantini huius discipula fuit sancta Hilda puella que requiescit in episcopati Trecensi."

8. The most important confirmation of the existence of the relics of a Saint Helen outside Constantinople immediately before the Fourth Crusade is found in the description of the city and its religious monuments by Archbishop Anthony of Novgorod, who visited there in 1200. Riant, in *Exuviae Sacrae* 2:230, quoted a Latin translation of the Russian edition of P. Sawaitov, *Puteschestive novgorodskogo archiep* (Saint Petersburg, 1872), 171, made for him by J. Martinov. The archbishop speaks of a Saint Helen virgin whose body lies outside the Golden Gate, a general location that could well fit Natura, i.e., Ἀθύρας, modern Buyuk Tchekmedje according to Jean Ebersolt, *Orient et Occident: Recherches sur les influences byzantines et orientales en France pendant les croisades* (Paris, 1929), 2:27.

that, as we shall see, was responsive to the needs of the diocese of Troyes. Progressively, the cathedral chapter was able to provide an identity for this unknown Saint Helen, develop a cult in her honor, and orient the devotion of the local laity through this cult to the pressing task of reconstructing the cathedral.

Saint Helen could not have chosen a more opportune time to take up her residence in Troyes than the opening years of the thirteenth century.[9] The demographic, economic, and political developments of the preceding century had not been kind to the bishop and his chapter. In the course of the twelfth century, Troyes had grown from an episcopal city bounded by the ancient walls of the *civitas* to a commercial and industrial community centered on the *forum* southwest of the old town, an area dominated ecclesiastically by the powerful monastery of Notre-Dame-aux-Nonnains.[10] Because the monastery was largely independent of the bishop and the cathedral chapter, it, rather than they, was the primary recipient of the increasing economic benefits of the great fairs held in Troyes. Not only was ecclesiastical control of the wealthiest section of Troyes largely beyond the cathedral, but the counts of Champagne and Brie had been gradually increasing their judicial control over the town at the expense of the bishop. By 1198 this process was substantially complete, and the jurisdiction of the chapter court was reduced to adjudicating certain cases involving the canons' servants.[11]

In spite of this erosion of episcopal resources, the bishop might have been able to preserve the status quo of his cathedral had no major crisis occurred to demand a tremendous outlay of capital in a short time. But on the night of July 23, 1188, fire, that great devourer of wooden medieval towns, swept through Troyes, destroying all its

9. Joseph and Frances Gies present a vivid image of thirteenth-century Troyes as a "typical" medieval town in their *Life in a Medieval City* (New York, 1973).

10. This shift is discussed by Elizabeth Chapin in *Les villes de foire de Champagne des origines au début du XIVe siècle* (Paris, 1937), 32–34. On Notre-Dame-aux-Nonnains see R. Rohmer, "L'abbaye bénédictine de Notre-Dame-aux-Nonnains des origines à l'année 1503," *Positions et thèses de l'école des Chartes* (1905), 123–129; and A. Prévost, *Le diocèse de Troyes, histoire et documents* (Dijon, 1923), 185–189. This abbey, founded between 651 and 656 by Saint Leuçon, nineteenth bishop of Troyes, was originally the mother parish of the entire southwest area of Troyes, and the abbess retained the position of *curatus* of the parish of Saint-Jacques-aux-Nonnains, which had grown up around the abbey; see Prévost, 186; and Troyes, Arch. dép. Aube, MS. G. 927.

11. Chapin, 19; Arch. dép. Aube, MS. G. 465.

principal buildings: the abbey of Notre-Dame-aux Nonnains, the collegiate church of Saint Stephen, the palace of the count, and the cathedral.[12] The abbey had its prosperous parishes from which to draw revenues to rebuild; the count would certainly be able to restore his palace and chapel; but the cathedral had little to fall back on but its rural holdings and the ingenuity of its canonical chapter. With the help of Saint Helen, the latter proved to be at least as important as the former.

Although no records remain of the total cost of the reconstruction and renovation project, it is possible to estimate roughly that construction costs were in the area of fifty thousand pounds.[13] This was a huge sum by any standard, and for a town that was experiencing simultaneously a decrease in the profitability of its fairs and marked financial irresponsibility by its lord, Thibaut IV, it must have been an enormous burden indeed.[14]

It is no surprise, then, that the thirteenth century saw Troyes's secular and religious institutions beset by financial crises: in 1242 the commune of Troyes was so greatly in debt to financiers of Reims, Laon, Arras, and other towns that it collapsed;[15] from 1262 until after 1267 the abbess of Notre-Dame-aux-Nonnains fought violently but futilely to prevent the establishment of a rival parish church within

12. *Chronicon Roberti autissiodorensis, MGH SS* 26:253; Théophile Boutiot, *Histoire de la ville de Troyes et de la Champagne méridionale* 1 (Troyes, 1870), 263.

13. The cost of construction of the church of Saint-Urban during the middle of the thirteenth century can be accurately determined from contemporary figures. The construction of the choir cost £24,145 19s; see Charles Lalore, *Collection des principaux cartulaires du diocèse de Troyes* 5 (Paris, 1875), lxxviii. The total interior length of the cathedral is 104.18 m, whereas that of Saint-Urban's is only slightly more than 50 m; the cost of the former must have been considerably more than that of the latter, although this is obviously a rough guess.

14. The gradual evolution of the fairs from centers of trade to centers of finance affected the profitability of hall rents. Moreover, between 1265 and 1273, ecclesiastical courts lost, to the courts of the count, the jurisdiction over disputes and suits arising from visitors to the fairs. On the Champagne fairs the article of Robert-Henri Bautier remains classic: "Les foires de Champagne, recherches sur une évolution historique," *Recueils de la Société Jean Bodin*, 5, *La foire* (Brussels, 1953), 97–147. On Thibaut's indebtedness and constant borrowing see Chapin, 167–168.

15. Charter of December 1232, ed. in Auguste Vallet de Viriville, *Les archives historiques du départment de l'Aube et de l'ancien diocèse de Troyes, Capitale de la Champagne, depuis le VIIe siècle jusqu'à 1790* (Troyes, 1841), 370–374; Chapin, 167–168. The reorganization after the collapse is presented in a charter of 1242, also ed. Vallet de Viriville, 370.

Notre-Dame's jurisdictional boundaries.[16] If even these institutions experienced such great financial difficulty during the century, things probably were even worse for the cathedral.

At any rate, even in 1188 it must have been evident to those concerned that rebuilding and enlarging the cathedral would require careful planning and long preparations.[17] Indeed the first concrete step was not taken until twenty years after the disaster, when Bishop Hervé received by exchange a piece of land for the rebuilding project.[18] Then, in 1213, the first indulgence for contributions to the reconstruction fund was issued.[19] The second followed in 1215,[20] and in 1218 the chapter acquired a stone quarry from which to get building materials.[21] When Bishop Hervé died in 1223, it appeared that he had begun a slow but sure program, like so many others across Europe, that would in time result in the completion of the new cathedral. But on November 10, 1228, a second natural disaster struck: a storm destroyed the partially rebuilt cathedral, making it necessary to begin again.[22] Significantly, while the head of Saint Philip

16. In 1262, Urban IV, a native of Troyes, decided to honor his own memory in that town by erecting a church in honor of Urban III on the site of his own birthplace and sent £29,007 10s, for this purpose. The objections of the abbess to this new foundation were clearly motivated by fears that Saint-Urban's would soon become a rival parish. See Charles Lalore, *Documents sur l'abbaye de Notre-Dame-aux-Nonnains* (Troyes, 1874), 191–192.

17. On this and every other point of detail concerning the construction of the cathedral, it is necessary to consult Joseph Roserot de Melin, *Bibliographie commentée des sources d'une histoire de la cathédrale de Troyes*, 1, *Construction* (Troyes, 1966), and 2, *Décoration, Ameublement* (Paris, 1970). Roserot de Melin points out that rebuilding the cathedral was less the problem than greatly enlarging the older edifice.

18. H. Arbois de Jubainville, "Documents relatifs à la construction de la cathédrale de Troyes," *Bibliothèque de l'école des Chartes* 23 (1862), no. 1, 217, in exact copy. This exchange took place in 1208; Roserot, 1:13.

19. Arbois, no. 2, 218; Roserot, 1:20.

20. Arbois, no. 3, 218; Roserot, 1:20.

21. Arbois, no. 4, 219; Roserot, 1:20.

22. *Chronica Alberici monachi Trium Fontium, MGS SS* 23:922: "Ventus validissimus extitit ante vigiliam sancti Martini et in plurimis nemoribus in multa quantitate ceciderunt quericus et fagi, et ecclesia Trecensis corruit et caput sancti Philippi [*other MS:* Stephani] apostoli in illo casu se mirabiliter abscondit." Roserot, 1:24, insists that the damage was not as great as one would assume from this description. See Elizabeth Carson Pastan, "The Early Stained Glass of Troyes Cathedral: The Ambulatory Chapel Glazing c. 1200–1240" (Diss., Brown University, 1986), 38–39, on the limited extent of the damage.

miraculously escaped destruction, the reliquary of that most obscure of Byzantine saints, Helen of Athyra, was almost totally destroyed.[23]

Creating the Cult

This debacle marked a turning point in the reconstruction program. To raise the funds for the construction, the chapter apparently decided that what was needed was a new object of devotion that would attract pious donors and pilgrims eager to contribute to the construction project. As the focus of this new devotion, the relics recently acquired from Constantinople were chosen. While the relics of Philip and James, as well as the sacred blood, the piece of the cross, and what later came to be venerated as the Grail were honored in the cathedral, the cult of Helen quickly overshadowed these others. It appears that the prominence given to Helen was intended by the chapter, and it is possible, I think, to suggest why they made this choice.

One might think that the relics of the Passion or the remains of such great saints as James the Greater and Philip might have been better suited to the elaboration of a far-reaching cult. But, as we shall see, these relics were used in a supplemental way to reenforce the cult of Helen. This choice must be understood in the context of thirteenth-century spirituality.

The head of Philip surely was an important relic. But the cult of Philip had been well established in Rome since the sixth century, and an uninterrupted tradition placed his remains in that city.[24] Moreover, many other places—Florence, Saint-Denis, Corbie, Bruges, and Paris, to name only a few—claimed relics of Philip acquired, like the head in Troyes, after the Fourth Crusade.[25] Obviously, though the possession of the head of the saint was a wondrous thing, it was not sufficient to allow Troyes, a relative newcomer to the Philip cult, to become the center of devotion to the apostle. The same difficulty was even more evident for the arm of James: Compostella could never be outdone as the center of his cult by a cathedral in northern France.

---

23. *Chronica Alberici*, ibid.
24. For a survey of the cults of Philip and James in Rome, see Francesco Spadafora, "Filippo e Giacomo," *Bibliotheca Sanctorum* (Rome, 1965), 5:711.
25. On relics of Philip see Riant, *Exuviae Sacrae*.

But even in the north, Namurs and Paris could also claim relics of James acquired from Constantinople.[26]

The relics of the true cross and the sacred blood were also widely distributed during the course of the thirteenth century.[27] Clearly they were not unique, and even in Troyes itself, there appear to have been at least two other relics of the sacred blood, one at Notre-Dame-aux-Nonnains and the other at the count's chapel.[28]

The supposed Grail presents a slightly more complex problem. The cathedral treasury contained a vase of green and black porphyry around which was a silver band inscribed in Greek.[29] The inscription, according to Charles Noiré, identified this vase as the cup used at the Last Supper.[30] The cup itself was destroyed during the French Revolution, but because of the inscription in Greek, whatever its actual text may have been, one may suppose that it did originate in Constantinople. Yet during the Middle Ages the chapter seems to have been unaware of the importance of the vase. In an inventory of the cathedral treasure of 1429 it is not mentioned, although a plate is described as "a certain large silver bowl whose bottom is from the bowl of the Lord."[31] Exactly what this object may have been is unclear, but apparently it was a paten believed to contain a portion of a plate used at the Last Supper. The inventory of 1611 does describe the porphyry vase but makes no mention of a tradition identifying it with the Last Supper.[32] What these two objects were considered to be in the thirteenth century it is impossible to say, but apparently neither of them was venerated as the Grail.

The advantages of the remains of Helen over these relics can be briefly summarized. The Fourth Crusade had apparently done for relics what shipments of New World gold would do for sixteenth-century European finances: while increasing the demand for relics, it

26. Ibid.
27. On relics of the cross see the remarkable work of A. Frolow, *La relique de la vraie croix: Recherches sur le développement d'un culte*, 2 vols. (Paris, 1961).
28. See M. l'abbé [Charles] Nioré, *Inventaires des principales églises de Troyes* 1 (Troyes, 1893), cix.
29. Ibid., cx.
30. Ibid.
31. Ibid., 2, ed. Charles Lalore, no. 514, 72: "Quedam scutella magna argentea, cuius fundus est de scutella Domini."
32. Ibid., no. 685, 88.

simultaneously caused a deflation of their value, particularly of relics of the more popular saints, by oversupplying that demand. The result was a skepticism of some magnitude and something of a feeling of indifference resulting from the confusion. This is not to say that relics of the true cross or the head of Saint Philip could not claim the devotion of a local populace, but it is doubtful that such relics could form the center of a wider devotion. The position of Helen's remains was quite different. First, the claim of Troyes to her body was unique. She may have been obscure, but at least no other church in the West had the slightest claim to her relics. Second, unlike the fragmentary remains of Philip and James, the body of Helen was entire, and Troyes was thus the natural center for the development of her cult.

But beyond the considerations of the relative importance of the other Byzantine relics in Troyes, there were particularly good reasons why such a saint might be popular in that town in the thirteenth century. The very name Helen could easily suggest two other devotions in Troyes: that of the hermit Helynus noted by the Bollandist Henskens,[33] and the cult of Helen, the mother of Constantine, who was also honored in Troyes.[34] This is not to imply that there was, at the official level, any confusion about whose body lay in the cathedral, but these preexisting Helen devotions may have predisposed the Champenois to yet another.

Moreover, the church of Troyes was already devoted to another virgin, Saint Mastidia, a most obscure local saint whose cult had been of great importance in Troyes since the ninth century and whose body was likewise to be found in the cathedral.[35] As the cult of Helen grew, the two saints were closely paired as the two patronesses of the cathedral.

There was yet another factor that contributed to the development of the cult of Helen: the account of her life and miracles. The *Vita beatae Helenae* was written, according to a letter that accompanied it, by John Chrysostom and translated into Latin in 1215 by a cleric in Constantinople. It presents difficulties at every point in its examina-

33. See above, note 7.
34. *El arte romano Exposición organizada por el gobierno español bajo los auspicios del consejo de Europea Catalogo* (Barcelona, 1961), no. 1127, 416, is an enamel of Helen in the Musée des beaux arts de la ville de Troyes of about 1170.
35. *AASS*, May 2, 141–145.

tion: its sources, the place and date of its composition, its original content and form.[36] Yet when these problems are examined, the results provide a clear indication of the significance of Helen in the religious life of Troyes.

The author of the letter, a certain Angemer, a native of Courbetaux in Champagne and a lector of the church of Chalcedon, claimed that he had translated the life into Latin at the request of John, a cleric of Troyes who arrived in Constantinople in 1215 seeking information on the saint. Giles Constable's discovery of the Latin texts of the letter and the prologue to the *vita* has increased the probability that both are contemporaneous with the *vita*.[37] It is still far from certain, however, under what conditions or where the *vita* was composed. Clearly, the attribution to John Chrysostom is an effort to provide authenticity to what is most definitely a thirteenth-century composition. But was this spurious text written in the East or in Troyes? Constable, encouraged by the rediscovery of the letter and prologue, tends to believe that it was probably written in Constantinople without, however, ruling out the possibility that "the *vita* and letter were both forgeries composed at Troyes to authenticate some traditional relics and that the mission of John and the labors of Angemer are all literary fictions."[38] As we shall see from an analysis of the three versions of the life, Constable is quite likely correct in his assertion that the *vita* was written in Constantinople, but it was probably "written to order" by Angemer to fill the requirements of the cathedral chapter in Troyes.

The *vita* itself is preserved in three different medieval versions, each of which seems to some extent incomplete. The first is the text printed by Nicolas Camusat in 1610, which recounts the life and miracles of Helen, daughter of King Agiel of Corinth and his queen, Gratulia, up to the death of the latter.[39] The abrupt end of the text before the passion and death of the saint herself is most peculiar in hagiographic literature and has led to speculation that the manuscript used by Camusat was incomplete, but a fourteenth-century

---

36. Nicolas Camusat, ed., *Promptuarium sacrarum antiquitatum Tricassinae dioecesis* . . . (Troyes, 1610), fols. 402v–410v.
37. See above, note 2.
38. Constable, 1041.
39. No such persons existed, and all efforts to discover them in other medieval literature, Greek or Latin, have so far been in vain.

manuscript containing the *vita,* Bibliothèque nationale 5614, provides no such indication.[40]

The second version of the *vita* is found in Vatican Reg. lat. 583. It is an abridged fifteenth-century version of the text in the Paris manuscript and is reproduced in the appendix at the end of this chapter. Unfortunately, at least one folio is missing at the end. It is theoretically possible, therefore, that more of Helen's life and death had been summarized in this manuscript and that in its original state this text would have provided an account of the *passio S. Helenae.*

This hypothesis is unlikely, however, given the evidence of the third and most problematic version of the *vita,* that presented in one of the windows of the high choir of the cathedral itself (Illustration 1). The window dates from the thirteenth century and would logically present the most important evidence for reconstructing the life of Helen as it was known at that time.[41] The traditional interpretation of the twelve scenes from the life of the saint would, however, indicate that the window is a most unsatisfactory source; for seven of the scenes apparently have no referent in either of the written versions of the *vita.* If this interpretation is accepted, then the restoration of the *vita* as it was known in thirteenth-century Troyes is impossible.

I suggest the contrary: that when the twelve scenes are placed in their original order and properly interpreted, they reflect accurately and completely the life of Helen found in BN 5614. They demonstrate that even in the thirteenth century all that was known of Helen was details from her life. The reason for this is to be found, I believe, in the circumstances under which her cult was originally developed and encouraged.

First, let us review the interpretation of the twelve scenes, in order

40. My examination of Paris, BN MS lat. 5614 has convinced me that Camusat probably used this manuscript for his edition.

41. The considerable debate over the completion date of these windows is summarized by Roserot, 1:29–40. It revolves around efforts to recognize in one of the windows the arms of Jean d'Auxois (1314–1316) or those of Blanche of Castille. André Marsat, *Cathédrale de Troyes: Les vitraux* (Paris, 1974), 60, after summarizing the debate, opts for a mid-thirteenth century date, pointing out that other bases than the arms must be used, given the numerous changes and restorations the windows have undergone through the centuries. Until art historians can offer more solidly based arguments for the later date, I accept that defended by Marsat. In all my references to the windows, particular scenes are numbered 1 to 12, beginning in the lower left and proceeding left to right.

Illustration 1. Cliché J. Philippot. © Inventaire général SPADEM.

from left to right and from bottom to top, as presented by Ch. Fichot and later by André Marsat:[42]

1–2. Gratulia receives her doctor in a prenatal consultation (not in BN 5614).

3–4. Birth of Helen; the doctor and his companion or student are present (not in BN 5614).

5. Gratulia carries Helen; the child reaches for a fruit from a tree, whose branches bend to place it in her hand (as in BN 5614); Marsat describes this scene as the education of Helen by her mother.

6. Baptism of Helen; a dove gives her a miraculous ring (accords with BN 5614).

7–8. Helen changes a pauper's cup into silver (this accords with BN 5614).

9. Helen instructs her father in religion (Fichot; not in BN 5614); Helen speaks with her father of the troubles of her heart (Marsat; not in BN 5614).

. 10. The death of Agiel (not in BN 5614).

11. Helen has a dream of the death of Bishop Evagarus (accords with BN 5614).

12. Helen receives the blessing of God as she prays (not in BN 5614).

Clearly, the window reflects a substantially altered version of Helen's life, the artist has taken considerable liberties with the account, or the interpretations of the scenes are inaccurate. The last alternative appears to be correct. The first scene is not a prenatal consultation but, rather, the first miracle performed by Helen. Before her birth she cries out "contradico" from her mother's womb. The figures in the second scene are not a doctor and his assistant (who would be most out of place in thirteenth-century maternity care); they portray the amazement of the people who witness this miracle. Likewise, the third scene represents her second miracle: A new church has been built, but no one knows to whom it should be dedicated. The infant Helen cries out "Mariae, Mariae," indicating that it should be dedicated to the virgin. Again, the figures in Scene 4 represent the witnesses to this miracle.

The middle rank of scenes is more accurately described by Fichot:

42. Charles Fichot, *Statistique monumentale du département de l'Aube*, 3, *Troyes, ses monuments civils et religieux* (Paris, 1894), 301–322; Marsat, 65–66.

the miracle of the palm tree (Scene 5); Helen's baptism, at which time she received her miraculous ring that calmed the fires of concupiscence of the desert fathers (Scene 6); and her kindness to the pauper (Scenes 7, 8) are quite clear.

The top rank of scenes is most problematic because they are out of order, evidently having been removed for renovation or protection and not replaced properly. The correct order of scenes is 11, 12, 10, 9. When this adjustment has been made, it is possible to reconsider the interpretations of the scenes; for they now fall in the same order as in the *vita* and correspond closely to it. Scene 11, as Fichot and Marsat point out, represents Helen's dream of the imminent death of Bishop Evagarus. Scenes 12 and 10 tell the story of Helen's miraculous handkerchief. In Scene 12, Helen's handkerchief (mistakenly identified by Fichot as a ray of light blessing the saint at prayer) is taken by an angel and then applied to King Agiel (Scene 10) to cure his toothache. The final scene, 9, represents Helen giving her father advice on the election of the new bishop, namely, to choose the one who arms himself with the Gospels and with a hair shirt.

It is clear, then, that even in thirteenth-century Troyes, no more of Helen's life was known than what is found in BN 5614. We are forced to conclude that the text we have now is as complete as it ever was. Still, one must explain why the story ends so abruptly with the death of Gratulia. Such an ending might indicate that the *vita* is in fact only one chapter and that a second chapter involving Helen's later life and death may have been lost. Surely, had the *vita* been written in Troyes, it would have included a *passio*, no matter how typical it might have been. Was the *vita* an adaptation of a fragmentary Byzantine saint's life? The details of Helen's childhood miracles suggest some relation to the infancy gospels of the Apocrypha, particularly the Protoevangile of James, but the widespread use of this and other apocryphal works makes it impossible to identify a proximate source. We can only conclude that the peculiar nature of the *vita* points to an origin outside of Troyes, and considering the provenance of the relics, Constantinople is a likely source. Should the letter of Angemer be taken at approximately face value, then, and should it be acknowledged that he did in fact translate a portion of a *Vita beatae Helenae* for John? I think not, because, when carefully examined, the letter accommodates closely, perhaps too closely, the specific needs of the church of Troyes. To demonstrate this I must return to the progress on the cathedral and the stages in the development of the cult of Helen.

Promoting the Cult

The possibility of associating the two virgin saints in the religious life of the church of Troyes was facilitated by the proximity of the feast days of these saints and those of other saints of the diocese. The feast of Helen was celebrated on May 4. Both the prologue of the *vita* and the letter of Angemer state that this was the day of her feast in Athyra.[43] Moreover, the letter says that it was on this very day that John approached him for information on the life and virtues of Helen.[44] Certainly this is excellent reason for celebrating the fourth of May in Troyes, but there are further considerations that lead one to suspect that the day was first chosen in Troyes and later incorporated into the prologue and letter at the request of the chapter.

The establishment of the feast of Helen combined admirably the preexisting feasts of Troyes, the feast of the empress Helen's discovery of the true cross and the feasts of the other saints whose relics were brought from Constantinople. The first week of May was the most significant religious period in the church of Troyes. May 1 was the feast of saints Philip and James the Lesser. As a fifteenth-century missal from Troyes explains, that day was particularly commemorated "because here rests the head of blessed Philip, and hence the commemoration of James is held the following day."[45] May 3 was celebrated as the feast of the Invention of the True Cross, thus providing a fitting occasion for the veneration of the relic of the true cross in the cathedral. But the evening of the same day was of even greater importance: it began the feast of the *other* Helen, with a

---

43. The prologue, ed. Jacques Severt, is found on 147–148 of his *Chronologia*, published in 1628. Constable chose not to republish it when he published the Latin version of the letter (1042).

44. Constable, 1042: " . . . quarto nonas Maii me inuenit et conuenit, ipsa videlicet die, qua tota Constantinopolitana Prouincia et praecipue Naturensis Ecclesia pretiosae Virginis Helenae solemnia cum multa deuotione de antiqua consuetudine celebrabat."

45. V. Leroquais, *Les sacramentaires* 3 (Paris, 1924), 171; Missel de Troyes, Paris, BN MS lat. 865, fol. 222.

procession in the cathedral to which were summoned all the clergy of Troyes.[46] The following day was the feast of the saint herself, celebrated, as Constable pointed out, "with the same pomp as those of the Assumption of the Virgin and of All Saints."[47] Three days later, May 7, was celebrated the feast of Troyes's other virgin, Saint Mastidia.[48]

Of course it is possible that this striking coincidence of feasts was the result of chance. But it would be more likely that the feast day was chosen by someone familiar with the calendar of saints of the diocese of Troyes. If, because of the apparently incomplete form of the *vita*, we are to look to Constantinople as its place of origin, we should probably conclude that some information was given to the author about the needs of the diocese and that he adjusted his account to these needs in the two least essential sections of his product: the prologue and the end.

What sort of saint was thus created to appeal to the devotion of thirteenth-century Champenois? To judge from the windows and the *vita*, the level of spirituality in the population of Troyes must have been considered remarkably low by Helen's publicists. There is nothing in her life of her virtues, no indication of an intense relationship with God or a passionate internal faith. Except for Scene 12, in which she is dressed in what might be described as the habit of a mendicant, nothing of the new movements in Christianity has been incorporated for popular edification—and this in spite of the fact that the Dominicans had been in Troyes since 1220 and the Franciscans since 1237.[49] In 1259, the year before the establishment of the procession in Helen's honor, the latter had obtained property for their church within the city itself.[50]

If the only accommodation to the new spirituality was purely external, this externality is in keeping with Helen's life. She is merely a

46. Riant, *Exuviae Sacrae* 2:141–142.
47. Constable, 1035.
48. The two saints are frequently associated in the litanies of the saints in Troyes, as in Troyes, BM MS. 1147, fol. 82v: S Iulia, Iuliana, Maura, Sacina, Siria, Mastidia, Helena, Eufrasia, Verena, Flora, Proba, Concordia; and MS. 51780, fol. 203: Helena, Mastidia, Savina, Syria.
49. T. Boutiot, *Histoire de la ville de Troyes et de la Champagne méridionale* 1 (Troyes, 1870), 312–313.
50. Ibid., 313–314. This establishment was made possible only by the intervention of the count, who gave the chapter an annual rent of £4 on the halles of Douai merchants as indemnity for the loss of revenue it would suffer owing to the presence of the friars; see Arch. dép. Aube, MS. G. 3633.

thaumaturge. Both in the window and in the *vita,* she simply works miracles, involving her ring and handkerchief, which respectively temper sexual passion and cure toothache. These magic objects are given prominence in the *vita,* in what remains of the abridged version of it, in the windows, and in the hymn for second vespers on her feast in the Breviary of Troyes.[51]

This extremely low level of spirituality may also be explained by the function of the saint in Troyes. The cathedral did not need a new saint who would inspire the faithful to the heights of spiritual reform; it needed a thaumaturge to appeal to the masses, who would ask her favor in return for offerings. The steps by which the development of Helen's cult correspond with the cathedral construction can be easily traced.

Progress toward adequate financing of the cathedral was apparently slow after the second damage of 1228. In that year, Cardinal Roman, papal legate to the ecclesiastical provinces of Sens and Lyons, granted an indulgence of forty days to those contributing to the project.[52] In the following year Pope Gregory granted a similar bull of forty days' indulgence.[53] In this same year the canons of Saint Peter's took action to help themselves. They agreed to set aside one-sixth of all prebends for the restoration of Helen's shrine.[54] This was surely an act of piety, but just as certainly an investment. Further papal help followed in 1240 when the legate to the province of Sens issued yet another bull of forty days' indulgence for the reconstruction.[55]

But apparently by the middle of the century the chapter was financially exhausted. According to Bishop Nicolas, the situation was so grave that it was necessary to increase financial levies from one rural church by as much as 1,000 percent in order to meet daily expenses.[56] In this dire circumstance, Helen was called upon to come to the

51. The hymn for second vespers, based on Aquinas's "Pange lingua," praises Helen's ability to temper the desires of the flesh, her prenatal conversation with her mother, her ending of the drought, and her choice of Mary as the titular patron of the new church. The text is in Riant, *Exuviae Sacrae* 2:50.
52. Arbois, no. 5, 220.
53. Ibid., no. 6, 221.
54. Riant, *Exuviae Sacrae* 2:LIII, 114; Camusat, fol. 27v.
55. Arbois, no. 6, 221. On the construction campaigns see Stephen Murray, *Building Troyes Cathedral: The Late Gothic Campaigns* (Bloomington, Ind., 1987), 1–17.
56. Arch. dép. Aube, MS. G. 2856. In 1262, Bishop Nicolas raised the annual payment due the chapter by the curates of Gérosdot from £2 to £20.

rescue of the project. In 1260 the procession in her honor was instituted, with all clerics of Troyes required to participate.[57]

In 1262, Urban IV issued a bull designed to promote this newly established procession by offering the much larger indulgence of one year and forty days to anyone who would visit the cathedral on the feasts of its titular patron, Saint Peter, or on the feast of Saint Helen.[58] Perhaps he was motivated by the recognition that his decision to establish a new church in Troyes could not help but affect the fund-raising efforts of the cathedral. The close connection between this procession and the fund-raising efforts is evidenced by the apparent extension of this indulgence the next year to anyone who would contribute to the cathedral reconstruction.[59] It is likely that the institution of this procession corresponded to the completion of the high choir and the windows portraying the life of Saint Helen and, below it, the chapel dedicated to her.[60]

The best indication of the important role of the cult in the reconstruction is to be found in yet another window of the cathedral, that representing the translation of relics from Constantinople (Illustration 2). This window too must be reinterpreted for the connection between the construction and the saint to be recognized, because at first examination it appears that Helen is not represented at all. Clearly identifiable are (Scene 1) the head of a saint, probably Philip, carried by Hugh, chaplain of Garnier de Traînel, (Scene 3) a cup, quite possibly the one later identified as the Grail, and (Scene 12) the tooth of Peter. Apparently missing are the arm of James and the relics of Helen.[61] It is probable, however, that these relics are in fact represented but heretofore not identified. Scene 4 is of a male saint, his right hand raised in blessing and his right arm bare. It is quite probable that instead of James's arm carried by another person, the

57. Riant, *Exuviae Sacrae* 2:141–142.
58. Arch. dép. Aube, MS. G. 2592: "Nos igitur ad prosequenda predicta gaudia causam dare fidelibus populis cupientes omnibus uere penitentibus et confessis qui ecclesiam uestram in honore beati Petri principis apostolorum fundatam in festiuitatibus ipsius principis et sancte Helene uirginis cum deuotione uisitauerint annuatim de omni potentis Dei misericordia et beatorum ipsius Petri et Pauli Apostolorum eius auctoritate confisi unum annum et quadriginta dies; illis uero qui usque ad octauas ipsarum festiuitatum ad predictam ecclesiam singulis annis accesserint centum dies de iniuncta sibi penitentia misericorditer relaxamus."
59. Ibid.; Arbois no. 8, 222–223.
60. See above, note 41.
61. This according to the description provided by Fichot, 321–324.

Illustration 2. Courtesy of the Bibliothèque du Patrimoine

saint himself was represented here. Helen appears to have been similarly treated. Scene 9 (Plate II, left) is a female saint carrying a cloth that Fichot wished to recognize as the robe of Christ. Scene 10 (Plate II, right) is likewise a nimbed woman carrying what Fichot described as a foot, possibly of Saint Marguerite.[62] Neither of these relics figure in the list traditionally said to have been brought from Constantinople. It is more likely that one or even both represent

62. Ibid., 324.

Helen herself, the first as she carries her handkerchief, the second possibly carrying her ring. This identification is not definitive, but the similarity of representations of the saint in the previously discussed window and in Scene 10 of this one strongly supports this identification. The close relationship between the arrival of these relics and the construction of the cathedral is graphically represented in Scenes 7 and 8: an architect supervises the construction while Bishop Hervé looks on.

In summary, it is clear that the cult of Helen was carefully introduced and elaborated over the course of the thirteenth century: her reliquary was restored after the damage of 1228; a *vita* was composed to appeal to a population seeking cures and miracles rather than spiritual reform; a procession in her honor was introduced to coincide with the time of the other major feasts of Troyes's patrons; her life was represented in a pictorial form accessible to the laity; and finally, her *vita* was incorporated into the public worship of the cathedral. Paralleling this process were the efforts to rebuild and enlarge the cathedral in the face of severe financial crises, both ecclesiastical and civil. Helen was called upon to help in these circumstances, most clearly in the indulgences for participants at her feast and in the iconographic homage paid her and the other relics brought from Constantinople, a homage reinforced by the juxtaposition of the translations and the construction of the cathedral.

It is of course impossible to estimate the precise extent to which Helen was actually successful in meeting the requirements of the cathedral.[63] But by the end of the century, the major portions of the construction were substantially completed.[64] Moreover, the diocese of Troyes had a new patroness, ranking, as Constable has pointed out, with its most illustrious patrons. And by the mid-fifteenth century, when her relics participated in a tour of the diocese to raise money for the final completion of the cathedral, her identity and importance were long secure.[65]

---

63. Murray, 24, notes that in the late thirteenth century, Bishop Jean de Nanteuil (1269–1298) had seized ten pounds raised by carrying Helen's relics, but he returned this sum to the fabric in his testament. His successor, Bishop Guichaud, again took the funds collected from relics.

64. Roserot, 1:51.

65. Arch. dép. Aube, MS. G. 2593.

Appendix

∽

A fragment of the Vita beatae Helenae in Vat. Reg.
lat. 583, fols. 3r–3v

Hoc tempore [ca. 1212] corpus beate Helene transfertur cuius uitam
Sanctus Iohanes Christomus descripsit. Hec a rege Corinthiorum
illustri Agiele et coniuge sua Gratula processit, de cuius ortu et tran-
situ Naturencium ciuitas gaudet. Hic rex clementissimus largius de
hostibus uisibilibus et inuisibilibus triumphauit, et labefactum regnum releuauit in gloriam et subiectum sibi populum pacifice guber-
nauit per iusticie disciplinam. Qui cum bella committeret sub lorica et
galea cilicio ieunio lacrimis et orationibus expugnabat inimicos. Re-
gina uero licet quandoque in uestitu deaurato tamen plus moribus
quam uestibus placens, in urbe residebat Naturensi. Que cum ges-
taret infantem, Sanctus Porphirius Naturensis episcopus spiritu pro-
phecie plenus indicata filie quam portabat predixit, et hibernio tempore ex latere regine manu eidem apposita lilia retraxit. Cum autem
pariendi tempus aduenisset, rex in partibus Thebanis agens uocauit
reginam ut Thebas properet. Que cum disponeret gressus suos, de
utero suo uocem audiuit dicentem sibi bis "Contradico," ex qua re
terrore concussa partum effudit, et Helene nomen Sanctus Euagrius
ei preposuit. Et cum pro tempore siccitatus populus clamauit et prius
natam infantulam omni populo sub diuo iacere precepit, et facto
mane pluuia erupit inebrians undique regionem, ut ne una quidem
gusta cunas Helene contingere presumpsisset. Mox episcopus, ar-
reptis ligone et cophino, in loco ipso ubi cuna recedit primus fodit, et
cum populo ecclesiam construxit; et ad cuius sancti ecclesia honorem
dedicanda sub hac ambiguitate, infantula dixit, "Marie, Marie," in
cuius dedicacione illa nec more puerili fleuit, nec uagitum edidit, nec
mammas suxit. Cumque beata Helena bimatum lustrum peregisset,
Rex cum maioribus regni in uigilia Penthecostes cum filia ad ecclesiam uenit. Helena uero magnatum manibus de curru desposita est et
sub umbra palme ante fores potuisset uidentibus omnibus subito
palme ramusculus inclinauit et edulio sibi ministrato in statum pris-
tinum se erexit. Quam ipsa die post misse celebrationem Aurisus
episcopus ex precepto regis baptisauit. Et tunc columba de celo de-

scendens anulum aureum et gemmatum coram omni populo in digito Helene in figuram sue desponsacionis proprio rostro defixit. Que sancto ipso confestim enarrat. Quem anulum cum honore Corinthiorum ciuitas consueruat, qui tante uirtutis esse dignoscitur, ut infixus digito carnis temperet incentiua, ueri penitentes et hermite per uastas Egipti et Grecie solitudines habitantes. . . .

12 The Magi and Milan

౦౦

In memoriam Roberto S. Lopez

One treasure that cannot be counted among the riches of the Milanese church—a treasure whose role in the development of Milanese art, liturgy, and architecture cannot be assessed, whose importance to the venerable Ambrosian tradition cannot be treated—is the tomb of the three kings, the Magi, whose appearance at Bethlehem has always fascinated Christians. This chapter is not, then, dedicated to the history of Milan and its cult of saints; it is the history of a void, of a nonpresence that, by its negation, has fascinated Milanese and others for over eight centuries.

The legend of how the Magi came to be in Milan is well known: According to the various versions of the anonymous *Vita Beati Eustorgii Confessoris*, they arrived from Constantinople, during the reign of Constantine, thanks to Saint Eustorgius, a noble Greek who had been Constantine's faithful adviser and agent. In this capacity he had visited Milan and there, because of his outstanding qualities, was elected bishop. The saint made his acceptance of the position dependent on imperial approval and returned to Constantinople. The emperor not only confirmed the election but presented Eustorgius with the remains of the three kings, which had been acquired by his mother, Helena. The bishop returned to Milan with the remains, transported in a massive marble sarcophagus, and erected a church to house them. In time he was buried in this same church, which thereafter carried his name. Even today the huge sarcophagus is displayed in the church of Sant'Eustorgio along with a figured capital from the ninth century, said to portray Eustorgius's transport of the saints' sarcophagus to Milan in a cart drawn by two oxen.[1] But the sarcophagus is empty.

The reason the tomb is empty is even more famous than the story of the translation itself: After the surrender of Milan to Frederick Barbarossa on the first of March, 1162, the city was systematically plundered by the imperial forces before being razed. As a reward for his great service, the imperial chancellor, Rainald of Dassel, archbishop elect of Cologne, was given relics pillaged from Milan's churches.[2] The most important of these were the remains of the Magi, which he brought back to Cologne for the glory of his city and his church. In the words of the near-contemporary *Gesta Frederici I Imperatoris in Lombardia* for the year 1164: "On the eleventh day of this month [June] Rainald, chancellor and archbishop of Cologne, took the bodies of the holy martyrs Nabor and Felicity and that of the holy confessor [Martin?] as it was said, and three other bodies which had been placed in a sarcophagus which was in the church of Blessed Eustorgius, and which were said to be those of the three magi, and he sent them to Cologne."[3] If the anonymous author of the *gesta* was somewhat uncertain about the identities of the three bodies (*que dicebantur*), later authors had no such doubts: the Annals of Disibodenburg, for example, say that in the year 1162, "Rainald, bishop of Cologne, transferred the bodies of the three Magi to Cologne, each in its coffin."[4] Rainald's journey home was not without difficulties, however. According to tradition, supporters of Pope Alexander III at-

1. On the various versions of the *vita*, which has never been the object of a critical edition, see Hans Hofmann, *Die Heiligen Drei Könige: Zur Heiligenverehrung im kirchlichen, gesellschaftlichen und politischen Leben des Mittelalters* (Bonn, 1975), 80–89.
2. Julius Ficker, *Reinald von Dassel: Reichskanzler und Erzbischof von Köln, 1156–1167* (1850; reprint, Aalen, 1966); Peter Munz, "Frederick Barbarossa and the 'Holy Empire,'" *Journal of Religious History* 3 (1964–1965): 20–37.
3. *MGH SSRG* 42:58: " . . . undecimo vero die eiusdem mensis [Iunii] Raynaldus canzellarius ac Coloniensis archiepiscopus tulit corpora Sanctorum Martyrum Naboris atque Felicis et Sancti Confessoris [Martini?], prout dicebatur, et tria alia corpora, que erant condita in archa, que erat in ecclesia Beati Eustorgii, et que dicebantur esse Magorum Trium, et exportavit Coloniam." Note that although Hofmann calls the *Gesta* "zeitgenössischen" (97), in fact they were written at least as late as 1187 and probably even later; see Wilhelm Wattenbach et al., *Deutschlands Geschichtsquellen im Mittelalter vom Tode Kaiser Heinrichs V. bis zum Ende des interregnum* 1 (Darmstadt, 1976), 85.
4. *MGH SS* 17:30: "Reinoldus Coloniensis episcopus corpora Trium Magorum . . . ad Coloniam singulis in loculis transtulit." See Hofmann, 100; and Wattenbach et al., 142–143.

tempted to recover the sacred booty from him, but he pretended that the three corpses were those of friends whom he was taking home for burial and thus escaped, making his way through Burgundy, Alsace, and then down the Rhine to his city.

The Magi became Cologne's most important patrons. Early in the 1180s, Nicholas of Verdun, the greatest goldsmith of the twelfth century, began the magnificent golden shrine in which they were placed, a shrine that became the goal of an important pilgrimage: preceding or following his coronation in Aachen, a German king would visit the shrine and leave gifts for the three kings. The image of the three kings made its way onto the arms of the city, its coinage, and the symbols of its corporations. Cologne became the city of the three kings, and the close association has continued to this today.[5]

From Cologne the cult of the kings spread out across the Empire and, owing in great part to the role that the city played in international commerce, even into France, England, Spain, and back into Italy. The first Italian to lament the theft was Master Boncompagno in Letter 5 of his *Boncompagnus* written before 1215. In this letter, written in the persona of an unnamed emperor, he castigates the Milanese for transgressing against the Empire. As a result they had lost their *carraccio* and "moreover your fathers lost the sacred bodies of the three Magi, which Cologne reveres today."[6] But while Cologne celebrated and disseminated the cult of its new patrons, Milanese authors remained virtually silent about their erstwhile Magi. This silence would first be broken in 1288 by Bonvesin de la Riva in his *De magnalibus Mediolani:* "A more grave and significant disgrace befell us, the bodies of the three Magi, whom Blessed Eustorgius had miraculously translated from the city of Constantinople to our city in the year 314, O sorrow! were taken away to the German city of Cologne

5. On the cult of the Magi in Cologne, see, in addition to Hofmann, Adam Wienand, ed., *Die Heiligen Drei Könige: Heilsgeschichtlich, Kunsthistorisch, das religiöse Brauchtum* (Cologne, 1974); and the essays in Rainer Budde, ed., *Die Heiligen Drei Könige: Darstellung und Verehrung*, Exhibition catalog of the Wallraf-Richartz Museums of Josef-Haubrich-Kunsthalle, December 1, 1982, through January 30, 1983 (Cologne, 1982).

6. "Amisserunt insuper tria magorum corpora veneranda, quibus hodie Colonia veneratur." I am grateful to Robert L. Benson for pointing out this text, which he published and discussed in his "*Libertas* in Italy, 1152–1226," in *La notion de liberté au Moyen Age: Islam, Byzance, Occident*, Penn.-Paris-Dumbarton Oaks Colloquia 4, ed. George Makdisi, Dominique Sourdel, and Janine Sourdel-Thomine (Paris, 1985), 191–213.

by the archbishop of this same city."[7] From that time on, interest in the
Magi grew in Milan. The great archbishop Charles Borromeo attempted to secure their return, and finally in 1909, Cardinal Ferrari
managed to have fragments of the saints' remains returned from
Cologne to Milan.[8]

But were the events of 1909 a return of long-lost patrons, or was it
only the first time the Magi had visited Milan? In other words, had the
reputed remains ever been in Milan, or was the entire legend, including both their translation from Constantinople and their subsequent
translation to Cologne, the invention of Rainald of Dassel? This is the
question this chapter addresses, not with the primary purpose of
establishing the "objective facts" but rather to arrive at an understanding of what the Magi were to the people of the twelfth century
and, subsequently, to such as Bonvesin de la Riva.

The Magi in Milan

No point would be served in repeating the enormous literature on the
origin and development of the numerous legends and cults of the
Magi in late antiquity and the early Middle Ages. Nor shall we examine the questions of how the *magi ab oriente* of Matthew 2:1 came to be
generally thought of as only three (the Gospel gives no number) and
how these three came to be identified as Caspar, Melchior, and Bal-
thazar. Instead, I limit my investigation to the nature of the cult of the
Magi in Milan before their translation to Cologne, so that we can see
what role they had, if any, in the cult and culture of the city.

Hans Hofmann, in his exhaustive study of the Magi, has demonstrated that all attempts to search out references to the Magi in
Milanese liturgical and historical documents from the period before
the twelfth century have come up with nothing but later interpola-
tions or outright forgeries. The most important text on the Magi in
Milan, the *Vita Eustorgii*, does not reflecting Milanese traditions; for it

7. Bonvesin de la Riva *De magnalibus Mediolani*, ed. and trans. Giuseppi Pontiggia,
   intro. Maria Corti (Milan, 1974), 120: " . . . quod in deterius et maius opprobrium
   nobis cessit, trium Magorum corpora, que in civitatem nostram anno .CCCXIIII.
   beatus Eustorgius ab urbe Constantinopolitana miraculose transvesit, proch dolor!
   Coloniam, Alemannie civitatem, per eiusdem civitatis archiepiscopum detracta
   fuere."
8. On the later cult of the Magi in Milan, see Hofmann, 218–259.

was apparently composed in Cologne in the later twelfth century. The earliest manuscript, Köln Stadtarchiv Codex W 320, was copied at Saint Panetlon in Cologne in the last years of the twelfth century. The earliest Milanese versions of the *vita*, found in Biblioteca Ambrosiana, Codex H 56 supplement and Codex D 26, date from after 1436. Hofmann concludes that both the Cologne and Milanese versions descended from a lost original, but he can find no compelling argument to conclude that this original was written in Milan. It appears that the tradition originated in Cologne and only later came to be accepted in Milan. Nor can there be found any authentic archival, liturgical, or literary sources from the period before 1158 which mention either a cult of the Magi in Sant'Eustorgio or the existence in Milan of any royal basilica in which they might have been venerated.[9]

The earliest reference to the Magi's presence in Milan dates, according to Hofmann, to shortly after 1158. In that year, according to *The Chronicle of Robert of Torigni* (ca. 1110–1186), the bodies of the Magi were found in an ancient chapel near Milan, from whence, out of fear of Frederick Barbarossa, they were moved into the city: "In the same year the bodies of the Three Magi who adored our infant Savior in Bethlehem were discovered in an ancient chapel near the city of Milan, and they were elevated and placed in that city out of fear of Frederick, emperor of the Germans, who had come to beseige that city."[10] If Hofmann is correct, this piece of information is the earliest—because it comes from a well-informed Norman abbot not directly tied either to Milan or Cologne—most reliable information about the existence of the relics in Milan before their translation in 1164. One might, then, conclude, with Hofmann, that although the exact date of the origins of the cult in Milan cannot be determined, by the twelfth century the relics were certainly believed to have been venerated in the city before the revolt of Milan and moreover to have been considered sufficiently important to be brought into the city for safekeeping.

9. Ibid., 89–90.
10. *The Chronicle of Robert Torigni*, ed. Richard Howlett, *Rerum britannicarum medii aevi scriptores*, Rolls Series 82 (London, 1882), 199: "Eodem anno, inventa sunt corpora Trium Magorum, qui Salvatorem nostrum infantem adoraverunt in Bethleem, in quadam veteri capella juxta urbem Mediolanum, et pro timore Frederici imperatoris Alemannorum, qui eandem urbem obsidere veniebat, levata et in civitate posita." Hofmann, 76.

Unfortunately, a careful examination of the information on the Magi in Robert of Torigni's chronicle does not support this thesis. As we shall see, Robert probably acquired his information in 1165, the year after the translation, and his source was none other than the infamous (to Milanese) Rainald of Dassel, archbishop of Cologne.

Robert of Torigni, abbot of the great Norman monastery of Mont-Saint-Michel, was ignorant concerning northern Italy in general but quite well informed about Frederick Barbarossa's expeditions against the Lombard cities and against Sicily. He was particularly well informed about the siege of Milan. He reports the start of the siege in 1159—"In this year, as in the preceding, Frederick, emperor of the Germans, besieged the city of Milan because the Milanese had rebelled against him. He destroyed the towers of Pavia and Placensia and subjected almost all of Lombardy to his will."[11]—and its fall and destruction in 1162—"Frederick, emperor of the Germans, captured and destroyed the city of Milan, afflicted by famine, which he had besieged for three years, except for the principal church and certain others."[12]

Under the year 1164 he describes in great detail not only the translation of the Magi to Cologne but even the condition of their corpses, which, according to a report given him by an eyewitness, were so well preserved that one could see that they were the bodies of men of approximately fifteen years, thirty years, and sixty years of age respectively. Moreover, he reports in the same account the story that would appear later in the *vita Eustorgii*, namely, that that bishop of Milan had brought the remains to the city:

> Rainald elect of Cologne, chancellor of Frederick emperor of the Germans, translated the bodies of the three Magi from Milan to Cologne. Their bodies, because they had been preserved with balsam and other spices, had remained externally incorrupt even to their skin and hair. The first, according to what those who had seen them told me, from what one could tell from their face and

11. Robert of Torigni, 201: "Hoc etiam anno, sicut et praecedenti, Fredericus, imperator Alemannorum, urbem Mediolanensem obsidet, quia rebellaverant adversus eum iidem Mediolanenses. Papae et Placentiae turres dejecit, et fere omnem Lumgobardiam ad libitum sibi subjecit."

12. Ibid., 213: "Fredericus, imperator Alemannorum, urbem Mediolanum, quam per tres annos obsederat, necessitate famis afflictam, capit et destruit, reservatis tantummodo matrice ecclesia et quibusdam aliis."

hands, appeared to be fifteen, the second, thirty, the third sixty years of age. Blessed Eustorgius, who had been given them by an emperor, brought them from Constantinople to Milan with an altar on which they had been placed, in a small cart which by divine power and will two cows had pulled. Rainald also translated the body of blessed Valeria, the mother of the holy martyrs Gervasius and Protasius, and the head of the martyr Nabor.[13]

Ought one conclude with Hofmann that these accounts should be taken as independent evidence, recorded in each instance shortly after the events, of the cult of the Magi in Milan? Clearly not. Robert continued to edit, expand, and revise his chronicle throughout his life. The chronicle was no mere seriatim record of events. Instead, the various versions of the chronicle show its author's constant effort to add or delete material. Thus, as scholars in the nineteenth century had already recognized, the manuscript tradition of the chronicle must be divided into a complex series of "editions." The first edition, represented by seven extant manuscripts, was begun before Robert's departure from Bec in 1154, and extant copies were continued, probably at Mont-Saint-Michel, until 1157, when one was returned to Bec and the others became the basis for further, revised versions that vary greatly in their inclusion or omission of whole paragraphs or sets of paragraphs. The most important of these, Avranches MS. 159, was apparently the copy made by the scriptorium at Mont-Saint-Michel and corrected and revised by Robert himself. This manuscript, which breaks off in mid sentence and which probably continued for another page, can be considered the author's final edition, and it continues until the year 1185.[14]

13. Ibid., 220–221: "Rainaldus, Coloniensis electus, cancellarius Frederici imperatoris Alemannorum, transtulit trium Magorum corpora de Mediolano Coloniam, quorum corpora, quia balsamo et aliis pigmentis condita fuerant, integra exterius, quantum ad cutem et capillos, durabant. Eorum primus, sicut mihi retulit qui eos se vidisse affirmabat, quantum ex facie et capillis eorum comprehendi poterat, quindecim annorum, secundus triginta, tertius sexaginta videbatur. Beatus autem Eustorgius, dono cuiusdam imperatoris, transtulit illos Mediolanum de Constantinopoli, cum quadam mensa cui superpositi erant, in quodam vehiculo parvo, quod duae vaccae divina virtute et voluntate trahebant. Transtulit etiam idem Rainaldus exinde corpus beatae Valeriae, matris sanctorum martyrum Gervasii et Prothasii, et caput Naboris martyris."

14. See Howlett's introduction, xxiv–lxix, esp. lix. See also Jacques Hourlier, "Les sources écrites de l'histoire montoise antérieur à 966," in *Millénaire monastique du*

Given this complex textual history, one cannot suppose that Robert
first heard about the Magi shortly after their putative discovery in
1158, entered this information in his chronicle, and then later, shortly
after 1164, heard about and described the translation. It is much
more likely that he heard the entire story after the translation and
then went back to his chronicle and inserted the information, along
with that concerning Frederick Barbarossa's war against Milan, all at
once. It is easy to imagine when and from whom he acquired the
story.

In 1165, Robert informs us, Frederick Barbarossa sent legates to
King Henry II of England, who was at Rouen, to negotiate marriages
for one of his sons and for Henry the Lion with daughters of the
English king. The principal legate was none other than Archbishop
Rainald of Cologne, freshly back from his victorious plundering of
Milan: "Likewise legates of Frederick emperor of the Germans, Rainald archbishop of Cologne, his chancellor, and many other powerful
men came, asking him on behalf of the emperor, that he would give
one of his daughters to duke Henry of Bavaria and another to his son,
who was then quite young."[15] We do not know for certain that Robert
of Torigni was present at Rouen and participated in the negotiations,
but as he was the godfather of one of the princesses, Eleanor,[16] we
may assume that he very likely had some part in them. Thus, rather
than supposing with Hofmann that Robert's account presents an
independent corroboration of the presence of the Magi in Milan
before its capture and of the details of Rainald's acquisition of them,
we see that the account is probably but one more version of the
tradition, which, like all the others, emanated from the archbishop of
Cologne.

Mont-Saint-Michel, 2, *Vie montoise et rayonnement intellectuel*, ed Raymonde Foreville
(Paris, 1967), 121–139, and "Robert de Torigni et 'Clio,'" in ibid., 141–153;
Marjorie Chibnall, "Orderic Vitalis and Robert of Torigni," in ibid., 133–139; and
Joseph M. M. Hermans and Elizabeth M. C. Van Houts, "The History of a Mem-
brum Disiectum of the *Gesta Normannorum Ducum*, Now Vatican Reg. Lat. 733 fol.
51," *Mededelingen van het Nederlands Instituut te Rome* 44–45 (1983): 79–94.

15. Robert of Torigni, 224: "Venerunt similiter ad eum legati Frederici, imperatoris
    Alemannorum, Rainaldus scilicet, archiepiscopus Coloniensis, cancellarius ipsius,
    et multi alii magni potentatus viri, requirentes eum ex parte imperatoris, ut daret
    unam filiarum suarum Henrico, duci Baioariae, et aliam filio suo, licet adhuc
    puerulo." On the negotiations see Ficker, 74–75.
16. Robert of Torigni, 211.

With the elimination of the witness of Robert of Torigni, we are forced to conclude that there is no evidence that a cult of the Magi ever existed in Milan before the translation of their remains to Cologne in 1164. The presence at Sant'Eustorgio of the huge sarcophagus and of the figured capital showing the oxen transporting a large box had already given rise to various local legends identified with the imperial past, but these did not apparently include the Magi.[17] The cult seems to have been the invention of Rainald: sometime between his departure from Milan with the relics given him by Frederick and his arrival in Cologne, these remains apparently took on the identity of the three kings. Only after the tradition had taken firm root in Cologne did it spread out from there, ultimately even returning to Milan, where, by the time of Bonvesin de la Riva, one could mourn the loss of patrons whose cult had never existed.[18]

Although this retroactive cult creation sounds preposterous by modern standards, it is not only possible in the Middle Ages but not uncommon; several saints were initially unknown in the locations from which they were said to have been translated. The closest parallel is that of Mary Magdalene, venerated at Vézelay. Her cult developed first at Vézelay in the course of the eleventh century. Initially her presence in Burgundy was explained by a variety of accounts of her translation from Jerusalem. By the early twelfth century, however, the *Vita apostolica Beatae Mariae Magdalenae* explained that after the ascension she and her brother and sister, Lazarus and Martha, had traveled to Marseille, where she had lived a life of solitude and penance. After her death she was buried at Aix-en-Provence, where, in fact, a devotion to her developed around the church where she was said to have been buried. But the Provençal tradition had not originated in Aix. It first began in Vézelay and traveled south to Provence, where it was incorporated into local tradition, even to the point that local clergy argued that though the legend of her arrival in the region

17. See Hofmann, 91–92.
18. Bernard Hamilton recognized the role of Rainald in the creation of the cult of the Magi and in particular in the relationship between this cult and the creation of the purported letter of Prester John to Manuel Comnenus. Not realizing, however, that Robert of Torigni's source was none other than Rainald himself, he assumed that the information Robert reported was independent confirmation of the discovery of the relics in Milan. See his "Prester John and the Three Kings of Cologne," *Studies in Medieval History Presented to R. H. C. Davis* (London, 1985), 177–191.

was correct, the account of her translation was not: they insisted that her body was still buried in Aix.[19]

Much the same apparently happened with the cult of the Magi. Only after their fame had spread out from Cologne thanks to the efforts of Rainald did interest in them develop in Milan itself. Why Rainald would have invented and developed such a tradition can be understood by an examination of the developing meaning of the cult of the Magi, which reached its climax in Cologne in the thirteenth century.

From Magi to Kings

For the early church, although the Magi were thought to represent the recognition of Christ by the Gentiles, they were not explicitly identified (except in one passage of Tertullian)[20] as kings. This identification was first made common by Caesarius of Arles at the beginning of the sixth century. The Magi were, already in the Gospel of Matthew, shown as embodying the recognition of Christ's lordship, however, so their adoration was thus a potent symbol of legitimate rule. This potency became increasingly pronounced in the Constantinian period, when the legitimacy of the ruling family was closely connected in imperial propaganda to the favor of the victory-giving Christ. The Magi were both symbols of the recognition by the nations of Christ's lordship and also, by their recognition, themselves symbols of legitimate, God-given kingship. The clearest example of the association of the Magi with earthly rulers is found in the sanctuary mosaic of San Vitale in Ravenna, in which the emperor Justinian and Theodora are portrayed as though Magi offering gifts to Christ, dressed as an earthly ruler. By presenting themselves as Magi, they are implying their right to be the earthly representatives of God.[21]

Precisely such a right was sought by Frederick Barbarossa and his chancellor, Rainald of Dassel, in the contest with Pope Alexander III.

19. Victor Saxer, *Le culte de Marie Madeleine en occident des origines à la fin du Moyen Age*, 2 vols. (Auxerre, 1959); idem, "L'origine des reliques de sainte Marie Madeleine à Vézelay dans la tradition historique du Moyen Age," *Revue des sciences religieuses* 29 (1955): 1–18; Geary, *Furta Sacra*, 74–78.

20. On the cult of the Magi in the early church, see Hugo Ludwig Kehrer, *Die Heiligen Drei Könige in Literatur und Kunst*, 2 vols. (Leipzig, 1908–1909); and Ernst Dassmann, "Epiphanie und die Heiligen Drei Könige," in Budde, 16–19.

21. Dassmann, 30.

The period that saw the destruction and pillage of Milan also saw the emperor and his chancellor working to develop a foundation for imperial legitimacy independent of the pope. "From whom, then, does he have the *imperium* if not from the lord pope?" had asked Roland Bandinelli, the future Alexander III, at Besançon in 1157,[22] and both Rainald and Frederick were eager to provide an answer.

For the emperor, the major source of this independent authority was in the cult of Charlemagne. On December 29, 1165, he had Rainald and Alexander of Liège elevate the remains of the great Frankish emperor and place them on a silver bier in the middle of the church of Saint Mary in Aachen. On January 8, 1166, Charlemagne was formally canonized by Rainald with the approval of Frederick's anti-pope, Pascal III.[23] These two measures were intended to establish a sacred basis for the position of the emperor and to confirm Aachen as the seat of power in direct opposition to Rome.[24] The basis for Aachen's particular role, as for the authority of the emperor, was to be seen as Charlemagne, the source of imperial legitimacy.

On first reflection, it seems only logical to imagine that the translation of the three kings to Germany was an integral part of this imperial propaganda. There is, however, no evidence that Frederick or his immediate Staufer successors made any use of the three kings in their propaganda war with the papacy. As Hugo Stehkämper has said, "It is astounding, actually incomprehensible, that Barbarossa, in accord with the various ecclesiastical justifications of the legal basis of his royal and imperial office did not reserve the remains of the three kings to himself and his successors."[25]

This failure to exploit the relics of the Magi is only astounding, however, if one believes that as early as 1164, Frederick and other

22. *Ottonis et Rahewini gesta Frederici I, MGH SSRG* 46:17: "A quo ergo habet, si a domno papa non habet imperium?" On the relationship between the Magi and the imperial cult, see Hugo Stehkämper, "Könige und Heilige Drei Könige," in Budde, 37–50.

23. Ficker, 91.

24. On the cult of Charlemagne under Frederick Barbarossa, see Erich Meuthen, "Karl der Groß-Barbarossa-Aachen: Zur Interpretation des Karlsprivileges für Aachen," in *Karl der Große: Lebenswerk und Nachleben, 4, Das Nachleben*, ed. Wolfgang Braunfels and Percy Ernst Schramm (Düsseldorf, 1967), 54–76; and Robert Folz, *Le souvenir et la légende de Charlemagne dans l'Empire germanique médiéval* (Paris, 1950).

25. Stehkämper, 38. Hamilton, 183, assumes, erroneously, I believe, that Barbarossa and Rainald together collaborated on the creation of the cult in Milan.

imperial supporters were convinced that Rainald had acquired the remains of the Magi. But, as we have seen, apart from the sources directly dependent on Rainald himself, there seems to have been no general belief that the Magi had in fact been translated to Cologne from Milan: such a story could be told convincingly in Normandy, but in the circle of imperial supporters who had been present at the siege of Milan, the legend may have taken longer to gain acceptance. As we saw above, the author of the *Gesta Frederici I Imperatoris in Lombardia* was not entirely convinced that the Magi had figured among the relics acquired by Rainald. Had there been universal belief in the authenticity of the relics in 1164, one could well imagine that, as Stehkämper suggests, Frederick would probably have sent them not to Cologne but to Aachen.

If anyone intended to develop the cult of the Magi in Cologne in a manner similar to that of Charlemagne in Aachen, that person was probably not Frederick but Rainald, who may well have hoped that he could thereby secure not simply the independence of the emperor but also that of the archbishop while establishing his city as the equal of Aachen. His letter to the church and people of Cologne, written from Vercelli on June 12, 1164, announcing his acquisition of the relics and ordering that their welcome be prepared, was the first articulation of this plan. In the letter he explains that among the gifts he has received, the most important are "the distinguished bodies of the most blessed three Magi and kings, who first from the gentiles, in type and prefiguration of the future church of the gentiles, brought precious gifts to Christ when he lay in the manger."[26] The letter goes on to announce the receipt, in addition, of the saints Nabor and Felix and to warn that the journey home may be blocked by enemies. If genuine, this letter was the first step toward creating a receptive atmosphere into which to introduce the new relics, to state the importance of the Magi as the figures of the peoples recognizing Christ, and to suggest that the relics were so valuable that "enemies" would probably attempt to stop their transport to Cologne.

It appears that Rainald's plan was not widely shared in imperial circles. The silence of other sources concerning Frederick's involve-

26. Giovanni Domenico Mansi, *Sacrorum Concilia* . . . 21.865: " . . . corpora insignia beatissimorum trium Magorum ac Regum, qui primitiae gentium, in typum ac praesagium futurae ex gentibus ecclesiae, jacenti adhuc Christo in praesepi munera pretiosa obtulerunt."

ment in the development of the cult of the Magi may reflect, in addition to skepticism about their identity, a disinclination to partici-pate in an attempt to compete with Aachen and its sacred king by supporting the sacred kings of Cologne.[27]

In time, of course, the kings in Cologne did become an important center of a royal cult, beginning with Otto IV of Braunschweig-Poitou, who had himself portrayed as the "fourth" king on the mag-nificent reliquary around the year 1200, a measure that recalls di-rectly the representation of Justinian in San Vitale. Through the thirteenth and fourteenth centuries, a firm tradition developed that, after their crowning in Aachen, German kings would travel to Co-logne to venerate the Magi. The intention of Rainald was finally fulfilled.[28]

"Back" to Milan

The introduction of the cult of the Magi in Milan was likewise closely related to the legitimacy of local rulers. Bonvesin de la Riva, the first Milanese to mention the alleged theft, equated internal strife in his own day with the absence of kings. The Visconti were quick to pick up on the potential value of the celebration of the Magi and became the principal supporters of the cult in Milan. The first reported celebra-tion of the pageant of the Magi in Milan was that in 1336 organized by Giovanne Visconti, then bishop of Novara.[29] This festival, whose climax was a procession of the Magi mounted on horses through the streets of Milan to Sant'Eustorgio, was at once a celebration of the kings and of the Visconti. Thus the Magi served to undermine re-publican values to the benefit of the Visconti, who were their princi-pal patrons. In the course of the fourteenth century, the Visconti were portrayed as the defenders of the Magi while their enemies, the Torriani, were presented as having betrayed the location of the saints' remains to Rainald.[30]

By the sixteenth century, in the Milanese version of the translation

27. Stehkämper, 38–39.
28. Ibid., 39–40; Odilo Engels, "Die Reliquien der Heiligen Drei Könige in der Reichs-politik der Staufer," in Budde, 33–36.
29. Rab Hatfield, "The Compagnia de'Magi," *Journal of the Warburg and Courtauld Institutes* 33 (1970): 112–113.
30. Hofmann, 13, 219.

to Cologne, Gualvagno Visconti, count of Angleria, was presented as
the principal patron and protector of the relics of the Magi before
their confiscation in 1162. According to the legend, Gualvagno was
Frederick's principal opponent in the uprising of the city and after its
fall was saved only by the cleverness of his sister, who told Rainald
where the remains of the Magi were hidden in return for her brother's safety.[31]

Similar political interests led to the spread of the cult of the Magi
throughout Italy and especially in Florence, where the Florentine
desire for legitimation and the burger society's longing for noble
status were exploited by the Medici, who became the principal patrons of the Company of the Magi.[32]

In summary, we can say that the cult of the Magi, long associated
with legitimacy of temporal lordship, probably did not exist in Milan
before the late thirteenth or early fourteenth century. After the capit-
ulation of the city to Frederick, his imperial chancellor, because he
needed to bolster the autonomous authority of the emperor relative
to the pope, transformed Milanese traditions associated with the large
sarcophagus at Sant'Eustorgio into a legend of the Magi. In Cologne
he and his successors spread the belief that the tomb had contained
the three kings and that he had brought them to the banks of the
Rhine. Although the legend found believers far from Cologne and
Milan, only after 1200 did the cult begin to serve the royal purposes
intended by Rainald, and only with the rise of the Visconti did the
Milanese begin to mourn their "loss."[33]

31. Ibid., 113.
32. Richard C. Trexler, "The Magi Enter Florence: The Ubriachi of Florence and
    Venice," *Studies in Medieval and Renaissance History*, old ser. 11, no. 1 (1978): 129–
    213.
33. And yet, though the Magi had never been in Milan to be lost, some relics surely had
    been taken from the city. Indirect evidence of this has appeared in a most tantaliz-
    ing form: studies of cloth fragments removed from the shrine of the Three Kings
    in Cologne in 1864 have recently proved, upon study, to have been woven in Syria
    in the first or second century. If these cloths had not covered the remains of the
    Magi, to which of the other relics stolen from Milan in 1164 did they belong? See
    Irmgard Timmermann, "Seide, Purpur und Gold: Untersuchungen zu den Ge-
    webfragmenten aus dem Schrein der Heiligen Drei Könige im Dom zu Köln," in
    Budde, 115–125.

Index of Published Sources

∽ↄɕↄ∾

This index lists primarily twentieth-century published works by author and title of reference, and the page on which a full citation of the publication appears. Footnote numbers are given when necessary.

General Index

හ

CPSIA information can be obtained
at www.ICGtesting.com
Printed in the USA
LVHW04s2227290618
582304LV00002B/150/P